A PREFACE TO POLITICS

A PREFACE

SECOND EDITION

TO POLITICS

David Schuman
University of Massachusetts, Amherst

D. C. HEATH AND COMPANY
Lexington, Massachusetts   Toronto

We are grateful to the following publishers and individuals for permission to reprint from their works:

Page

v © 1974 Paul Simon. Used with the permission of the publisher.

xv "I'd Have You Anytime"—Copyright © 1970 by Big Sky Music and Harrisongs Music, Ltd. Used by permission. All rights reserved.

53, 79 From Studs Terkel, *Working: People Talk About What They Do All Day and How They Feel About What They Do* (New York: Pantheon Books, Inc., a division of Random House, Inc.), 1974.

143–44 From Perry Miller, *Errand into the Wilderness* (Cambridge, Mass.: Harvard University Press), 1975.

183, 205, 221–22 Reprinted with the permission of Farrar, Straus & Giroux, Inc. from *The Electric Kool-Aid Acid Test* by Tom Wolfe, copyright © 1968 by Tom Wolfe, copyright © 1967 by the World Journal Tribune Corporation.

196, 199–200 From R. D. Laing, *Knots* (New York: Random House, Inc.), 1972.

207 Copyright © 1939 Chappell & Co., Inc. Copyright renewed. Used by permission.

215 "Happiness Is a Warm Gun" (John Lennon, Paul McCartney). © 1968 Northern Songs Limited. All rights for the United States, Canada, Mexico, and the Philippines controlled by Maclen Music, Inc. Used by permission. All rights reserved.

International Standard Book Number: 0–669–00348–4

Library of Congress Catalog Card Number: 76–20831

Now I sit by my window
And I watch the cars
I fear I'll do some damage
One fine day
But I will not be convicted
By a jury of my peers
Still crazy
Still crazy
Still crazy after all these years

PAUL SIMON

Foreword to the First Edition

Such an honest book deserves an equally honest foreword. However much it may strain the reader's credulity, that is what I attempt here.

This book must be either a dramatic success or a complete flop. It is deadly serious and outrageously funny, a "textbook" that is a delight to read and yet provocative of the deepest insights. It is *about* politics, but it is emphatically *not* traditional political science. It may be that only students can appreciate it, but I hope that other teachers will be curious enough to try it in their classrooms. If they do—if the gatekeepers are bold or foolish enough to let it in—I am convinced that it will have electric impact, and that the introductory course will come alive as it has not for years. I shall try to state quite simply my experience with the book and what I conceive to be its strengths—and weaknesses.

I urged this book upon the publisher after listening to David Schuman's students exult about his introductory course and teaching a course with him out of masochistic curiosity. When the manuscript was finally delivered, I let it gather seniority, alternately on my office desk and living room coffee table, in my usual dilatory fashion. On at least four occasions during this week or so, students or other friends poked into it idly, not knowing the author—only that it was another book for political science courses. In every case, they either refused to put it down or insisted upon taking it with them to read through, emerging from periods of wild laughter and profound silence to insist that it be published immediately. Piqued at this repeated disruption of the normal sobriety of my surroundings, I decided it was time to read the damned thing myself. Of course, my young friends were right again. It *is* hilarious, *and* profound. And best of all, it is what education can and should be—people learning with and from each other through sharing personal experiences and reactions. It thus came as no surprise to me, though it was a bit disconcerting for some editors, that the same incidents occurred in the publisher's offices. The fact is that this is a book with immense human appeal to young people, and perhaps to others as well. It speaks not only *to* them where they are today, in terms that are real and important and never condescending, but also *for* them. Identification between author and audience is immediate, and complete rapport is established as together they dispose of hypocrisy and quickly begin breaking the mental constraints that our society has induced us to impose upon ourselves.

The focus of the book is on the nature of politics. I used to think that the introductory course could be counted a success if it communicated a sophisticated sense of the nature of politics. Then I realized that it would be nice if the ten or more courses of an undergraduate major in political science would just add up to an understanding of the same thing. I finally realized that the question of the nature of politics was the core of the *whole* problem—the problem of political science, of teaching about politics, and of politics itself. If we just understood politics. . . . Now, I wonder if David's book might not enable us to go back and delve deeply into this question, and at the proper beginning, in the introductory course. It does not have all the answers, of course, if only because they are found in people and not in books. But it should help us to begin with the right approaches to the question.

The essential ingredient that this book offers to the understanding of politics is to shift the focus from "out there" to "in here." Politics is not just the acts of officials, nor even the totality of events, attitudes, and behavior in the objective world. It is also the thoughts and feelings of people as they relate to each other and to their political environment, and their accumulated experiences over time. To understand this interpenetrated world of subjective and objective experience, analysis must begin with oneself and not with external matters. As David shows in his delightful cartoon quote, "We have met the enemy, and he is us", insight into the problems of the United States today must begin with us. This means that we must first understand the way we think—our political consciousness—and why we think that way, and whether there might not be other ways to think about ourselves, our politics, and our world. The book uses a variety of means, some highly innovative, some quite familiar, to show the many ways in which our thinking is shaped to prevent us from addressing problems in truly new and creative ways.

But this is not a book of answers. The whole thrust is toward learning how to become aware of one's own self-imposed blinders, and that places the bulk of the burden on the student—where it belongs. The materials and the provocation are ample, but the real teaching takes place below the surface, when the student *feels* the problem and forces himself or herself to break through it to new concepts and approaches. Students are obliged to confront themselves and think things out. Then they can help each other. Throughout, the book is the source, but not the solution.

Some may think this book subversive. It is. Not politically, but of the accepted modes of thinking, and perhaps of teaching. It will take a certain self-confidence, a willingness to try something actually different, to bring teachers to employ this book. I suppose this is a weakness, but I am told that nothing new and interesting and important is achieved by doing the same old things. The weaknesses that concern me more are not pedagogical or discipline-grounded, but political. With all its achievements, there are some things that this book does not do. Key elements in the understanding of politics are ignored completely. Absolutely essential things remain to be learned. Fortunately, there will be time for David's students to take courses with me and find out what these things are. Isn't that what we are all about?

Kenneth M. Dolbeare

Contents

Reintroduction

...you think this is too horrible to have really happened, this is too awful to be the truth! But, please. It's still hard for me to have a clear mind thinking on it. But it's the truth even if it didn't happen.

KEN KESEY

The world, of course, is different. I'm not and you're not and the world is not 1971.

The world, of course, is a whole lot the same. Me and you and the world are basically much like we were in 1971.

If I understand correctly, *both* of the things you just read are true. Part of the tension of being a student or teacher is learning how to sort out what is *really* different and what is *really* the same. To rewrite this book is an exercise in trying to come to terms with what has changed; how I have changed and how a changed me looks at a changed out there.

I'm still wearing the same glasses, but the prescription has changed.

No matter what goes on, there are certain things which seem to be true. For example, James Madison[1] quit changing and revising *Federalist* No. 10 some years ago. It seems reasonable to assume that the *Federalist* No. 10 which was printed in the first edition is the same one which will appear here. Bureaucracies have just gotten bigger, organizations more complex, science more powerful, and the military able to kill us more times over. And, with regularity, people keep trying to be elected to some office or another, and other people keep encouraging them by voting.

The basic undercurrents of our culture are still powerful, and what was true a few years ago is true today. The critique then is the critique now.

Knowing that, we know about half of what is necessary to

---

[1] Good old Madison. My friend Ken Mayers was more than amused when he pointed out that the heart of the real-world-of-selling-America is called . . . Madison Avenue.

get at what is going on. Like it or not, this generation acts out American themes in ways different from the last generation. This generation does not have to deal with a whole lot of things: there is no big, up front, obvious, "hot" war (I hasten to say there is none *tonight,* as I write this); no President in office who is in need of a pardon (I hasten to say, etc.). In other words, there is no great national trauma in the news every night . . . unless you want to count the Bicentennial.

Of course there is terrible unemployment, we are polluting ourselves to death, and discrimination is still an everyday fact. But those are *hidden* things. Not news. Not dramatic. They are just facts without much reality for us.

They're just there.

No more marches. Sit-ins. Non-negotiable demands. Up against the walls. Day-Glo. Hippies or revolution. The Movement moved.

All kinds of different ways of trying to come to terms with America have come into being. While a lot aren't strikingly unique, these ways have distinct characteristics of this generation. This generation? What does *that* mean?

The older brothers and sisters (and I mean blood ties) were people who belonged, if not participated, in long-hair when it was a political statement, dope when it was national news, and war—in it or against it. They dropped out, and all that.

This generation saw the hurt and the fun and some of the successes and failures. Apparently, they disapproved and/or they wanted an identity of their own. It was their turn to come to terms with America. "Generation gaps" apply almost as well to successive generations as to the space between parents and children.

The eighteen-year-old turns his or her back on the twenty-eight-year-old. The classes in business are now over-enrolled. God has made a comeback. One suspects people even wash behind their ears. Change, indeed.

But, of course, we all get tugged by a lot of the same forces, and because of all the big and obvious things—like language and schools and TV—we have much more in common than we often admit. We're a whole lot alike. That is the truth of it. Our environment, physical and cultural and mythical, seeps in and affects us all. In real ways we are where and when we live.

If we want to do it right (makes more sense than to want to do it wrong), if we want to be smarter and better than we are, part of what we have to do is understand how others have dealt with their times. Clear but bad advice may be helpful, even if it is said as good advice. Part of what older generations should do is to put their knowledge into forms which younger generations might learn *something* from. The other part is that younger generations should try to listen.

Given all that we know, with an amazing amount of hard work and good intentions and clean hands and a pure heart and all that—given all those things—sometimes we get lucky and get a little smarter and better.

Besides, there are some things that can't be the truth even if they *did* happen.

KEN KESEY

Thanks Again

All I have is yours
All you see is mine
I'm glad to hold you in my arms
   to have you anytime.

GEORGE HARRISON

I'm writing this *Preface* on a different side of American than when writing the other *Preface*. That's only a vague hint of what's been going on. From the shadow of snow-capped mountains to the shadow of Jonathan Edwards and his Puritan fury means that, while I'm still in the dark, it's a different kind of dark. In lots of ways I want to thank those involved in the move.

Had I not moved I would not have met Barbara. Had I not met Barbara, the world just would not be the same. She conspires to make life wonderful and even stops her work to help me with mine. She understands, and stays with me during the hard times. An extra special thanks is simply terrible understatement.

This, like the last edition, has much to do with students and friends and classes of both.

For two years at Washington I worked with extraordinary teaching assistants. We did a kind of Introduction-to-Politics-

and-American-Thinking course in which we tried to make a virtue out of the diversity of huge numbers of students. The TA's
did a remarkably good job, and taught both the students and
me a great deal. There was also an American theory class from
which none of us will soon recover. They were patient, if nothing else.

My former colleagues, of course, taught many things.

My friend Ken Dolbeare was again very helpful. It is impossible to thank him adequately for all of his aid and kindness.
Doug Amy taught with me, and talked with me, and did research for the book. Doug often taught me—or reminded me
—of important matters.

Robert Waterman, John Voekel, Linda Medcalf and the folks
in the house—big and small—added special kinds of help.
I thank them all.

David Schuman
Spring, 1976
Northampton, Mass.

A PREFACE TO POLITICS

About Textbooks in General, and This One in Particular

It seems sensible to begin by saying something that most people already know if they have taken the time to think about it. These first pages have to do with textbooks whose purpose is to introduce people to political science and to politics. To understand some of these attempts is to begin to understand how uninviting—and in some cases how misleading and dangerous—these attempts *may* be.

Anyone with reasonable intelligence and enough courses in political science can outline an introductory textbook.

First, there is the secret language to explain. This means that at least one chapter must be devoted to defining terms. "Politics is . . .; science is . . .; therefore, political science is. . . ." That is fine. It certainly *seems* reasonable to expect people who use the same language to have similar words mean similar things. So, our ideal textbook strains toward purity of definition. It strains toward standardization.

On with the text. After definitions—after laying the parameters—there seem to be at least four things we must try to do. First, we should give examples of the system proving that it is good or bad—*but giving tacit support in either case*. Second, we must give as many "facts" as possible. Third, perhaps we should include a couple of case studies to make the whole thing more "real" and appealing. Finally, we should consciously integrate material from other fields to show the interrelationship of all the social sciences.

Worthy aims, all.

There are, of course, little things that ought to be done. We might discuss how a bill becomes a law, and/or how power is spread less or more evenly around, and/or how elections count. We should, of course, find an appropriate quote from old Abe Lincoln. If we can manage to do this, and work up a teacher's manual with true-false questions of medium difficulty, then we will have succeeded in writing a standard—and possibly even successful—textbook.

These elements a text doth make.

It seems difficult to fault our ideal/typical textbook, because it sounds so reasonable, so obvious, so normal. It is what was, what is, and what always will be. Basically, there is nothing terribly wrong with the notion of an introduction to a field— nothing wrong, that is, unless it goes unquestioned. Certainly we should know about the political system, be introduced to "facts," and involve ourselves with word definitions. All these things may, at some point, be critical to the student. Nevertheless, there is work that must go on before this begins. The investigation of the obvious may *not* be the obvious place to begin. There are questions that are logically prior to the "facts" of the empirical world. Let me try to explain.

Built into our typical text are assumptions about politics, about the system, and about knowledge. Our book would be correct if we were agreed on the ultimate "truths" of the empirical facts of the "real world." If we could agree not to question these "truths" and not to question what they meant or whom they benefited, then such a book would be a fine one. We would have to agree that politics was pretty well limited to elections and representatives, that it was generally an activity which was neither noble nor had any immediate effect on our lives.

There is, of course, no good reason to accept these assumptions. Politics, in a real sense, affects everything we do. To begin to understand politics, we must begin by understanding the range of politics and the power of ideology. To look at politics in this manner is to open up a whole series of problems—problems which do not seem to be political, but which really are. Politics—in spite of what we have been taught to believe—may have something to do with how we think about happiness or with why we seem to be lonely. It may have a great influence on how we view each other, or on how we react to rules, or on what we think is important. For certain, politics is more than voting, and to understand it requires much more than trying to integrate the social sciences.

What I want to argue is that what you do means something, that your actions are connected with what you believe—or were taught to believe—and that these actions are important for at least two reasons. First, most of our learned behavior supports the status quo, supports what is. Our political system —in fact, Political Systems—are geared to self-survival. This is achieved, in no small measure, by teaching the people who live under that system to support it. No great news in that. Second, our behavior is important because it defines who we are. If you act like an ass, but think like a saint, you are still an ass.

The task of this book is immodest: to begin to explore how we think and act, why such behavior is political, and what all that might mean.

There is little reason to assume that all I write is true. Of course it is not. Politics is often unsure and sloppy, a lot like life. To write a textbook—indeed, almost any book—using only those things we can all agree upon would be as boring as it would be useless. To begin to understand politics is to begin to understand how we got to where we are—as individuals and as groups of individuals and as a society. This has to be incredibly complex, and must be made up of many different truths.[1]

There is an order to this book, an effort to explain a position and then to explore it. A "model" of politics is contained in the initial chapters. Simply stated, this is an attempt to understand the kind of individual our system tries to shape; how that individual is taught to look at the world (how he or she knows what he/she knows); and what kind of societal structure is constructed in the image of that individual. These chapters are most clearly understood after the others have been read.

---

[1] There are many problems an ordinary text deals with which are not covered in this book. The most obvious example is the set of problems (complicated by racial bigotry) minorities face in a nation. In a sense, this book concentrates on the problems of those who have lived in America for any length of time and who have been socialized—or victimized—by our particular ways.

In an important sense, the rest of the book deals with the texture of a person's life. It attempts to explore some of those problems which seem to require only natural, everyday, common sense answers, but which actually deserve much closer attention. Somehow, we all live in groups and seek to be free, but we do these things without thinking about what they mean or about how we have been taught to understand them.

We must understand the *context* of our actions, both from the outside in and from the inside out. We must begin to be aware of the transactions between our selves and our society.

We will begin with what we know best—ourselves. Everyone of us is the system, we have it in our heads, and we act it out in our everyday lives. To learn about the system is to learn about ourselves—and, of course, the reverse. To think about making the one better, we must know about both and about how they are related. Who knows, maybe Charlie Brown was right: "We have met the enemy, and he is us."

When?

Perhaps in time the so-called Dark Ages will be thought of as including our own.

Sometimes you just want to sit down, sigh, and wish you knew how you got where you are. After another sigh, another question occurs: Just where are you?

Don't look at me, I don't know. It is possible to pinpoint the century we're in. We may learn more than we want by just knowing that much.

As Friedrich Nietzsche wrote and grew older and his thought matured, he became more aware of what great limitations societies placed on individuals. His work became a chronicle of repressions and restraints; of the loss of a person's creative energy in the modern state.

So he developed an image of an individual who understood what was happening—a kind of superman—who was condemned to the sad realization of the blandness of the current state of affairs. The superman wandered Europe telling those he met the horrible truth of their lives. Far from being a Germanic conqueror—an Arian goose-stepping in formation—Nietzsche's truthsayer did not seek conquest, but rather education. He took no pleasure in victory, but rather shared the individuals' pain of loss.

Zarathustra lived on the mountain top for ten years. He then came down full of wisdom and joy, knowledge and sadness. He walked the earth with his destructive yet creative message.

Freud lived in Vienna and did his work seated silently behind a blank screen. His message was to a whole different point.

Think of the world as it was in 1850—and then make it more fully developed. The industrial era was a fact. It won. Governments and industries and societies were fully involved in becoming much bigger and more complex. The way to handle complexity was to organize it; the way to handle people was to make them fit into those organizations.

5

There were, of course, some pretty obvious losses.

For example, as roles became more explicit, more specialized, the range of human activities became more limited. The paradox is a nice one: As the whole society becomes more complex, the individual in the society has been forced to become more simple. As the industry produced more and faster, the individual produced greater volume but fewer things. The world was working, but the people in it seemed to be breaking down. Even Victorian morals weren't doing their job in keeping society stable and people stable.

If the aim of Nietzsche was to go beyond the present by understanding the past, Freud's aim was to help people adjust to now . . . to make it work. What Freud worked with was each individual; each of us doing his or her own thing. Freud knew we were more than we appeared to be. He listened to our words and tried to understand our dreams. He made myths for us to believe.

Freud wanted to save people by understanding them—he wanted to understand by quietly listening to someone talking on a couch.

When Nietzsche wandered, Freud sat; Nietzsche spoke, Freud listened and took notes; Nietzsche defied—Freud was paid to befriend:

Nietzsche died in 1900.

Welcome to the twentieth century.

Politics as Evil People

1

Although I know very little of the Steppenwolf's life, I have all the same good reason to suppose that he was brought up by devoted but severe and very pious parents and teachers in accordance with that doctrine that makes the breaking of the will the cornerstone of education and upbringing . . . in so far as he let loose upon himself every barbed criticism, every anger and hate he could command he was, in spite of all, a real Christian, and a real martyr. As for others and the world around him he never ceased in his heroic and earnest endeavor to love them, to be just to them, to do them no harm, for the love of his neighbor was as deeply in him as the hatred of himself, and so his whole life was an example that love of one's neighbor is not possible without love of oneself, and that self-hate is really the same thing as sheer egoism, and in the long run breeds the same cruel isolation and despair.

HERMANN HESSE

... and the past not uncommonly takes a while to happen, and some long time to figure out.

KEN KESEY

About Being a Person in a World with Other People

There are, I believe, a number of essential questions we each have to ask ourselves in order to even begin to sort out who we are and why we do what we do. Most often, for most of us, we assume answers without knowing the questions, propose solutions without understanding the problems, and take actions without thinking about the consequences. We believe and act on myths: the American Dream, Christian ethics, or an insight induced by dope. For us, these are valid. Unexplored, but valid. We obey. A principle is a principle—do it and like it, maybe even love it, but always without knowing exactly why it is being done.

What I want to argue is that, basically, we live in a society that thrives on its citizens' self-ignorance. Of course we know who the senator from our state is; we may even know our representative. I mean something different. Our political system runs best in an atmosphere of one person's inability to know and relate to other people. In essence, we live in isolation, according to others' rules. We might be what we are taught, or we may be as we were trained. Either way, we are what others want us to be—and that seldom includes much self-knowledge.

There is a passage in a book by J. P. Donleavy that concerns a young man who is very kind to many people. He says: "... at a distance, people look different but when you talk with them they all become the same."[1] At some point, it may be important to look around and to remember conversations.

For a moment, let me argue that, indeed, we are all much alike. Further that the sameness is nothing new, but simply the natural result of our political ideology. To cut away our past, to be blind to things that have gone before, is an almost sure method of being trapped in a world that is impossible to understand. The question, now, has to do with being an individual.

---

[1] The quote is from J. P. Donleavy's fine *The Beastly Beatitudes of Balthazar B.* (New York: Dell Publishing Co., 1968).

An obvious place to begin talking about a person is in terms of the roles he or she plays. A person may be what that role is. To try to understand that role is to try to understand parts of the core of our culture. To begin to understand who we are, we must examine the role our government wants us to play in relationship to it. It seems obvious, then, that any truly helpful self-knowledge must incorporate an understanding of how our government wants us to act and what kinds of rules it wants us to follow.

We are taught to ignore this. The "political" process is something that is abstract and vague, something that others are involved in. It is, for some reason, dirty. So we do not involve ourselves in any kind of active relationship with the government nor do we pay much attention to the dues we are made to pay. Instead, we involve ourselves with individualism, never thinking about what that might mean.

For reasons of sanity, we all seem to argue that we are individuals. Indeed, being an individual is very important. We are unique. We think our thoughts, we do our thing. We are what we are and can be no one else. But that may well be a static, potentially suicidal approach to being one's self. Deep down inside, if we ever bother to go there, is probably the fear that we are not terribly unique. We are not different. Our thing is their thing, and we are they.

This state is built on the sameness of people who do not know themselves. Read James Madison and marvel; read James Madison and ask: Are we as evil as he believes, as incompetent as he thinks? Ask what it means to act as if he were right.

As Americans, we all know that people cannot really have freedom unless they are individuals. To think otherwise is to be some kind of fool, or worse. Ours is a culture of a people wronged who go out and kill the villain. Can't count on the cops, and there may not even be honor among thieves. Can't count on anyone else. The hero or heroine is not only good, but also alone. The hero has the freedom to go anywhere but to stay nowhere. America is flooded with Walden Ponds. We each want—and often grow to need—our own shack by a pitiful pond that is within walking distance of town. We must, after all, remind people that we are individuals, lest they forget.

Neither the image nor the meaning needs much elaboration.

To be an individual is to be free, and to be free is to be free *from* things. This is neither new nor startling. It is, if you will excuse the term, a fact. Our freedom is freedom from.[2] We often take our identities from the groups we are in, and then refuse to participate in those groups. We are in, but not of; we are defined by those very institutions and people we refuse to acknowledge. We seem to be free from dirtying our hands, but not free to cleanse ourselves.

To repeat, to be an individual is to be free, and that freedom is negative. It is the freedom of the freeway. People kill themselves by jumping off mountains with wings tied on ... but they do it *themselves*. Ours is an alone freedom.

But things are much more complex than that. Much more complex than beginning to understand the relationship between the State and the individual and freedom. It is more complicated than saying that our concept of freedom may lead to a kind of political impotence.

There is another powerful myth that is important to mention. We are the great leveling country. Read Walt Whitman. We are the land of the common person. Noble, proud, practical, and common. More than that, we have a government that can be run by anyone. It was carefully planned to run rationally, according to principles that assumed each human element was replaceable and interchangeable. It demands that, while we may think of ourselves as individuals, we must fear being different. Further, we must fear those who appear different.

So we elect people who are common, or some close approximation. Somehow we feel safe that way. To elect common people to stereotyped roles in an impersonal political system reminds us of something like democracy, and has something to do with equality, and makes us feel a little safer from corrupt politicians. The idea is simple: We trust our government to those common, and continue to think of ourselves as uncommon.

And that is the whole point, isn't it?

There is, of course, no particular reason why you should accept what I have written. It is vague and abstract and not

---

[2] For distinctions of freedom, see Chapter 7.

flattering at all. For the rest of this chapter, I shall try to show why I argued as I did. Let me begin at the beginning, with James Madison's *Federalist Paper* No. 10. A background on the paper seems in order.

James Madison attended the Constitutional Convention. For a number of reasons, he stands out. It is Madison who informs us of that convention; he kept an informed and intelligent diary of the convention debates. More importantly, along with Alexander Hamilton and John Jay, he wrote a series of papers defending the Constitution for the citizens of New York State. The papers—*The Federalist Papers*—are brilliant propaganda which do much to explain the Constitution. The following is *Federalist* No. 10, in which Madison writes about our citizen's relationships with each other, what they should be and how they should be handled.

Two suggestions: Read it at least twice—one for what it says and again for what it does not say. Omission is important (if one knows just what to look for).[3]

> Among the numerous advantages promised by a well-constructed Union none deserves to be more accurately developed than its tendency to break and control the violence of faction. The friend of popular governments never finds himself so much alarmed for their character and fate as when he contemplates their propensity to this dangerous vice. He will not fail, therefore, to set a due value on any plan which, without violating the principles to which he is attached, provides a proper cure for it. The instability, injustice, and confusion introduced into the public councils have, in truth, been the mortal diseases under which popular governments have everywhere perished, as they continue to be the favorite and fruitful topics from which the adversaries to liberty derive their most specious declamations. The valuable improvements made by the American constitutions on the popular models, both ancient and modern, cannot certainly be too much admired, but it would be an unwarrantable partiality to contend that they have as effectively obviated the danger on this side as was wished and expected. Complaints are everywhere heard from our most considerate and virtuous citizens, equally the friends of public and private faith, and of public and personal liberty, that our governments are too

---

[3] *Federalist* No. 10 can be found in various places. Clinton Rossiter edited a complete version of the Federalist papers, and Bobbs-Merrill has reprinted some of the papers individually.

unstable, that the public good is disregarded in the conflicts of rival parties, and that measures are too often decided, not according to the rules of justice and the rights of the minor party, but by the superior force of an interested and overbearing majority. However anxiously we may wish that these complaints had no foundation, the evidence of known facts will not permit us to deny that they are in some degree true. It will be found, indeed, on a candid review of our situation that some of the distresses under which we labor have been erroneously charged on the operation of our governments; but it will be found, at the same time, that other causes will not alone account for many of our heaviest misfortunes, and particularly for that prevailing and increasing distrust of public engagements and alarm for private rights, which are echoed from one end of the continent to the other. These must be chiefly, if not wholly, effects of the unsteadiness and injustice with which a factious spirit has tainted our public administrations.

By a faction, I understand a number of citizens, whether amounting to a majority or a minority of the whole, who are united and actuated by some common impulse of passion, or of interest, adverse to the rights of other citizens or to the permanent and aggregate interests of the community.

There are two methods of curing the mischiefs of faction: the one, by removing its causes; the other, by controlling its effects.

There are again two methods of removing the causes of faction: the one, by destroying the liberty which is essential to its existence; the other, by giving to every citizen the same opinions, the same passions, and the same interests.

It could never be more truly said than of the first remedy, that it was worse than the disease. Liberty is to faction what air is to fire, an ailment without which it instantly expires. But it could not be less folly to abolish liberty, which is essential to political life, because it nourishes faction than it would be to wish the annihilation of air, which is essential to animal life, because it imparts to fire its destructive agency.

The second expedient is as impracticable as the first would be unwise. As long as the reason of man continues fallible, and he is at liberty to exercise it, different opinions will be formed. As long as the connection subsists between his reason and his self-love, his opinions and his passions will have a reciprocal influence on each other, and the former will be objects to which the latter will attach themselves. The diversity in the faculties of men, from which the rights of property originate, is not less an insuperable obstacle to a uniformity of interests. The protection of these faculties is the first object of government. From the protection of different and unequal faculties of acquiring property, the possession of different degrees and kinds of property immediately results; and from the influence of these on the sentiments and views of the respective proprietors ensues a division of the society into different interests and parties.

The latent causes of faction are thus sown in the nature of man, and we see them everywhere brought into different degrees of activity, according to the different circumstances of civil society. A zeal for different opinions concerning religion, concerning government, and many other points, as well of speculation as of practice; an attachment to different leaders ambitiously contending for pre-eminence and power, or to persons of other descriptions whose fortunes have been interesting to the human passions, have, in turn, divided mankind into parties, inflamed them with mutual animosity, and rendered them much more disposed to vex and oppress each other than to co-operate for their common good. So strong is this propensity of mankind to fall into mutual animosities that, where no substantial occasion presents itself, the most frivolous and fanciful distinctions have been sufficient to kindle their unfriendly passions and excite their most violent conflicts. But the most common and durable source of factions has been the various and unequal distribution of property. Those who hold and those who are without property have ever formed distinct interests in society. Those who are creditors and those who are debtors fall under a like discrimination. A landed interest, a manufacturing interest, a mercantile interest, a money interest, with many lesser interests, grow up of necessity in civilized nations and divide them into different classes actuated by different sentiments and views. The regulation of these various and interfering interests forms the principal task of modern legislation and involves the spirit of party and faction in the necessary and ordinary operations of the government.

No man is allowed to be a judge in his own cause because his interest would certainly bias his judgment and, not improbably, corrupt his integrity. With equal, nay with greater reason, a body of men are unfit to be both judges and parties at the same time; yet what are many of the most important acts of legislation but so many judicial determinations, not indeed concerning the rights of single persons, but concerning the rights of large bodies of citizens? And what are the different classes of legislators but advocates and parties to the causes which they determine? Is a law proposed concerning private debts? It is a question to which the creditors are parties on one side and the debtors on the other. Justice ought to hold the balance between them. Yet the parties are, and must be, themselves the judges, and the most numerous party or, in other words, the most powerful faction must be expected to prevail. Shall domestic manufactures be encouraged, and in what degree, by restrictions on foreign manufactures? are questions which would be differently decided by the landed and the manufacturing classes, and probably by neither with a sole regard to justice and the public good. The apportionment of taxes on the various descriptions of property is an act which seems to require the most exact impartiality, yet there is, perhaps, no legislative act in which greater opportunity and temptation are given to a predominant party to trample on the rules of justice. Every shilling with which they overburden the inferior number is a shilling saved to their own pockets.

It is in vain to say that enlightened statesmen will be able to adjust these clashing interests and render them all subservient to the public good. Enlightened statesmen will not always be at the helm. Nor, in many cases, can such an adjustment be made at all without taking into view indirect and remote considerations, which will rarely prevail over the immediate interest which one party may find in disregarding the rights of another or the good of the whole.

The inference to which we are brought is that the *causes* of faction cannot be removed, and that relief is only to be sought in the means of controlling its *effects*.

If a faction consists of less than a majority, relief is supplied by the republican principle, which enables the majority to defeat its sinister views by regular vote. It may clog the administration, it may convulse the society, but it will be unable to execute and mask its violence under the forms of the Constitution. When a majority is included in a faction, the form of popular government, on the other hand, enables it to sacrifice to its ruling passion or interest both the public good and the rights of other citizens. To secure the public good and private rights against the danger of such a faction, and at the same time to preserve the spirit and the form of popular government, is then the great object to which our inquiries are directed. Let me add that it is the great desideratum by which this form of government can be rescued from the opprobrium under which it has so long labored and be recommended to the esteem and adoption of mankind.

By what means is this object attainable? Evidently by one of two only. Either the existence of the same passion or interest in a majority at the same time must be prevented or the majority, having such coexistent passion or interest, must be rendered, by their number and local situation, unable to concert and carry into effect schemes of oppression. If the impulse and the opportunity be suffered to coincide, we well know that neither normal nor religious motives can be relied on as an adequate control. They are not found to be such on the injustice and violence of individuals, and lose their efficiency in proportion to the number combined together, that is, in proportion as their efficacy becomes needful.

From this view of the subject it may be concluded that a pure democracy, by which I mean a society consisting of a small number of citizens who assemble and administer the government in person, can admit of no cure for the mischiefs of faction. A common passion or interest will, in almost every case, be felt by a majority of the whole; a communication and concert result from the form of government itself, and there is nothing to check the inducements to sacrifice the weaker party or an obnoxious individual. Hence it is that such democracies have ever been spectacles of turbulence and contention, have ever been found incompatible with personal security or the rights of property, and have in general been as short in their lives as they have been violent in their deaths. Theoretic politicians who have patronized this species of government have erroneously supposed that by reducing mankind to a perfect equality in their political rights, they would, at the same time, be perfectly equalized and assimilated in their possessions, their opinions, and their passions.

A republic, by which I mean a government in which the scheme of representation takes place, opens a different prospect and promises the cure for which we are seeking. Let us examine the points in which it varies from pure democracy, and we shall comprehend both the nature of the cure and the efficacy which it must derive from the Union.

The two great points of difference between a democracy and a republic are: first, the delegation of the government, in the latter, to a small number of citizens elected by the rest; secondly, the greater number of citizens and greater sphere of country over which the latter may be extended.

The effect of the first difference is, on the one hand, to refine and enlarge the public views by passing them through the medium of a chosen body of citizens whose wisdom may best discern the true interest of their country, and whose patriotism and love of justice will be least likely to sacrifice it to temporary or partial considerations. Under such a regulation it may well happen that the public voice, pronounced by the representatives of the people, will be more consonant to the public good than if pronounced by the people themselves, convened for the purpose. On the other hand, the effect may be inverted. Men of factious tempers, of local prejudices, or of sinister designs may, by intrigue, by corruption, or by other means, first obtain the suffrages and then betray the interests of the people. The question resulting is whether small or extensive republics are more favorable to the election of proper guardians of the public weal; and it is clearly decided in favor of the latter by two obvious considerations:

In the first place, it is to be remarked that, however small the republic may be, the representatives must be raised to a certain number in order to guard against the cabals of a few, and that, however large it may be, they must be limited to a certain number in order to guard against the confusion of a multitude.

Hence the number of representatives in the two cases not being in proportion to that of the two constituents, and being proportionally greater in the small republic, it follows that, if the proportion of fit characters be not less in the large than in the small republic, the former will present a greater option and consequently a greater probability of a fit choice.

In the next place, as each representative will be chosen by a greater number of citizens in the large than in the small republic, it will be more difficult for unworthy candidates to practice with success the vicious arts by which elections are too often carried; and the suffrages of the people being more free will be more likely to center in men who possess the most attractive merit and the most diffusive and established characters.

It must be confessed that in this, as in most other cases, there is a mean, on both sides of which inconveniences will be found to lie. By enlarging too much the number of electors you render the representative too little acquainted with all their local circumstances and lesser interests; as by reducing it too much, you render him unduly attached to these and too little fit to comprehend and pursue great and national objects. The federal Constitution forms a happy combination in this respect: the great and aggregate interests being referred to the national, the local and particular to the State legislatures.

The other point of difference is the greater number of citizens and extent of territory which may be brought within the compass of republican than of democratic government, and it is this circumstance principally which renders factious combinations less to be dreaded in the former than in the latter. The smaller the society, the fewer probably will be the distinct parties and interests, the more frequently will a majority be found of the same party; and the smaller the number of individuals composing a majority, and the smaller the compass within which they are placed, the more easily will they concert and execute their plans of oppression. Extend the sphere, and you take in a greater variety of parties and interests; you make it less probable that a majority of the whole will have a common motive to invade the rights of other citizens; or if such a common motive exists, it will be more difficult for all who feel it to discover their own strength and to act in unison with each other. Besides other impediments, it may be remarked that, where there is a consciousness of unjust or dishonorable purposes, communication is always checked by distrust in proportion to the number whose concurrence is necessary.

Hence it clearly appears that the same advantage which a republic has over a democracy in controlling the effects of faction is enjoyed by a large over a small republic—is enjoyed by the Union over the States composing it. Does the advantage consist in the substitution of representatives whose enlightened views and virtuous sentiments render them superior to local prejudices and schemes of injustice? It will not be denied that the representation of the Union will be most likely to possess these requisite endowments. Does it consist in the greater security afforded by a greater variety of parties, against the event of any one party being able to outnumber and oppress the rest? In an equal degree does the increased variety of parties comprised within the Union increase this security? Does it, in fine, consist in the greater obstacles opposed to the concert and accomplishment of the secret wishes of an unjust and interested majority? Here, again, the extent of the Union gives it the most palpable advantage.

The influence of factious leaders may kindle a flame within their particular States, but will be unable to spread a general conflagration through the other States. A religious sect may degenerate into a political faction in a part of the Confederacy, but the variety of sects dispersed over the entire face of it must secure the national councils against any danger from that source. A rage for paper money, for an abolition of debts, for an equal division of property, or for any other improper or wicked project will be less apt to pervade the whole body of the Union than a particular member of it, in the same proportion as such a malady is more likely to taint a particular county or district than an entire State.

In the extent and proper structure of the Union, therefore, we behold a republican remedy for the diseases most incident to republican government. And according to the degree of pleasure and pride we feel in being republicans ought to be our zeal in cherishing the spirit and supporting the character of Federalists.

In many important ways, *Federalist* No. 10 gives away most of the plot, a plot we have accepted with almost no reservations, accepted almost unknowingly. As it seems to have worked out, we, bright and brave college students; we, bright and brave future businessmen and women; we, Americans, really do not like or trust each other very much. At least we are not supposed to. We do not relate to each other well enough to make mutual decisions. *Federalist* No. 10 is the story of mistrust. Madison speaks of the rabbleness, of the potential evil doings of public meetings and democratic practices. He poses the essential question: How can we trust government to the people when we have no faith in them?

People, self-serving, self-centered, selfish people, are the raw material for our state. We are encouraged to be a private, materialistic people. We are essentially an uncommunitarian, anti-

political people who may act differently in spite of—certainly
not at the urging of—the state. Harsh words, these. Let me try
to explain.

Madison knew something that we must learn. He knew that
there was a close connection between how people relate to
one another and the structure in which that relationship takes
place. It is important to understand Madison's argument in
different terms.

If the problem is how to create a system that will continue
regardless of the basic inability of citizens to rule themselves,
the answer is deceivingly simple. Structure the system so that
its citizens will become mired in a self-grabbing, self-gratifying
way of life. Make it so that petty people, materialistic people,
will be allowed, whether acting singly or in small groups, to
go about the task of robbing the poor, robbing the rich, robbing the consumer, or even building a better mousetrap. Madison, in all his political wisdom, worked it out so that we could
pursue our own private, material interests. The plan was not a
stupid one; for certain, it has had lasting effects.

Have you ever seen a fairly large group of children "playing"
on a playground? There are balls and bats and fields and courts
and sandboxes and toys. Here, these young citizens of the future grab and kick and cry and fight over the toys or games
they are to play. Sometimes groups form and play their own
game—are able to play their own game—but sometimes they
just make nasty remarks to other groups. The critical element
in the playground is that the whole hassle is pretty harmless.
The children are being looked after, taken care of, and ultimately directed by adults. Theirs is a choice of what to do in
the sandbox. If Madison is correct, that is good training for the
system, good practice for the future.

The point is obvious: Do we make decisions of any more
importance than the toys we are going to play with? Houses,
cars, boats, big motorcycles, little pills—what difference does
it make? Face it, we are playing by their rules on their playground. The strategy of *Federalist* No. 10 is to divide and make
politically impotent; it does and we are.

The idea of a political state built on the evilness—and, hopefully, the powerlessness—of its people sounds pretty silly. It
should. Regrettably, to consider what students are taught about

the system is to consider just such thoughts. The following questions are quoted from a very reputable textbook.[4]

　1. "How is it possible to maintain a real equality of influence and power over government?" (In other words, won't a minority of people gain power?)

　2. "If everyone is to have an equal say, how can the decisions of government be made with sufficient knowledge and expertness?" (How can we expect "ordinary citizens" to understand?)

　3. "How can a popular government act vigorously, speedily, and decisively, particularly in crises?" (Citizens are just too slow.)

　4. "How can a system of popular government ever cope with . . . larger groups . . . tyrannizing smaller groups?" (We count on the worst in people coming out.)

　5. "Can a system really operate with the consent of *all?*"

These are not abstract questions but live issues. . . . In one way or another every popular government must surmount these problems. . . .

There is no doubt but that these are hard questions. While not exactly in the same class as "Have you stopped beating your wife?", they are close. At the root of these questions lies an unarticulated, seemingly reasonable bias: How do we form a popular government in spite of the weaknesses of people? Look at those five basic questions and at what they assume about you: that, among other things, you are probably not able to understand the complexities of government; that you will probably get more power than others if you are able; and, finally, that if you have the power, you will tyrannize others.

The beauty of it all is that we have been taught that *we* are not like that—but that *they* are. The self-protective mechanism is simple: "If others were only as good as I, then I could begin to act as kindly and generously and good as I really am." Score another one for Madison.

Maybe that is being too harsh, maybe we do have faith. Faith in a few, at least. There is another text, another book about American politics, which does add some fun to texts. It is *The Irony of Democracy* and the irony of *Irony* is that it is elitist. Simply stated, there is a faith in people—but only in some of them. A sample of faith . . .

---

[4] Robert Dahl, *Pluralist Democracy in the United States* (Chicago: Rand McNally & Co., 1967), pp. 10–11.

How Does Democracy Survive?

. . . survival of a democratic system does not depend upon a consensus that penetrates to every level of society. It is apparently not necessary that most people commit themselves to a democracy; all that is necessary is that they fail to commit themselves actively to an anti-democratic system. . . . It is important to keep in mind that although the masses may have anti-democratic attitudes, they are also inclined to avoid political activity . . . although *the masses can usually be counted on to leave politics to the elites,* we should not necessarily assume that our freedoms are safe in the hands of the elites. . . .

One is tempted to attribute the stability of American democracy to the actions of the elites. . . . This conclusion would be inaccurate . . . for in times of crises, the leadership of the elites has failed to provide a protective bulwark against anti-democratic forces. Ironically, it is to the poorly educated masses . . . that the stability of American democracy is to be attributed. Although the poorly educated tend toward authoritarianism, violence, and prejudice, they are also apathetic; they fail to take action on their beliefs.[5]

Impersonal Versus Material Me

Students Of Politics, the world is complex if we are to accept this "irony." The masses, the most of us, are potentially dangerous. We are full of violence and prejudice and had better not be trusted with deciding things for ourselves. Our virtue is in our inactiveness. We are act-less, therefore we are. But the analysis is more complicated. The elites are not to be trusted, either. This vision of politics—the Madisonian one—reminds us over and over again that government is a necessary evil. It is necessary, in part, because of our own evilness.

Because we have no faith in ourselves, we must place our faith somewhere else. Usually it is in those things we can see. Cars, clothes, boats, buildings—each a measure of wealth, each a measure of our own worth. Because we become isolated personally, we begin to relate impersonally. We relate in terms of things: first in terms of how many things there are, next in terms of how expensive we think those things may be. If we are all evil and materially consuming, it is only

---

[5] Thomas Dye and Harmon Zeigler, *The Irony of Democracy* (Belmont, Calif.: Wadsworth Publishing Co., 1970), pp. 137–38.

natural that we put our values into making, advertising, buying, and comparing material objects.

Henry Ford knew that, and so did Dale Carnegie. Build a
whole lot of things—in masses—and sell them with a smile.
We are what we own, or what we are making payments on.

This means, in large measure, that we must protect what
we have. We must fully understand privateness, and especially
the concept of private property. If we are in a measure defined by our property, then that property must be ours. I own
things, and you own things, and the state owns things. What
we are denied is joint ownership. What we seemingly cannot
do is control those things we "the people" own in common.
Let me give an example.

The Park

This example is actually an historical example. The fact is the
"Park" is not a very live issue to more than maybe twelve people in the world. Then, again, neither is *Federalist* No. 10. The
point is that we *should* be able to learn from more things than
just those current.

Three blocks from the University of California campus in
Berkeley there was a University-owned lot. There were plans
for the lot—a playfield and eventually student housing—but
budgets were being cut, and the projects were continually put
off. In 1968–69, the lot was mud in rainy weather, dirt in dry,
and a place to park for free if one got to school early. It was,
in other words, an urban eyesore. So far, there is nothing
unique about the example.

A fellow named Mike Delacour had the idea that the ugly
lot could be turned into a park—to be obvious, a Peoples'
Park. In the name of the Costinoan Indians, from whom the
land had been taken originally, students and street people
and anyone else interested began to build a park. Land was
cleared, grass was planted, and playthings were put up. The
University was asked to join; it was asked to provide some
tools to make the work go more quickly; it was asked, finally,
to leave the people alone. The University did none of these
things.

On May 15, 1969, workmen, guarded by gas-masked police

built a tall wire fence around the park. By the end of the day, city police, county deputy sheriffs, and National Guardsmen protected the fenced property. The whole day was bloody. The Alameda County Deputy Sheriffs killed one man, blinded another, and wounded scores of people. The police won, if we are to believe numbers: forty-three demonstrators hospitalized versus eighteen police. That was just the first day. Ultimately, that lot was to be "protected" by gas dropped onto a plaza of the University of California campus (and hospital, incidentally) from a helicopter as well as by the seemingly indiscriminate arrest of 482 individuals in downtown Berkeley.

The University built a field on the lot which no one used. A company was allowed to build a small parking lot on part of the former park. For at least a year, almost no one parked there. The point is not that the incident happened, the point is not even the brutality: the point is that the property of the state was being protected from the citizens who wanted to use it, and further, that what the state did seemed perfectly normal and right. The state had bought that land and it seemed only fair that it should use it in any way it saw fit. Casual empiricism indicated that the position of the state was supported.

The example of the Peoples' Park is adequate, yet just misses the point. What we might wonder is why we understand the position of the state. It seems very defensible to argue that the state simply reflects the views of its citizens. In other words, we can understand and even sympathize with the materialism of the state because we are geared to act in much the same way. If we could understand what we are doing, we might be able to see the point more clearly.

In many ways, we are much like our parents. Maybe there are style differences: drugs, dress, and the like; but, the basics are similar. We know we must train ourselves to be private, to get ahead, if we are to fit into this land of the free. So, we go to college to learn a trade, to become a professional, to prepare to be rich. Education for increased earnings. Education in how to live a life geared to privacy. We must learn to listen to and follow directions well. We must produce when told.

The structure of college is the structure of society, and the ends are the same. We go from class to class, learning truths contradicted by truths. We write our own exams and our own papers. Those who can best compartmentalize truth, who can learn most of what they are told, and who can do so alone get prizes. To excel is to be super average. To excel is to be rewarded materially.

That is like the state and our parents. We all agree on ends and on how they are to be judged and rewarded. We understand—at a subtle, sophisticated, gut level—why the state protects its property. Our institutions and our ideology are geared to similar principles. In important ways, we agree with what is. We agree to mistrust ourselves with our own ruling, we agree to judge ourselves, in large part, in terms of what we buy, and we agree on the basic rules of materialism, "capitalism," corporate wealth, and the like. James Madison would be proud.

Some problems are obvious. Because we mistrust others, we have lost control of all those things we might have in common. Every issue, every topic, every decision which might include all of us, is denied most of us because we have so little faith in the ability of people to make political decisions. Let us review what the Federalists, as exemplified by Madison, believed:

1. People could not be trusted to rule themselves. Indeed, the only thing worse than a few people trying to rule themselves was many people trying to rule themselves.

2. The morality of the system was in almost no sense public. Morality was a private thing, a commodity of the individual based on self-interest.

3. Citizenship was based upon an individual's remaining private. The system depended upon materialism, self-seekingness, and self-interestedness, and the citizen became trapped in this self-view.

4. The system was created by people of the Enlightenment who believed that if only the right (read rational) set of institutions were discovered, then the system could run indefinitely, in spite of people.

But Me?

Built into what the America of Madison means is that each of us acts in certain kinds of ways. We are, in truth, often threatened folks. It is, after all, a way to relate to the world we've come to know and—I mean this—to love.

I guess you don't hear it anymore, but for quite a few years there was a phrase used in politics that never failed to tickle me. To a then young lad like myself, it sounded like a cumbersome, slow moving, and slightly terrifying beast. It was, of course, *creeping socialism*. My impulse was always to look around to see if it was near, to prepare to stomp that dreaded creep right into the ground.

As it turned out, neither socialism nor capitalism were much to get excited about, but that's not the point.

In too many instances we seem subject to a lot of similar sounding evils. While we've learned what to like and dislike about socialism (creeping or not), we've had trouble identifying other things. The world, for an uncomfortably large number of people, is a threatening place. Think of a day in college: grades, money, popularity, professionalism, sex, roommates, etc., to better see the fear.

School is spring training for life.

Why are you in school? Just what are your motives? In an amazingly optimistic way, let's start our list with something nice. It is possible that people go to college to gain wisdom. Or (less grand and noble) we fear ignorance; or (more accurately probably) we don't want to appear stupid. That, of course, is the top of our list—the most impressive of our motives.

Why the hell are you in school? For future money? Maybe. For a wife or a husband with a college degree? Maybe. 'Cause your friends or parents silently (or not so silently) demanded it? Could be. Just a terrific set of reasons. But they are, in the end, not the most important or interesting topics. What counts —at least two things which count—are what you see and what you do.

We know, as one of those "facts," that college or university can put you through changes. Personal changes, value changes, social changes, which you will probably like, and which are for the good. It has been known to happen before. There is even a kind of secret history of people who have gotten wiser and better and who started that process in school. In spite of a whole lot of mindless effort and action, learning can and does go on. It is a learning that has to do with serious and important questions.

But two things seem to get in the way: students and teachers.[6]

We are painfully aware that there is a very good chance that any class you walk into will be fairly shallow, uninteresting, and destructive to your good mood and desire to learn. After all, the university is peopled by those who have, in a strange way, done the very best in the most ordinary way.

More precisely, if we learn from example it is important to remember that people in the university are often malignant forms of what is normal and ordinary. That a person made good grades and got high scores on standardized tests means nothing more than this: a person made good grades and got high scores on standardized tests.

There are an amazing number of other reasons why teachers aren't good at teaching, but what I wanted to say was they are mostly just normal—malignantly normal.

Students aren't much better, in some cases. What has always been most curious to me are those who *know* what's wrong; who *know* their compulsions, and who are so "sophisticated" they laugh at themselves.

We announce our anxieties about grades or money or whatever—we then explain why the anxieties are silly and talk about how we are "stuck" with them. After this formal announcement we then go about being anxious, unhappy, unpleasant, or the like.

That kind of self-analysis doesn't really do much good. In fact, it is often little more than a self-delusion which we "smart" people do. It works in a wonderful way: as we make fun of ourselves in sophisticated ways (but still act out those myths we are supposed to act out) we just make fools of

---

[6] I am not even strong enough to get into administrators at this point. They, like the rest of us, are a problem.

ourselves. We're simply much less witty and insightful than we think we are.

So we all walk around threatened by one thing or another. We are forced to miss many things—like an education in college—because we fear either looking for the truth or looking at ourselves. Every time we step back, or turn our head, or close our eyes to those things, we have only ourselves to blame.

Being threatened is another way of saying we are afraid, and that is another way of acknowledging the force of the system in which we live. If we can go to school and be scared enough to avoid being educated, what chance do we have when we go outside of college and try to do good?

If· you're scared now, you're on your way to becoming a dynamite citizen.

Politics

But we must understand more than what the Founding Fathers wrote. We must go beyond their words and even our own actions. We must begin to get at what was not said. We must try to figure out what the world of James Madison lacked.

What Madison excluded, what he feared and so eloquently attacked, was politics. Those things shared, the things we have in common, to him were not best served institutionally. The idea of community is not mentioned—only the idea of "interests." If politics were a science, then there could be a fairly accurate definition of those things political. But regrettably for accuracy, politics seems to be beyond the precision of science, and the impurities of language. The best that can be done at this stage is to discuss a few of the concepts involved in politics.[7]

Politics, to overgeneralize, is the activity by which people

---

[7] For various, but obviously related, discussions of politics, one might see Max Weber, "Politics as a Vocation," in Hans Gerth and C. Wright Mills, eds., *From Max Weber* (New York: Oxford University Press, 1958); Hannah Arendt, *The Human Condition* (Garden City, N.Y.: Doubleday & Co., 1959); and Sheldon Wolin, *Politics and Vision* (Boston: Little, Brown and Co., 1960).

live together. It is the process of adjusting aims and activities between you and others: the one and the many. Aristotle believed that it was Society's highest form of activity. It was, he thought (and I believe rightly), through citizenship—through people deciding how to act and then acting that way—that an individual could develop his or her capabilities to the fullest. Through this participation, people helped define themselves.

This definition implies much. It is meant to make politics have something to do with morality. What is implied is that politics means taking a stand, being passionate about something, defining what you believe to be right or wrong, good or bad, and then acting on that belief. It is not an easy kind of activity, especially when one is taught to reject just such propositions. But it seems to me that politics involves the inner tension of trying to figure out—and then doing—good in a world where we do not know what good is and where no choices seem clear-cut.

Politics, then, is something profoundly human, something with its roots in morality and its sources of action in a deeply felt inner tension.

Through political action, the individual becomes responsible. To either destroy or check the power to act is to destroy an individual's capacity to do good. By destroying the personal responsibility for power, one destroys its moral roots. It is precisely this kind of equation that Madison failed to acknowledge. We were denied the possible joys of making joint decisions, yet seem to be responsible for the actions of others. Politics includes the possibility of sharing happiness or unhappiness—but not so the Federalist state.

Finally, there must be some place for politics to take place. Politics needs an arena, a public space. There must be arenas, terms of issues and ideas and even physical space, where citizens can come together and work out courses of action. Space is both psychological and physical. Thus far, our only public space is the ballot box, which is neither public nor really space. There is always the idea of going into the streets, or of sitting in a building, or of bombing monuments. Those are only the choices of how to create space, a problem which is ahead of where we are now. To deny the citizen a public space is to suffocate political activity. That is very close to the precise state of our political life.[8]

But we have a tradition, a view of ourselves that denies us the opportunity to share. Certainly we give something to charity, or buy Girl Scout cookies, or avoid littering. But we do not involve ourselves in those decisions that control our lives. Madison talks about dividing power, pitting it one against the other; he talks about the selfishness of people, pitting them one against the other.

We are structured not for cooperative acts but for private ones; we are given a form of government that calls not for the best in people but only for the minimum in them. What we must realize is that we are living a self-fulfilling prophecy: that by founding a government geared to selfishness, we can maintain it only by being selfish. By participating within the structure, we are acting out Madison's belief that we are unworthy.

To repeat, Madison outlines a life alone; a life of technical skills, of savings bonds, and of mini-vans which carry our hopes for happiness. A common life without community, a public life without politics, and popular decisions without people.

What I am arguing is that our basic view of humanity condemns us to an autistic public life. We are powerless over ourselves. We are mute. We consider ourselves an evil people condemned to a life without trust, without power, without politics.

> I know a place where you can sometimes sing along with yourself . . . "Row, row, row your boat, gently down the stream . . ." —and just when you get to your merrily—merrilies, the echo comes in "Row, row, row . . ." right on cue. But you must be careful in choosing your key or your tempo . . . because an echo is an inflexible and pitiless taskmaster: you sing the echoes away. And even after you have left . . . you cannot help feeling, for a long time after, that any jig you whistle, hymn you hum, or song you sing is somewhere immutably turned to an echo yet unheard, or relentlessly echoing a tune long forgotten. . . .
>
>   KEN KESEY

---

[8] Hannah Arendt, *On Revolution* (New York: Viking Press, 1965), discusses the idea of political space and why it does not exist in the United States.

Politics and Knowledge

"But even worse was the way he talked about science—in which he did not believe . . . . It was a belief, like any other, only worse, stupider than any; the word science was the expression of the silliest realism, which did not blush to take at their face value the more dubious reflections of objects in the human intellect; to pass them current, and to shape out of them the sorriest, most spiritless dogma ever imposed upon humanity. Was not the idea of a material world existing by and for itself the most laughable of all self-contradictions?"

THOMAS MANN

Truth is always in poetic form; not literal but symbolic; hiding or veiled; light in darkness. Yes, mysterious. Literalism is idolatry of words; the alternative to idolatry is mystery. And literalism reifies, makes everything into things, these tables and chairs, commodities. The alternative to reification is mystification.

NORMAN O. BROWN

Knowing and being are opposite, antagonistic states. The more you know, exactly the less you *are*. The more you *are*, in being, the less you know.

D. H. LAWRENCE

Knowing Things

All of us act as if we know things. Moreover, we act as if we know *how* we know things. Every society is built, in great measure, on a method of knowledge gathering, on a way of knowing things. This is normal enough, but what does it mean? How much do we really understand about how we know things, about why a fact is a fact, and why knowledge is knowledge? What if our approach to knowledge is more closing than opening, more confining than freeing—in essence, more mechanical than human? What if our "facts" are unclear, misleading, or false?

In an important way, this chapter is simply an extension of the first. We now know something about Madisonian people, about ourselves. In this chapter, we will consider how we look at the world, what we know, and how we know what we know. To know about knowing is to begin to fill out our knowledge of politics.

The Madisonian person is, in a sophisticated sense, scientific. Put most simply, the link between the two is materialism; the link is an extraordinary reliance on the reality of objective things. We have a notion of what is real, of how to analyze reality, and of what that analysis means. It is that method—science—and its accompanying myths which form the basis of this chapter. It is "evil" people in a scientific, material, objective world who will be our main concern.

In essence, our society's knowledge gathering rests on what has been called (and I believe correctly) the myth of objective consciousness. It is the kind of myth that needs to be looked at in pieces, as well as a whole, to be fully understood. For a start we might say that the myth of objective consciousness assumes that the only "facts" in the world—the only things that are real—are those things that are apart from us. According to this myth, things have a reality if we can perceive them objectively.

A fact is a fact, in and of itself. Without help. A rose is a rose.

All that, simple as it is, sounds reasonable. Certainly it is what we have been taught. Indeed, it sounds so right that we rarely examine the assumptions upon which it rests. We think that all facts are objective things, but we fail to realize that we tie facts with moral codes. We seldom see that the result of our myth of objective consciousness may be trauma-filled. Yet the myth fills our lives in many ways, in many ways we are often unaware of.

The myth makes scientists of us all—we become counters; the more sophisticated of us, statisticians. We add and subtract reality. We use our fingers and toes, calculators and computers, to find facts, facts which become truths. This is our style: precise, calculating, objective.

Certainly, there are those who will object to this whole attack. It would be foolish to deny that this style has led to a great many things. After all, somehow those numbers are able to make airplanes fly and bridges span, and offensive and defensive missiles project. Science does produce a kind of magic; but the problem is more complex than that. To quote Theodore Roszak, "If we believe there is some place to get and if we believe it is important to get there very, very fast —despite the dangers, despite the discomforts, despite expense, despite the smog—then the automobile is an impressive piece of magic." [1]

The tension is obvious enough: Objectiveness is the stuff of science; but is it the stuff of politics?

Science: Real and True and Its Application

Science, in its approach to knowledge, in its gathering of it, and finally in its view of what is real, is little more than a value system of impressive proportions. To get at these values, we

---

[1] Theodore Roszak, *The Making of a Counter Culture* (Garden City, N.Y.: Doubleday & Co., 1969), p. 259. For an interesting work on the nature of scientific discovery, see Thomas Kuhn, *The Structure of Scientific Revolution* (Chicago: University of Chicago Press, 1962).

must get at the elements which make up science. We must study what it studies, approach its approach in a critical way, and try to make a judgment about the reality it produces. We might begin by clarifying objective reality, and then go on to the method of science.

It is important to realize that what is being discussed is not an isolated phenomenon which may or may not be personally interesting to me.[2] Again to quote Theodore Roszak: "Objectivity as a state of being fills the very air we breathe in a scientific culture; it grips us subliminally in all we say, feel and do. The mentality of the ideal scientist becomes the very soul of society." He continues to say that the stuff of this soul is objectivity and that the belief in objectivity becomes myth:

> The myth of objective consciousness is to cultivate a state of consciousness cleansed of all physical distortion, all personal involvement. What flows from this state of consciousness qualifies as knowledge, and nothing else does . . . . [Scientific knowledge] is a verifiable description of reality that exists independent of any purely personal considerations. It is true . . . real . . . dependable. . . . It works.[3]

It is real. Better yet, it is concrete. Yes, science is just what we can believe in because it deals with the real world, and if there is one thing we have learned to agree on, it is the real world. Of course, that is part of the myth—that we *think* we know what the real world is. Let us not accept that we know what the real world is, let us not accept the definitions that underlie science. It seems reasonable to begin to understand the myth of objective consciousness by trying to understand the term "real." [4]

What I would like to argue is that it is no easy thing to

---

[2] For example, see Floyd Matson, *The Broken Image* (Garden City, N.Y.: Doubleday & Co., 1966), or Abraham Maslow, *The Psychology of Science* (New York: Harper & Row, 1966).

[3] Roszak, *The Making of a Counter Culture,* pp. 208, 216. To skip ahead a bit, objective consciousness is the consciousness of the corporate liberalism of the Pentagon.

[4] This is taken, in large part, from J. Peter Euban, "Political Science and Political Science," in Philip Green and Sanford Levinson, eds., *Power and Community* (New York: Vintage Books, 1970), pp. 3–59.

know what is "real." To say that what one sits on is a real chair does not tell us quite enough. Are other kinds of chairs "real," or are they false? If we worked at the silly example of the chairs long enough, we might get to the point of knowing exactly what was included in, and *excluded from,* the phrase "real chair."

When we go from chairs to the "real world," everything gets more complicated. Maybe the "real world" consists of only those things that one can see, touch, or count. If that is so, and scientists as well as most social scientists would have us believe that, then we should know something about that reality.

To believe solely in the scientism of our time is to believe in a fairly static and, to me, fairly boring, state of affairs. To begin with, the bias is clear: If the scientist studies the "real world," then presumably the rest of us study the "false world." They have hard "facts," we soft; indeed, they have facts, we only values. The scientific method, as we all know, insists that all of its experiments be repeatable and that all of its hypotheses be verifiable.

Think about a world in which everything that is true (could there be a "true fact") must be able to happen again and again and again. If that is what "true" is, and if it comes from things that are real, then "real" is nothing more than what we already have. To put it differently, to accept the scientist's vision of reality is to accept a world in which change is neither probable nor perhaps even possible, and is certainly not desirable.[5]

Part of what I would like to argue is that politics is an art, a practice, a part of life that is beyond the validations of the scientific method. Maybe an example will help make my case more clear. Scientists build reality carefully, finding those "facts" in the "real world" that are "true" and making them into hypotheses that are potentially verifiable. Simple enough —just find enough truths, find enough facts, and one can build a real world.

Several years ago, someone studied how people voted in

---

[5] Thomas Kuhn, in *The Structure of Scientific Revolution,* discusses what changes in views have occurred and how they can happen.

Congress.[6] What he wanted to do was to build a model which would predict how each legislator would vote. The work was impressive, sophisticated science. There were numerous tables and charts and models of the most advanced type. Correlations were made and statistically things were at an important level of significance. With all this work, the author was correctly able to predict how each member would vote 87 percent of the time. Pretty impressive—87 percent.

Of course, an 87 percent correct prediction rate is not all that impressive. As an unsophisticated (methodologically, that is) student, you could predict outcomes almost that well. By knowing whether a legislator was a Democrat or a Republican, you could accurately predict his or her vote 84 percent of the time. The point is simple enough. The politics of the Congress takes place in that 13 percent of the vote which cannot be predicted. Most of the really interesting votes concern precisely those issues which are in doubt, those issues on which Republican and Democrats do not vote a straight party line.

In part, I am suggesting that to be successful in science, one must necessarily be limited to very ordinary, repeatable events. To have a social science is to think in rather limited, sometimes unimaginative ways. To use the words science would imply for us, maybe we should consider more carefully the "unreal world."

A Warning and a Suggestion

Before the attack on science continues, a couple of things should be made clear. First, just because a person is a scientist, or a social scientist, there is no obvious reason to believe that he or she is a conservative son-of-a-bitch who is hopelessly involved in wasted effort and useless endeavors. That would be foolish. All I am trying to argue is that the world in general, and politics in particular, is much more complicated and involved than science is able to comprehend. Second, I

---

[6] The following figures are suggestive of a very complex model found in Michael J. Shapiro, "The House and the Federal Role: A Computer Simulation of Roll-Call Voting," in *The American Political Science Review*, 62 (1968): 494–518.

am *not* suggesting that we, personally, are the source of everything; or, more precisely, that what each of us thinks is right, or that what we say is accurate, nor even that what we do is *not* good simply because *we* think, say, or do it. To ignore science entirely would be about as bright as to accept it entirely. Enough warning.

What I would like to suggest now, and to explore later, is the idea that the distinction between objective and subjective reality may not make sense.[7] Indeed, one does not make sense without the other. A more reasonable formulation of the world might be this: The interaction between our conscious selves and the world—the relationship between the objective and the subjective—makes what we know as reality. This view implies that science and objectification are simply less significant, less accurate ways of dealing with the world than is the more unconventional, and yet well explored phenomenological view.

Science: Compartmentalization, Objectification, and "Political" Style

We are problem solvers, we Americans. We think about something, analyze it, and then do it. We think of all the different ways we can do it, but we rarely consider the reasons for what we do. Values? Ethics? We God-fearing citizens get these every Sunday. But we practical people are mostly "manual" oriented: how to fix our own VW, how to make a killing in the stock market, how to have sex. What I want to suggest is that this emphasis on technique is a natural by-product of the emphasis that science places on method; moreover, that somehow we get divided—method from feeling, parts from the whole. To describe the techniques of science may help clarify the point.[8]

To begin with, we are taught that everything is a problem

---

[7] This approach is called phenomenology, and was first explored by Edmund Husserl around the turn of the century. It was furthered by his student, Martin Heidegger. Phenomenology is extraordinarily difficult to read, but there are explanations of it which do make sense. For example, one might read the introduction to William Barrett and Henry Aiken, eds., *Philosophy in the Twentieth Century*, vol. 3 (New York: Random House, 1962).

[8] Kenneth Keniston, *The Uncommitted* (New York: Dell Publishing Co., 1965), p. 254.

(therefore solvable) and that each problem is to be analyzed. So we do. We analyze. We take our lives or our problems or our relationships and break them down into manageable parts. We seek units of analysis. We make components; we compartmentalize. We ignore the whole. We dissect; we cut up; we make small.

What happens is clear. We have the impulse to *reduce* complex things to simple ones. Science urges us to devalue the rich —which we find difficult to understand—so that we can get to the common—which we might easily understand. We sacrifice the unique. To quote Kenneth Keniston: "Theories of learning frequently proclaim that human learning is essentially no different from animal learning—that Michelangelo in his studio is to the cheese-seeking rat merely as the large computer is to the small." [9] We are intellectual dis-integrators. For the most part, we perceive only pieces of problems.

The obvious way to go about problem-solving is by counting and comparing. We measure, we total, we add up the sum. Then we can *compare reality* and see *which* is the most, *which* is the best. Quality is too difficult to measure, or to compare; but horsepower, income, and grade averages are not.

And all the adding depends upon what one thinks reality is. To count depends upon those things that are external, that are objective. It is firmly rooted in the metaphysic that individuals must always turn outward, never inward. Insight is worth nothing if it cannot be made tangible. Science shuns the invisible: magic, art, religion, love. By doing so, we split our knowing from our being, our knowledge from ourselves. To do that enough is to be crazy. People who are able to divide themselves well are often considered successful; people who do not do it well are diagnosed clinically as schizophrenics.

"Crazy" is a later topic. For now, I would like to argue that this gathering, quantifying myth of objective consciousness gives us an odd perception of anything public, of anything that should be political. We have a public style of numbers. A politics of volume. For example, each week we were given the number of people killed in Vietnam. Body counts, they are called. It is instructive to think about what they mean.

---

[9] Ibid., p. 256.

To look back on that war is not very happy. While the obvious lessons of what war does have been repeated and repeated, it seems important to look at *how* we learned about what was going on. Where one starts helps explain just where one can expect to go.

With each fact, there is an implied value. As Americans were reported to have killed more Vietnamese than Vietnamese killed Americans, we were led to believe at least three things: 1) God was on our side; 2) we were better fighters than they; and 3) we were winning the war. However, this turns out not to be the case. All we know for certain is that these figures— these objective "facts" of the war—cannot be trusted, that they do not tell the whole story, and that they are absolutely incapable of conveying what is really happening. By objectifying reality, an effort is made to reduce war and killing to numbers and to measure success in columns. Surely insane. But we kept getting facts—real facts from the real world—and were led to believe that there were related values.

Back to war, this time to the massacre at My Lai. After a time, it appeared obvious that Americans really had shot innocent people, in fact, a whole village of them. But the U.S. Army (after trying to suppress the information on My Lai for a year and a half) informed the public that the Viet Cong had killed *three times* that number of civilians during the Tet offensive. The intent of the fact was obvious, the moral clear. The Army intended to show that the Viet Cong were three times as bad and guilty as we were, and it had the facts to prove it. Somehow our numbers were more impressive than theirs, so we must have been right.

All this, of course, sounds foolish. We know that the examples are a bit overdrawn, and are probably wrong—somehow. It is offensive to think that we can be given a list of numbers and then expected to find meaning and social value in them. Upon reflection, it is an outrage to believe that those numbers represent anything meaningful, except perhaps to an individual who is insecure personally and must relate impersonally; who is less interested in understanding the "why" of values than in being almost wholly dependent upon material worth.

The point is *not* that facts should not be used as ingredients in any moral argument. Facts and values are dependent upon one another. Each helps to inform and define the other. The point is *which* "facts" we look at, study, and are given, and *what* we imply from them. The point is that for us—Madisonian people in a scientific, objective world—more is better than less and that we regularly make qualitative judgments from quantity.[10]

The sad truth seems to be that the example offers a fairly clear vision of the world we inhabit and provides insight into the way we view reality. The scientist is closer to truth than the magician—at least, that is what we are taught to believe. But we must question our knowledge.

Is it possible that there is a kind of knowledge which is not objective, but which is nevertheless real? Must we measure everything—ourselves and our environment—in material terms? Can there be a better kind of politics that is related to a different kind of knowledge? Can there be an "us" which responds to a less gross ethic? What are the kinds of questions we can ask that will lead us to a different, and maybe better, set of answers?

Something Else

I suppose it is tempting, if the only tool you have is a hammer, to treat everything as if it were a nail.

                                                    ABRAHAM MASLOW

In a simplified way, I have argued that objects are facts, that lots of facts seem to imply value, and that these values appear to indicate moral worth. The conclusion, stated just as simply, is that there is a kind of insanity in that view. It seems to me that we must begin to understand ourselves as makers of both fact and knowledge, as makers of both value and morality. To make the world more understandable, indeed to recapture some personal power and meaning, we must think in terms that supersede the coldness of rationality and the sterility of science. It is necessary to go back and seek an explanation.

At the base of every social system—and ours is no exception

---

[10] For a full description of the psychological process involved, see Murray Edelman, *Symbolic Uses of Politics* (Champaign-Urbana, Ill.: University of Illinois Press, 1964).

—there is a series of rules which most people follow. Many of the rules are not obvious, but nonetheless they are remarkably binding. For example, most of us either do not know why we are in college or are here just because it seemed the thing to do. Either our parents wanted us to go or all our friends were doing it. More self-consciously, we are here to find a wife or a husband or so that we can land a better job.

In all these cases, we are getting ready to fit into the system. We are following its laws, obeying its rules. But what if our arguments have been correct, what if these laws are based on a reality that really is not human? It is unpleasant to think that the system is based on a kind of magic which can produce cars more easily than it can handle human cares; which spends more on bombs than little babies; and which is tuned more to the values of science than to the good of humanity. The argument, so far, has led us to the point of generalizing that to have a basic view of the world as being only objective can produce the kinds of rules and laws which function not to help a person grow, but only to produce more material reality.

Our politics are as sterile as our reasons for being in college or our experiences in high school or—in all too many cases—our own lives.

There are thinkers who believe that knowledge is the result of more than objective reality, more than those things we can touch. They argue that knowledge is the result of the interaction between the object and the individual; a kind of mingling of the "what is" with the "what might be"; the personal and the impersonal; the I and the thou. Let us begin with two individuals who meet and talk. They are strangers who view each other with what we know as typical insecurity and fear—two Madisonian people in our modern world. Each views himself or herself as "I" and the other person as an "it." There is no real exchange of anything between them. Each has his or her own little social act, own game to put on the other. Both become dehumanized, both objects. People become things; politics becomes impersonal and impossible.

What seems necessary is to begin again. Objective reality is not the only place to begin and science—when you get right down to it—is science. Just as there is knowing and knowing, so there is science and science.

What our sciences have to teach is truly amazing. Part of what is truly amazing is that it doesn't teach us what we generally expect it to.

Just see.

Science and Science

Now it's time to further an understanding of nature's order by re-assimilating those passions which were originally fled from. The passions, the emotions, the affective domain of man's consciousness, are a part of nature's order too. The central part.

ROBERT PIRSIG

One of the critical political tasks ahead of us is to understand that life is at least as strange as science fiction, if we do it (life) the right way, maybe even stranger. Before you argue that I have misunderstood, that "strangeness" not only does not seem a critical task but certainly *is not* a critical political task, let me try to explain myself.

Science fiction and similar kinds of fantasy can be interesting and instructive and even good escape. There are lessons to be learned from "Star Trek," and *Dune,* and what passes for the future on TV and in the movies. But an amazing amount of "science" "fiction" is pretty light-weight stuff. Fun for sure, and certainly a way to play, but it is generally just a logical extension of what we have and know.

Science fiction *is* instructive for showing ourselves as we are. It often looks strange because, if you happen to be in the mood to see it, much of what we do *is* strange. We worship gods and machines and things; we kill others and our earth and ourselves; we do marvelous and wonderous things for no reason beyond the fact they are right. In the end, it all makes only a very limited amount of sense—at best—and our science fiction really doesn't do much to help us. It's a lot like angel food cake: I never pass it up—it's good and light and fluffy, but all I get is a good taste in my mouth and a pimple or two.

What I want to argue is that it makes sense to understand the world in a way and do life in a manner that puts the particular "fantasy" of science fiction in the limited box where it belongs.

It seems necessary to take seriously the multiplicity of meanings of any event or of "facts." We are faced with a curious situation in the twentieth century. It is our legacy, in part, to be emotional heirs of a kind of despair and ultimate meaninglessness which has been powerfully argued for the last hundred years or so. Until that time, there were the twin assurednesses of religion and science. Philosophers took on religion and, in many important ways, seemed to have won. We know that by the turn of the century, scientists had begun to make the theoretical breakthroughs which forever removed science from the realm of Truth with a capital T, and removed it from Certainty.

With Einstein's theory of relativity, you literally had to triangulate your position in the universe just to know where to hang your hat.

It is a misleading and a cheap shot to say that because there is no certainty, then everything is relative. In a technical sense, that may be a fact—but that does not necessarily make it true for us. There are categories, concepts, and human convictions which do not easily fit into the casual name-calling style of being "relative."

Multiple meanings mean multiple meanings. The trick is that each of us—at some pre-conscious, inarticulable place—has a sense of the rightfittingness of the world.

To know about knowing is to begin to know why we see what we do, why we ask the questions we do, why we may be "right" and why those who disagree with us may also be "right." We must both look and act as well as look at looking. Things must mean *and* mean.

Let me try to sort that out.

False Stuff, If Wholly Believed

Between cockroach and codfish there were only structured differences—their substance was the same and *this substance itself* was a lie.

He saw the entire Universe wheeling, made of a fine shimmering pattern, a lie of such grand and incredible artistry his own vain dream of political empire collapsed—the White House was a doll house played in by childish fibbers. He left the University that morning, disappearing without forwarding address, becoming a nameless wanderer.

WILLIAM KOTZWINKLE

The effort of this section is not to say all science is wrong. (In "correct" writing, I'm told no one should begin a paragraph *that* defensively. The truth is, I simply don't want people to misunderstand that point.) What I want to argue is that there is an amazing amount of stuff which science either cannot deal with, or which science mishandles, or which science ignores, or which science tries to destroy. If possible, I would like to begin to work us out of the binding myths of science. That work will include some stuff which will make something between limited and no sense to you.

That's all right. Work at it, think hard about it, but relax. None of us, after all, really understands.

This is the order to what follows. We will consider science, our heads, what things might just possibly be, and some of the implications of change. Put differently, fiction is stranger than life—but not very often.

It makes sense to go about knowing in several different ways. Since I'm convinced and will argue that there are intensely individual aspects to how we see the world, it would be foolish to believe one argument would satisfy all folks. One could say, quite rightly, that if there is a "system" in our country, at its base it is a *system of thought.* The genius for politics —or the villainy of it—is located, at first, in our heads. It is how we see and structure our world. Our system of thought may well be our first unnatural act.

That is one way to begin our argument. Better, we could begin with a man described by his biographer as possessing "authentic magic," we could start with Albert Einstein. Read this: ". . . Einstein's physical intuition, though not infallible, had certainly stood him in good stead. *All science is based on faith.* The many strange developments that we have already seen . . . should have convinced us by now that great science is not built on cold logic." [11]

As we have seen, our science wants us to believe in a predictable universe. Not only is that bad life, it is even wrong science. The logic of the argument about how to get from predictability to chaos is fun; it is also useful to know.

---

[11] Banesh Hoffmann, *Albert Einstein: Creator and Rebel* (New York: The Viking Press, 1972), p. 193.

The classic function of science is to "discover" those few elementary laws from which the universe may be built up by pure deduction.[12] This, as we know, comes from the careful following of the scientific method. The method, in shortened form, is (1) stating a problem, (2) stating a hypothesis to explain the problem, (3) designing tests for the hypothesis, (4) predicting the results of each test, (5) conducting the tests and observing the results and, finally, (6) making conclusions from the results.

Fair enough. We are taught to believe that if the same results occur each time a particular test is given, it may be a "law."

In repeatability we trust.

What we are not taught are all of the problems with this method, or with the method's relationship to the truth. Einstein: "Evolution has shown that at any given moment out of all conceivable constructions a single one has always proved itself absolutely superior to the rest."[13] Let's accept that, and then look at what we have just accepted. In essence, we are accepting the idea that truth, in part, is a function of time.

No pretense about it. Something is true, in measure, because we are *who* we are, and live *where* we live, and exist *when* we exist. Those are odd kinds of criteria for truth.

But there's more. The scientific method is great, in those physical things to which it can be applied, only *after* the problem has been stated *and* the hypotheses have been formulated. The part we never seem to remember is that there are an infinite number of hypotheses for any given phenomenon. The whole basis of the scientific method rests on our own imaginations. We make up problems and tests and truths; we base our science on our myths.

Listen to Einstein: ". . . the concepts and fundamental principles that underlie [theoretical physics] are free inventions of the human intellect, [and they] form the essential part of a

---

[12] As an aside, the Greeks invented classical reason, but they knew some of the limits of its usefulness. For example, they listened to the wind and predicted the future from that. The way most life is, that is as reasonable a way as any. See Robert Pirsig, *Zen and the Art of Motorcycle Maintenance: An Inquiry into Values* (New York: William Morrow & Co., Inc., 1974), p. 171.
[13] Pirsig, *Zen and Motorcycle Maintenance,* p. 115.

theory, which reason cannot touch." [14] When we get to the nub of the most central of our sciences—theoretical physics— we see a group of people who believe in something more basic than logic, who often think in terms of beautiful pictures and of how they believe the physical world *may be*.[15]

The heart of science is not Reality, but one or another Myth.

We may do the argument another way. Even if you don't know or understand the details, you probably know that there is Euclidian and non-Euclidian geometry. For that matter, there are several of the non-Euclidian kind. What is interesting (are you listening hard-core-science-types, you left-over believers in the absoluteness of science?) is that these geometries contradict each other.

All of them, as it turns out, are "right," but some just happen to be more convenient than others. To quote: "Geometry is not true, it is advantageous." [16] That, at one level, is just outrageous. With little trouble, we can get to the same outrageous point with math as we did with the concepts of physics the math is used to "prove." Mathematical solutions have a harmony, a beauty, an elegance to them, and are often chosen for those reasons. It seems that our most hard core, hard science, high-powered magicians are not seekers of truth, but of beauty.[17]

What is astounding is that we keep the myth of scientifically verifiable truth. The system in our head is systematically wrongheaded.

If one pushes science, if one sees the way hypotheses multiply until there are too many to keep track of and too many to test, if one sees that scientific "truth" keeps changing at an increasing rate, and that the half-life of truth keeps getting shorter and shorter, or if one sees that underlying the basic principles of science are people's senses of beauty, one can come very close to seeing the obvious: the most impressive product of modern science is anti-science.

---

14 Hoffman, *Albert Einstein,* p. 170.
15 In 1916, a distinguished astronomer reported on Einstein's general theory of relativity. In part, he wrote, "Whether the theory ultimately proves to be correct or not, it claims attention as being one of the most beautiful examples of the power of general mathematical reasoning." Ibid., p. 129.
16 Pirsig, *Zen and Motorcycle Maintenance,* p. 264.
17 I think I like them better for that.

By understanding the work of our science, we can understand our world as chaos.

Real Stuff

William James tells us that the world "is a turbid, muddled, gothic sort of affair, without a sweeping outline and with little pictorial nobility."

Terrific. Start with knowing about knowing and end up with the idea of chaos. You want facts and you get beauty.

Think of it this way: When working out how you know what you know, and reality, there may be no simple answers. Equally possible, there may be no complex answers. There are ways to get into all of that, and what seems necessary is to sketch at least one way *other than* science.

Let me be specific about a thing or two: I am not suggesting that theoretical physics be our model for politics. All I want to argue is that if we are really hung up on the Truth of our science, we may as well admit to ourselves that some time ago science admitted its fundamental relationship to magic. Equally important, human lives and events are much more complex than "physical" events. Trying to live a day, much less a lifetime, with some meaning and social "goodness" makes discovering elementary particles of the universe seem like a piece of cake.

To get on with the topic, we will take up just where we find ourselves, what that might mean (or *not* mean, in this case), and how we can begin thinking about it.

We live in a world which quite literally never stops. While myths and often social institutions stay fixed for limited times, our world just keeps changing. Reality, in part, consists of all of the "facts" of our existence, *plus* relationships, functions, motives, ideologies, and the like.[18] Reality, to put it a little dif-

---

[18] To quote William James, "Life is in the transitions as much as in the terms connected; often, indeed, it seems to be there more emphatically, as if our spurts and sallies forward were the real firing line of the battle, were like the thin line of flame advancing across the dry autumnal field . . . Mainly . . . we live on speculative investments, or on our prospects only." *Essays in Radical Empiricism and a Pluralistic Universe* (New York: E. P. Dutton, 1971), pp. 46–47.

ferently, simply keeps becoming. Jean Paul Sartre writes: "For us, truth is something which becomes, it *has* and *will have* become. It is a totalization which is forever being totalized."[19]

We are what we were and what we will be in situations which will not stay set. As we will see, we became creators and definers in the context of our times and our surroundings.

The world in which we find ourselves—and now I'm talking about the physical world, the one science "deals" with—may well be, in its essence, just stuff. Basic, primal stuff. No few basic particles from which to create or recreate the world. Stuff. The stuff in our head is the same as the stuff of a desk, a car, or a flower.

Our universe, if we care to look deeply enough, is fundamentally chaos. The argument goes further. Each of us begins from that general chaos; we sort things out and make distinctions which help make sense of the world and which allow us to have some communications with those around us. We try to understand—more to the point, often we invent—the world around us. We often do well at it, but we fool ourselves if we believe we tap into anything more ultimate than our own myths—our own ghosts, as Robert Pirsig would say.

Part of what I want to warn about is that we should be careful of what we take as "given." For example, we know that there are many people in the world who really do see ghosts of one kind or another: old friends, dead relatives, supreme spirits. We have just a terrible time seeing those ghosts. But, fear not, we have our own ghosts. We can, for example, "see" the law of gravity, which is a ghost many others simply cannot envision. In any lived day one ghost is no more real (or false) than the other. After all, when we finally admit it, the world is relative and we really don't even know which way is up.[20]

Here we sit, in the midst of chaos, ultimately understanding that even the "basic" split between the objective and the subjective is a distinction we make. Please don't misread that. It was written to say that, originally, everything simply *is*, and we

---

[19] Jean Paul Sartre, *Search for a Method* (New York: Random House, 1968), p. 30.
[20] It makes sense to try and imagine a good, scientific "law." So far, I've come this close: What goes up must come down, most of the time, if we just knew which way was up. I'm attracted to the law for its preciseness.

continually add meaning to it. That does *not* mean everything is subjective or objective, but rather, just is.

And each day, each instant, we are confronted with objects and actions and events. Confronted with much more than we can deal with or sort out or make sense of. Much passes us by —or, we pass by much—because our world is cluttered and chaotic. We memorize whole lists of things (a pen is a pen, a desk is a desk) which helps us in the world a great deal. However, we are left with two critical points: What we do choose to consider, and how we put it together.

In the messy world, we are constantly experiencing and that experience immediately becomes a part of our past. From that past, we choose to recall parts, grant meaning to those parts because we pay attention to them, and we give them added meaning by thinking about them the way we choose to.

Nothing—no part of our experience—has self-evident meaning.[21] Once we are conscious of something, we add meaning to it. Not only that, we *get* those meanings from our surroundings. The myths of our society, the values of our parents and peers, the kind of day we're having, all contribute to how we make sense and meaning of the events around us. We make meaning *within* in the context of meaning; we make history *within* history.

That is half of it, the choosing-of-the-events half. The other half has to do with how those events are arranged in our heads. There are scientists (maybe they are really pseudo-scientists) who would have the inside of our heads look something like a great pyramid—things (blocks) arranged neatly, in a hierarchy, in a way that reflects the way *they* arrange the world on paper.

Life, and learning, for those scientists, is a matter of stacking up reality in a prescribed order. I suspect when some people speak of the building blocks of knowledge they aren't speaking figuratively at all.

A way to think of the world which seems more useful—even more accurate—is to envision the arrangement of the events of our lives as a mosaic, not a pyramid. Each of those events, those happenings, those striking elements finds a place in our

---

[21] For much of this, see William James, *Essays in Radical Empiricism.*

mosaic; each finds a place in our understanding of the arrangement of the world.

But the events, the tiles, of our mosaic are just part of our reality. Equally important is the glue which holds the tiles together; the relationships which place events in order in our heads.[22]

In important ways the key is in those relationships—in that glue. Much of how we do our arranging has to do with what we are taught both to see and to value. The more rigid we are about our reality, the more fixed the relationships, the less likely we are to change, to rearrange. We all know someone—a friend or relative or teacher—who just cannot "see" something very obvious to us.

In politics (more accurately, in our "public" affairs) we run into that non-seeing, that "blindness," all the time. People who have bought into the myths so deeply, who have set their mosaic so firmly, that change for them seems out of the question. Later, there will be a chapter on voting. It is, in a way, a tile in *your* mosaic. My guess is that it is a tile well set, and that whatever age you happen to be, you will resist rearranging your mosaic *even* if you agree with what I say.

If we arranged chaos in a pyramid based on *firm scientific data,* then change would really be incredibly difficult. We would probably have to replace one huge edifice with another. No wonder that damned hierarchy is so tough to get rid of; not only is it taught to us as Truth, it is taught in a way that makes it replaceable only with another Whole System. That, in short, is bunk.

In a mosaic, change is still difficult but certainly possible. With it, we can rearrange, "see," play a little with the facts of our life. I am not saying that fundamental change (whatever that means) is an easy thing, but it is possible.

Our—or any—culture constantly provides patterns of commonly held relationships. We just know what is expected of

---

[22] The eloquence of Einstein: "I am grateful to destiny for having made life an exciting experience so that life has *appeared* meaningful." (emphasis added); or, "Approached rationally that fear [of death] is the most unjustified of all fears, for there is no risk of any accidents to one who is dead or not yet born. In short, the fear is stupid but it cannot be helped." Hoffman, *Albert Einstein,* p. 261.

us, either in a classroom or drinking beer or being in a serious discussion. From the pattern of our speech to the pattern of our political and economic system, we are silently (and sometimes not so silently) given directions on how to put our act together in fairly particular ways. We are told of the "proper" relationships of events.

The world is chaos and we're forced to make meaning out of it. But it's more complicated than that. We want to be members of society, and society tells us how to order that chaos while being chaotic itself. How do we live in a way that satisfies both ourselves and our society and still remember the chaos?

We must continually consider a world of multiple truths and realities, and on-going social-political-economic truths and realities, all of which help us form powerful and inter-related facts. To keep the tension and chaos close at all times is tough, but really necessary.

All of that, it seems to me, provides the conditions of optimism.

It seems about time we do a little "politics." We can do it in laundry list fashion. If some of the tasks of politics are 1) living together in a way in which important decisions are decided in a collective way, 2) in which each of us has both responsibility and power when it comes to actions we each take, 3) in which dignity and justice and excellence are alive with meaning for decisions made—if those are some of the tasks, then it seems fairly obvious we have to rearrange the way we know the world.

Since our world is not set, does not rest on any ultimates, does not rely upon scientific methods to be verifiable—since our world is in constant motion and is given shape by each of us individually as well as collectively—then our job is nothing short of this: We must re-form and re-inform ourselves, and then work to have our society reflect that re-formation.

All of that doing and re-doing is political. It is, in its essence, the basis of politics.

I am convinced that each of us has a sense of how the world fits together in a good—and beautiful—way. That sense, or picture, or whatever, should be the touchstone of our mosaic.

There is no reason to believe that each of us will share the same sense of the rightfittingness of the world. Not only that, there *is* reason to believe that these differences will not be simply of taste or beauty, but will extend from our moral values to how we wish to arrange ourselves organizationally, to what we understand as politics.

As the monolith of our scientifically socialized heads and then society begins to break up, we should look forward to an America of united states or cities or towns or neighborhoods or blocks. A place where we can begin with our own self-conception of the way the world looks best; a place to join like-others to create an environment in which that sense can be worked out; in which we have a duty to be our best selves because the whole community will depend on it.

If we are creatures of myth, it makes sense to take it seriously and choose to live with the myths of our choice.

One could, I suppose, imagine whole groups of people who choose to think of themselves and others as evil, who will base their reality on the science of a hundred years ago, and who will wholly believe in the myth of objective consciousness.

How weird.

Politics and Knowledge: A Tie

Classically, one is supposed to state what is about to be said, then say it, then tell what has just been said. In a funny way, that is what I'm about to do. Let me repeat in different words and a little more to the point.

In order to challenge the amazing accumulation of facts lying between us and significance—the world of body counts and grade points—we must know ourselves and our actions well enough to teach and learn from others. An I-thou relationship is, in many ways, revolutionary politics.[23]

---

[23] There are certain things I am fairly clear about. For example, I believe consciousness-raising is one of the more pompous, elitist, arrogant concepts around. Either you *are* conscious (I think that includes *all* of us) or you're not. People are conscious of different things, and we can fight about what's best . . . what our choice happens to be. But *levels* of consciousness builds in an amazing bias which translates out—more often than not—White Middle Class Vision Is Best.

It may be best for the white middle class, but fairly silly (or much worse) when given the weight of some incredible psychological law.

The burden of the argument is clear: How one understands knowledge and how one does politics is interrelated. If by knowledge we mean only those things which are objective, then we may never have politics—but only an *elite* of science, a mythology of numbers. We will be organized as a bureaucracy and each of us will be reduced to a statistic of the state. Ours will be a well-ordered, rational world where rules replace revelation.

But knowledge is neither entirely objective nor rational. We must insist that those who lead share their knowledge with us; moreover, that those who lead follow us as we share our knowledge with them. One task of political science is to make clear as many different ways of living as possible. To do this, there must be a whole new series of questions we might ask. We must understand our present as well as our potentials. Henry Kariel has written that by "postulating functions which have the effect of shifting our perspectives, we expose previously unseen institutional forms. We perceive a new reality— lives *not* lived (or not lived decently) because of decisions not made. When the empty space in which potentialities might have been realized is bared, we become aware of our losses."

> Weakness is true and real . . . faking only proves weakness is real, or you wouldn't be so weak as to fake it. No you can't fake being weak. You can only fake being strong.
>
> KEN KESEY

Politics as Rules: The Enemy as Organization

3

As he struggles in this jungle, every position he's in, he's terribly lonely. He can't confide and talk with the guy working under him. He can't confide and talk to the man he's working for. To give vent to his feelings, his fears and his insecurities, he'd expose himself. This goes all the way up the line until he gets to be president. The president really doesn't have anybody to talk to, because the vice presidents are waiting for him to die or make a mistake and get knocked off so they can get his job. . . .

The executive is a lonely animal in the jungle who doesn't have a friend. Business is related to life. I think in our everyday living we're lonely. I have only a wife to talk to, but beyond that . . . When I talked business to her, I don't know whether she understood me. But that was unimportant. What's important is that I was able to talk out loud and hear myself—which is the function I serve as a consultant. . . .

I have a goal. I want to end my life in a home for the aged that's run by the state—organizing people to fight 'em because they're not running it right. (Laughs.)

STUDS TERKEL

Robots have no future. They merely have a past that has not yet occurred.

ROBERT BOGUSLAW

If how we think of the nature of people means something to politics and to our personal lives, and if how we view the world and knowledge means something, then it seems pretty obvious that the way we organize is also important. The way we organize ourselves and the accompanying ways those organizations dominate our behavior are the concerns of this chapter.

One way to begin to understand the effects of organizations, to understand their ideology, is to look at a concern central to political science: power. One of the debates of scholars of American politics is who has power; Who Rules? Do The People Rule, or An Elite, or Elites? The optimists say "The People" rule, the pessimists, "The Elite." Personally, I think either position may well be optimistic. If someone is in charge, if someone has power, if someone has control, then that someone can be changed. To believe that one or a few or many have power is to have faith that human beings are making decisions about the future. That is optimistic.

What if, ultimately, nobody is in charge?

The whole idea that no one is in charge, that we have a tyranny without a tyrant, is an unhappy one.[1] It is an idea tied directly to large organizations and how they work. To begin to understand how large organizations operate, to understand the rules by which they operate and the rules they impose on our world, is to begin to recognize that a large organization is greater than the sum of its human members.[2]

There is a tendency, a very natural one, to believe that because people work in organizations, organizations are simply the reflection of all those people. Such a tendency ignores the point of this chapter: that a large organization may easily set

---

[1] For an excellent discussion of this, see Hannah Arendt, *On Violence* (New York: Harcourt, Brace & World, Inc., 1969).

[2] Probably the most clearly spelled out statement of why organizations act as they do is to be found in James Thompson, *Organizations in Action* (New York: McGraw-Hill, 1967).

the rules for our society, and those rules will be geared towards organizational—not human—ends. That may be a description of our reality. To understand what it means to be involved in this kind of reality, this kind of societal/governmental machinery, is to understand what it means to be little more than a small cog in an impersonal machine—a cog that is interchangeable with other cogs, one that wears out and is replaced with no loss to the machine.

Before describing and analyzing large organizations, it might be useful to make this point: To understand what is going on, we cannot ignore the study of large organizations; they exist, they are "real," and they seem unwilling to go away.

Organizations as a Historical "Fact"

It is my intention to argue that many problems facing us today are related to the size and workings of complex organizations. Right now, all I want to show is that to look at history and the dynamics of organizations is to understand that these problems will increase with time.[3]

It is not news to be told that from the middle of the last century to now, organizations in America have gotten bigger and more complex. Indeed, bigger and more seem the dominant organization themes: *Bigger:* According to one investigator, "The American Telephone and Telegraph Company controlled 'more wealth than is contained within the borders of twenty-one of the states.' " [4] *More:* "The A & P chain, which had some 5,000 stores in 1922, had added 12,500 more by 1928." [5] *Bigger and more:* In 1903, when Ford Motor Company produced its first car, it had 125 people employed, and authorized capital of $150,000. It took Ford six months to conceive and produce the first automobiles. In 1964, when the Mustang was introduced, after three and one-half years preparation, Ford had assets of $6 billion, employed 317,000 people, spent $9

---

[3] This discussion draws heavily on Robert Presthus, *The Organizational Society* (New York: Vintage Books, 1962).
[4] Ibid., p. 71.
[5] Ibid., p. 72.

million on "Engineering and Styling" costs, and $50 million on tooling costs for the new car.[6]

The history of growth—of industrial consolidation and mergers—means that we are all becoming more involved in big organizations and bureaucratic conditions. The facts are these: Large organizations are more likely to survive than smaller ones, and people are now likely to be employees, not their own bosses. To quote Robert Presthus: "Huge capital resources, experience, and good will enable established firms to survive. Failure rates support this interpretation, showing that small firms have a very high failure rate, while big enterprises rarely fail. In time such a pattern probably increases concentration."[7]

This means, in part, that we are all a part of it; ours is an organizational environment.

Eighty-five percent of us are directly involved in the organizational apparatus and are susceptible to an organizational ideology. It is an ideology of impersonality, rules, interchangeability, and productivity. The history of organizational growth seems to indicate the following: *What we have Now is an extension of What Was; what Will Be will be a bigger and more Now.*

We must begin at the beginning and try to understand what bureaucracies and large organizations can do and might do.

Bureaucracy

There was only one catch and that was Catch-22, which specifies that a concern for one's own safety in the face of dangers that were real and immediate was the process of a rational mind. Orr was crazy and could be grounded. All that he had to do was ask; and as soon as he did, he would no longer be crazy and would have to fly more missions. Orr would be crazy to fly more missions and sane if he didn't, but if he was sane he had to fly them. If he flew them he was crazy and didn't have to; but if he didn't want to he was sane and had to. Yossarian was moved very deeply by the absolute simplicity of this clause of Catch-22 and let out a respectful whistle.

---

[6] John Kenneth Galbraith, *The New Industrial State* (New York: Signet Books, 1968), pp. 23–24.
[7] Presthus, *The Organizational Society*, p. 74.

"That's some catch, that Catch-22," he observed.
"It's the best there is," Doc Daneeka agreed.

JOSEPH HELLER

Most automobile manufacturers, certainly the Department of Defense, and any Big State University qualify as bureaucratic organizations. In each, there are few at the top and many at the bottom, the leaders and the led, those with positions of power and those without. The point of a bureaucracy is that those at the bottom feed information to those at the top, and those at the top give orders to everyone. Information up, orders down—that is the simple story of bureaucracy. It makes sense in a perverted kind of way. But that is getting ahead of where we are.

The first point I want to make is that when dealing with a bureaucracy, there is at least one vital lesson to learn. The lesson is simply that information is the stuff of power; the stuff to control organizations.

People who study organizations seem to be fascinated by charts and graphs. They are, in fact, picture drawers. So, to illustrate the "information is power" point, picture the following. As a student at Big State U, something bad has happened. The administration has somehow messed up your record. You expected to graduate in June, but now the computer print-out card from the registrar says that you lack units. That rude news could mess up your plans to go to Europe, to hitch across the country, or to retire to a villa; so you decide to see someone about it. Where would you go? [8]

Begin at the top of the organization chart. At many universities, there is a Board of Regents, or a Board of Trustees, which has a great deal of power. One could try to go to them, but common sense suggests that that would be a wasted trip. Below the regents, there might be a President, a Chancellor, some Vice-Presidents, and some Vice-Chancellors. But again, they seem a bit too high up. Theirs are problems of millions

---

[8] The story of school as bureaucracy is an oft-told one. In my opinion, one of the best and most complete analyses of the problems confronting the student and the university in contemporary society is found in Sheldon Wolin and John Schaar, *The Berkeley Rebellion and Beyond* (New York: Vintage Books, 1970).

of dollars or whole faculties or new buildings or doing politics with state legislatures or huge private corporations. None of these are of direct relevance to a person who simply wants to graduate.

Next on the chart, next down, is an administration of deans and assistant deans and various divisions and an incredible number of secretaries. Lower yet, but a little more accessible, are department chairpersons, vice-chairpersons, administrative assistants, undergraduate faculty advisors, undergraduate secretaries, faculty, junior faculty, graduate students, and, finally, undergraduates. Where does one go? Whom does one see?

Reasonably, one should see a secretary. The business of the Secretary is to know, to have information about how things work, to know whom to call to find out important facts. In an important sense, secretaries are everyone's best friend in beating the bureaucracy. While Deans and Presidents, faculty members, and graduate students pursue a variety of goals the Secretaries help human beings with the workings of the organization. Characteristic of bureaucracies, those at the bottom of organizational charts—the very individuals who are in direct contact with the public—are those members of the organization with the least formal power.

To repeat the point of the story: Information is power.

Government as Bureaucracy

"No, you can't go home," ex-P.F.C. Wintergreen corrected him. "Are you crazy or something?"

"Why not?"

"Catch-22."

"Catch-22?" Yossarian was stunned. "What the hell has Catch-22 got to do with it?"

"Catch-22," Doc Daneeka answered patiently . . . "says you've always got to do what your commanding officer tells you to do."

JOSEPH HELLER

This section of the book is the one that comes closest to dealing with what is traditionally considered the governmental process. While it does not exactly deal with "How a Bill Becomes a Law," Congress and the President and the Pentagon are mentioned. The following story is not meant to represent a complete and accurate account of what happens. What it is meant to do is to abstract the process, to cut through much of what is of public prominence but of only lesser importance, in order to see just how information is power and how bureaucracies effect important decisions.

Let us take a "hypothetical" decision, one which involves a great deal of money for a group of individuals but which has little effect on the lives of most of us. The example selected involves the decision by Congress to build the B1 bomber. The B1 bomber was supposed to replace the B52 as our strategic bomber. As I write this, it seems certain many B1's will be built.

The Pentagon as Bureaucracy

It is easy to start with the Pentagon, with the U.S. Army, because it represents the most obvious, the biggest, and possibly the most "ideal" bureaucracy anywhere (with the exception of other armies and maybe the Catholic Church). A word about the Pentagon.

Every few years, new people are put in charge of the military. If a bureaucracy is a pyramid, then every so often the top of the pyramid is lopped off and a new top put on. The President appoints civilians to head the armed forces, which is probably a good plan. One problem, an obvious and big one, is that the civilian head of the military never knows a great deal about the defense establishment. Further, the leaders are wholly dependent on the bureaucracy in gathering information that might be beneficial to the military.

At some point, well before the public became aware of it, the military was working on ideas for the B1 system. A task force, probably headed by a major or a general, was in charge of the research. That individual's future, in many ways, became linked with the future of the B1. The more successful it could be made to appear, the more necessary for the sake of our air defense it could be shown to be, the more he would know about it and consequently the better off he would be. As the B1 project grew, that somebody's importance would grow.

The dynamics of this revolved, in *part*, around certain important issues. First, there were the environmentalists' arguments that the high-flying bombers would muck up the ozone layer. (The military reply was classic: "Make no mistake about it," said one official, "I am just as much concerned about the environment as the Sierra Club." But, it is not to worry says the military . . . most of the time the B1's would be on the ground.) Second, the cost. The first prototype models were said to cost more than their weight in gold. As of now, a production model will cost $377,000,000. Third was the issue of nuclear warheads. If B1's carried them, there would be one-third more in our arsenal—13,000—more than the number of cities on the face of the earth.

But we are really dealing with bureaucratic questions. There would be no great desire to make public any information that reflected badly on the B1. Also, it meant that when a new Secretary of Defense was named, there would be a huge effort on the part of the military to sell him or her on the B1 program. Information in a bureaucracy goes up; information in a bureaucracy is power. In other words, why wouldn't the new Secretary of Defense be convinced that the project was worthy of billions of dollars and millions of working-hours? The B1 means institutional growth, glamor, and stability.

Finally, the dynamics indicate that a bureaucrat in one bureaucracy will seek out a counterpart in another to help promote a similar goal.

The B1 case helps us to understand an interesting process. One part of the process is how a bureaucratic aim becomes a sacred aim. Frightening but true. Moreover, in this particular case, there were those in the military who were opposed to the B1. Yet the fighting that went on was kept mostly *within* the organization itself. The military, as represented by the Secretary of Defense, presented only those "facts" to the public which favored the B1. One can wonder aloud why political decisions are made from private debates.

Congress

On to Friends of the Bureaucrats—this time the Congress. Congress is set up so that it is possible for an individual to get more, rather than less, power. It helps for an individual to work hard and to follow the rules and to be intelligent. But it helps most to be re-elected over and over and over again. The longer a congressman or congresswoman lives and continues to be re-elected, the more power will be accumulated.

Almost as foolproof as that.

Congress, like any complex organization these days, is set up to produce specialists. This means that committees are formed, and then each committee is broken down into sub-committees. If a legislator or senator is interested, he or she can become a specialist, an expert in an area, and control the information having to do with that area. The longer the person lives, the more powerful his or her word becomes on matters in the area of specialty.

The late Senator Robert Kerr of Oklahoma illustrates the point. Kerr was all those things we have talked about: hard-working, rule-following, long-lived, and often re-elected. After some years, he became Chairman of the Subcommittee on Rivers and Harbors. That God had provided Oklahoma with so few rivers and harbors mattered little in the logic of the Senate. Kerr was a Senior Senator, and Rivers and Harbors was a powerful subcommittee. Every river dredged or harbor built or dam constructed went through Kerr's subcommittee. Kerr could get these projects for any state—for any senator—but in return he could expect favors. A dam for a vote on an important matter, or some such calculation.

A committee is important in the Congress in part according to the monies it controls. The Appropriations Committee is more important than the one that helps rule Washington, D.C. Power in committees often revolves around expertise in expensive projects.

The point should now become more clear: There were individuals in Congress who would benefit politically if the B1 were passed. Its passage would mean more control over more expensive projects. It could mean more bargaining power with other members of Congress. It is precisely this group of people who became allied with their counterparts in the Pentagon, with all those individuals working on the B1, supporting the B1, and selling the B1 to their leaders and to the nation.

The interested legislators and military people found help from those individuals in "private" industry who worked on war-related goods. To learn just how much of the economy is supported by building goods for the armed forces is to learn how effective this industry is as a pressure group. Its Washington operation is generally very well financed, has much experience, and is able to supply information to those individuals in Congress who are considered friendly.[9]

There is an informal rule of politics that organized groups are more effective than unorganized ones. Certainly what is known as the Military Industrial Complex is a very well-organized group. To conceptualize it another way, think how easy it would be to gather an effective group of people from industry, the Pentagon, and Congress to work for the B1. They could virtually control the public's access to information about the B1. Think how difficult it would be to gather anti-B1 forces. At best, it would be a group of strangers with no obvious connection to important sources of information, no money with which to publicize or pressure Congress, and no on-going organization.

There are all kinds of "fictional" stories we could offer. Pretend our democratic country financed a very huge and expensive bunch of spies. Make up a name. Call them, say, the CIA.

Pretend like they made mistakes (like not even hinting at the Tet offensive or the 1973 Yom Kippur War) and spent time figuring out how to kill "enemy" Heads of State. Just pretend.

What about the person in charge of the House Oversight Committee—Lucien Nedzi—who knew those things? Simply construct an iron curtain called "national security" so we citizens need not worry about problems of "our" interest. Nedzi keeps his mouth shut.

What about William Colby, head of the CIA? His idea was that in order to answer the questions the Congress and the Rockefeller Commission asked him, he should tell the truth. Only one solution: Fire him for being too "candid."

But that wouldn't really happen here.

This would: Bureaucracies need bureaucracies. The CIA is an amazing example.

In the Senate hearing about the CIA, it was learned (read

---

[9] One might see Robert Heilbroner, "Military America," *The New York Review of Books*, July 23, 1970; or Seymour Melman, *Pentagon Capitalism*.

revealed) that the Russians, by using antennae on their missions in the United States and by using orbiting satellites, can spy (Something—if not Body—really is up there looking at you). The Russians monitor and record thousands and thousands of telephone conversations carried by microwave.

It turns out we're doing the same thing in Russia.

What's interesting is that we could jam the Russian interception of our microwave communication. Of course we don't because then *they* would jam ours in Moscow. Bureaucracies need bureaucracies. The CIA needs the KGB. They do, after all, see the world in the same way.

Information is power in a bureaucratic world, and bureaucrats from different organizations share knowledge if they share a common aim. What we must understand now is just what kind of style bureaucratic politics has, what the bases of its decisions are, and what the built-in limits of its organizational structure are. What underlies, what motivates, the actions of a bureaucracy?

Bureaucracy: The Ideology

Ideally, a bureaucracy is a hierarchy, with few at the top, many at the bottom. Those at the top—ideally—have the authority to make decisions; the others have the responsibility for carrying out those decisions. As we know, information from the outside world comes in through the bottom and is sent up the organizational ladder if it seems important. Decisions stem from this information.

A bureaucracy is supposed to be a human machine. Each position in it is defined, described as to function, and limited in its freedom of action. The position becomes standardized; as a piston does only the work of a piston, so a clerk does only the work of a clerk. When either malfunctions, it is replaced.

The human machine is geared toward productivity. It must produce something, and that something must be measurable. Whether it is measured in terms of profits, sheer quantity of goods produced, or number of diplomas granted, the output of a bureaucracy must be able to be measured. So the basis of information for a bureaucrat is objective reality. That which is

objective can be counted, and that is precisely what bureaucracies are good at. It is very important to understand that
bureaucracies are too gross, too inexact, too unsubtle to comprehend quality. Huge organizations like our bureaucracies
function "efficiently," and are capable of understanding that
functioning only in terms of how many in how short a time
and at what material cost.

Like any machine, a bureaucracy works best when it is well
insulated from the outside, well protected from different elements. In a real sense, bureaucracies are afraid of the outside,
afraid of the public sector. Paranoid, if you will. So they grow.
They keep trying to occupy more space and to control more
sectors so that their internal workings will be protected. The
larger a bureaucracy grows, the more the world will look like
a bureaucracy. The more the world is like that, the greater the
likelihood is that more decisions which should be made publicly will be made privately and that the criteria used will suit
organizational demands rather than societal ones. The style is
production-oriented, paranoid, and private.

The dynamics of the B1 fit this style. So does the style of the
CIA.

The Future

When man invented the machine, for which there is no external
model in nature, he invented it in his own image. The machine does
not come from nowhere—it mirrors man's mechanical head.

PHILIP SLATER

There is a logic to large, complex organizations that we must
understand. In question form, it is this: If a bureaucracy is a
human machine (and, therefore, vulnerable to human mistakes), wouldn't it be better to develop machines that would
eliminate many of those mistakes? This kind of thinking has
led to a technology and an organizational style with implications far beyond organizational efficiency.

Large organizations are coming to rely more and more on
the centralization and standardization of information gathering. This is particularly true in the case of the military. As
the technology, as computerization, becomes more central

to an organization, that organization begins to change its operations. To quote Judy Merkle:[10]

> Because the computer does not process general information in the same subconscious manner as human commanders, and because errors are incredibly costly, computer technology forces an immense clarification of thought and a precision of action in preparing computer inputs. The rules governing the operation of organizations and the decision process must be determined, the routine business must be separated from functions requiring human judgment, and the procedures for computerized functions must be laid out before actual computer calculations. In creating a man-machine network to process information, more and more effort must go into the precise definition of organizational requirements.... Technology has not merely merged with organization theory, it has become organization theory.

Thus, as technology begins to control information, it begins to change the world to fit its categories. "The core technology," continues Merkle, "because it is computerized, has no means of handling ambiguity, and so its inputs of information, equipment and manpower must be regularized according to its requirements and stripped of ambiguity, which requires in turn that the same process be carried out on the inputs to *those* inputs, and so forth." [11]

The point we must make is that computer technology has already and will continue to change the nature of society. It requires a particular kind of behavior with which we are just beginning to become familiar. The following example from Merkle pushes us into the not very distant future. It deals with the "successful" use of a police data bank. The

> policeman stops [a] speeder (or drug suspect, or whatever); policeman detains suspect while contacting data bank; data bank, within minutes, informs policeman that suspect is wanted in another state for armed robbery; arrest is made. This speeding up and filling in of information gaps appears to be a real improvement, with no particular drawbacks. However, the continued use of such a system will actually tend to change the nature of crime itself. That is, the computer will soon eliminate the amateurs,

---

[10] Merkle, Judith A., *Command and Control: The Social Implication of Nuclear Defense* (General Learning Press, Morristown, N.J. 07960). © 1971 General Learning Corporation. Reprinted by permission of Silver Burdett Company.
[11] Ibid., p. 16.

leaving two types of crime untouched—spontaneous crime, thought of and executed on the spot, and organized crime, which to escape detection will become more tightly organized and more technically capable. Individual criminals cannot afford the services of computer technicians, but the Mafia can if it discovers that this is the path to survival. The computer has simply eliminated individual crime in favor of ever more highly organized crime. Criminals must know the location of data banks and redundant facilities as well as sophisticated techniques of sabotage and circumvention.[12]

That is fairly easy to understand. Organized crime really will become organized. But the example only sets the stage for the more important point: It is easy to substitute politics for police.

An intensive use of such systems [political data banks] to handle urban riots would essentially change the nature of civil disobedience. First of all, it would eliminate the "amateurs." The public meeting speaker, letters-to-Congressman writers, and presidential threateners could easily be rounded up at the first signs of trouble (signs to be interpreted by the military, of course). Any person or organization foolish enough to publicize complaints against the established order would be eliminated from the political game. Two kinds of political potential cannot be registered before-the-fact by computers: first, genuinely spontaneous mass action . . . and second, tightly organized, technically competent, politically uncompromising . . . opposition groups, which will be the only political action groups able to withstand the onslaught of the computer. Given the right historical circumstances, this is a much finer recipe for revolutionary violence than any of the potentially inflammatory situations which the technology is programmed to pacify.[13]

Bureaucracy in a More Personal Sense

"Did he tell you how I could ground you?"
"Just by filling out a little slip of paper saying I'm on the verge of a nervous collapse and sending it to Group. Dr. Stubbs grounds men in his squadron all the time, so why can't you?"
"And what happens to the men after Stubbs does ground them?" Doc Daneeka retorted with a sneer. "They go right back to combat status, don't they? And he finds himself right up the creek. Sure, I

---

[12] Ibid., pp. 23–24.
[13] Ibid., p. 24.

can ground you by filling out a slip saying you're unfit to fly. But there's a catch."

"Catch-22?"

"Sure. If I take you off combat duty, Group has to approve my action, and Group isn't going to. They'll put you back on combat status, and then where will I be? On my way to the Pacific Ocean, probably . . . all they've got in the Pacific is jungles and monsoons. I'd rot there."

"You're rotting here."

JOSEPH HELLER

Although not an extraordinarily precise way to present an argument, I would like to introduce one with a physical law: For every action, there is an equal and opposite reaction. That is the sense of what I should like to argue. While the following contains a good deal of speculation, there seems to be enough truth in it to take it seriously. If possible, accept what is right and reject the rest, my feelings will not be hurt.

Basically, bureaucracy develops only half of an individual. It so concentrates on some personality factors that it wholly ignores others. What I shall argue is that as we become more highly skilled bureaucrats, we develop urges equal and opposite to those skills. For example, as we become more developed "rationally," we may also become more anxious to be "irrational." Simply stated, bureaucracies may be driving us crazy. We may be going mad in part as a result of the organizational imperatives which have such a disproportionate effect on our lives.

It may be easiest to understand what I mean by visualizing how one learns to diagram a compound sentence in ninth-grade English. As I recall, it looked something like a straight line that was split into two lines. What I want to argue is that in the beginning an individual has some kind of wholeness, some kind of merging of qualities. At some point—indeed, we seem to have reached that point—bureaucracies overdevelop certain of these qualities, while leaving others underdeveloped. The individual with integrated skills slowly becomes an individual divided. Like our diagrammed sentence, the person is split in two. There are three areas which help illustrate the point: rationality, time, and relationships.

A basic assumption of this whole line of thought is that a

healthy individual is able somehow to integrate the various factors of his or her personality. To a greater or lesser degree, the rational and the emotional would mix. One would not always be employed; nor would either be used alone. Our undivided individual would not be concerned for the future at the expense of the past or the present. Indeed, each would hold importance. Finally, he or she would not participate in relationships exclusively on the basis of roles, according to the positions held by each person. Nor would all relationships be of the encounter-group type: extra-tense, personal, and in a sense, tyrannizing. Somehow, a middle ground should be sought.

But bureaucracies develop extremes. I mean, the human cogs in the organizational machine are forced to divide their feelings, emotions, and actions into extremes. Let us begin with rationality.

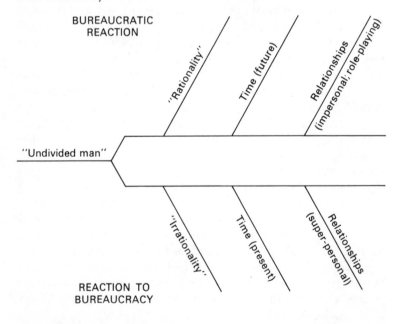

Rationality

There is a certain rationality that a bureaucy fosters. Most of its parts we understand, for in a sense the logic of bureaucracy is the logic of science. It assumes an objective reality, one that is "real" and quantifiable. The aim of the bureaucracy is to produce a countable product at the lowest possible cost. The most for the least—just so it is objective. All questions must be technical, all problems soluble in terms of costs and benefits. To build a house or an atomic bomb cannot be judged as "good" or "bad" *per se;* it can be judged only in terms of organizational credits and debits.

So the bureaucracy constructs its own world and makes its own rules about what is real. For a person to get ahead in that world, that person must act according to its rules and its rationality: keep within the framework, produce and behave, stay in step to get ahead. If one believes in the outputs of bureaucracies, one is forced to admit that it functions effectively. But the point is that it seems to be very difficult for a human being to be so confined for very long, difficult to leave one's emotions at the front door in exchange for wholly rational thought.[14]

The idea of a human machine in which human beings are confined to the rationality of cogs means inevitably that in some part of life "irrationality" must come out. If an individual is rational eight hours a day, we certainly should expect signs of something different when he or she is not at work.

We can begin to understand our irrationality by exploring the ideas of religion and violence in America.[15] Religion first.

There are, of course, all kinds of religions and all kinds of worshipers and "faithful." From polite Episcopalians to Jesus Freaks (read *Children of God*), people take their religion with differing degrees of intensity. It seems that we Americans have a rather singular expression of conviction: We are the land of the Revivalists. Always have been—from one fire-breathing hell-talking preacher to the next, and almost gladly we vent our emotions at a good revival. A good Sunday revival seems

---

[14] The use of the words rational and emotional are, I am afraid, a bit sloppy. While I am using them as most people do, it is important to remember that relating to the world "rationally" is simply one kind of emotional stance. To put it differently, rationality is at its root only another emotion.

[15] For an example of how dysfunctional bureaucratic organizations are in France, see Michael Crozier, *The Bureaucratic Phenomenon* (Chicago: University of Chicago Press, 1967).

as good for the pent-up, rational person as a good Saturday night drunk. Maybe the best of worlds would be to have both.

A minister named Albert Barnes once said: "The religion of forms is the stereotyped wisdom or folly of the past, and does not adapt itself to the free movements, the enlarged views, the varying plans of this age." [16] The age in which he spoke was 1844, and his idea was to return to the pure conditions of primitive Christianity, to get back to the basics. In a land where social movement is in unique combination with the confinement of work, people naturally looked for a release. They turned to God with a vengeance—or, if not with a vengeance, at least with an emotional intensity that would help ease the rest of the week. Redneck religion for the confined. A perfectly rational response to a "rational" life.

Moreover, it is good business. Billy Graham, Oral Roberts, and T. L. Osborn are in the noble tradition of evangelists in America. From the days of tent revivals to contemporary TV, revivalists are not only saving souls but making a little money too. For example, by the 1880s, Dwight L. Moody was into the God business the way Andrew Carnegie was into steel and P. T. Barnum into circuses.[17] It was big business and hard sale. Moody had "expenses" for his meetings: $32,000 for Boston, $30,000 for New York, $140,000 for London. Once there, he would give his pitch: "Who'll take Christ now? That's all you need. With Christ you have eternal life and everything else you need. Without Him, you must perish. He offers Himself to you. Who'll take Him?" [18]

The point I am trying to make is *not* that all religion is insane, or that every evangelist should be institutionalized. All I am suggesting is that we are attuned to a particular kind of religious experience. We have a kind of therapy, a societally approved place in which to be emotional, to be "irrational." The bureaucrat and the evangelist may be the two sides of our selves.

The other and obvious reaction to rationality, at least ob-

---

[16] Richard Hofstadter, *Anti-Intellectualism in American Life* (New York: Vintage Books, 1963), p. 137.
[17] Ibid., p. 110.
[18] Ibid., p. 111.

vious in our experience, is violence. It takes no keen insight or imagination to argue that violence in America is not a new phenomenon. There is no need to list examples from the Old West, or from television's version of the Old West. The on-going violence in the South, where it was always open season on blacks, included burnings, beatings, rapes, and hangings. White men in white robes, being irrational, relieving their frustrations in an American tradition.

There is also the violence of the lonely: The seemingly senseless killings in almost every community, done by a person alone, and now so commonplace as not to "make" the national news.

The violence of war is generally not surprising. Yet the violence of the Vietnam War somehow was. The violence was "hidden" by words. For example, "rooting out the infrastructure" meant essentially that you no longer kill only soldiers carrying weapons but "every citizen who might be related to or sympathetic to those soldiers. Since in a civil war there is no way of telling this at a glance, it comes to mean killing everyone in a specific area." [19] We take it for granted. War is hell, and all that. The motto of some pilots engaged in defoliation was "Only You Can Prevent Forests." We admire their wit and ignore their acts. Their acts were almost commonplace, their wit refreshing.

But the war may be too easy an example of violence. As we know, not all violence is acceptable. "Innocent" violence is all right. Acts that are obvious reactions to the confinement of normal existence, such as the return of panty raids or eating goldfish, are permissible. What is not acceptable is violence against the "rational" system. It is all right to relieve oneself of the tedium of the day—even irrationally—just so long as one is willing to return to that tedium. But when violence begins to mean something, when it becomes a weapon instead of a release, an important political act instead of just a childish prank, then it becomes dangerous.

So we are allowed meaningless (save to those we harm) violence in order that we may be good bureaucrats during

---

[19] Philip E. Slater, *The Pursuit of Loneliness* (Boston: Beacon Press, 1970), p. 32.

the day. It is one way in which we can be emotional, have a little fun, feel unconfined. Our violence is as normal a reaction as it is "irrational." While it would be foolish to claim that bureaucratic rationality was responsible for all violence, it would be equally foolish never to make that connection.

Time

It was Ezra Stiles who in the 1700s came to believe that the "multitudes were seriously, soberly, and solemnly out of their wits."

There is a fairly definite view of time that a bureaucracy creates. As a large, ongoing organization, it points to the future, it plans on contingencies; it is problem-solving. It lives not in the Now but in the Will-be. There is no real end in sight for a bureaucracy. The compulsion to produce, the ideology of production, means that the organization will continue to look ahead until there are no more raw materials to consume. In other words, bureaucracies live in the future until there is no more life to destroy.

This fits well with our Christian heritage. It goes well with the idea that if we work hard now, if we continue to deny ourselves in the present, then we will go to heaven. Heaven is the ultimate bonus, the best fringe benefit. So we live in the future. Let me try to explain it in a different way.

My example is really a comparison between the French view of time and the American view. Imagine a truck traveling along a road. On the back of the truck, facing the road just traveled, sits the Frenchman. His ability to see clearly from there is like a perception of time. The past is most clear, the present is whizzing by so fast that it is a blur, while the future, the road before him, is simply unknown.

Now the American sits in the cab, facing front. The future, for that American, is most clear. The present is a blur, while the past is behind him, completely unknown. Our vision is best when we anticipate. We live there, not here. For example, we go to high school in order to get into college; to college in order to get a job; get a job in order to have a family; and have a family so that our children can have those things we never had. We have an endless future, as does a bureaucracy. That is what we are taught; yet we know the reaction to that vision of time has been almost "irrational."

What some have done—and this was probably most clear a few years ago with the hippies—is to completely reject both the past and the future. The emphasis became the Now, the Here and Now. Everyone wanted to be current, or hip, or with it. Time became the present and just those things the senses were currently sensing. Plans were a middle-class hang-up, the past was old-fashioned. Even nostalgia became the "current rage," with no connection to history or the past. Old might have been funky, but it surely wasn't meaningful.

Bureaucracy condemns us to the future, while we react by claiming the present. Neither the richness of the past nor the lessons of tradition are in much evidence in such an arrangement. To reclaim ourselves from the demands of a hectic, meaningless now or a never-to-be-reached future, we might consider understanding the past. Learning about the culture which produced us, and the varieties of styles which are so different from our own.

Relationships

"Well say, buddy, is this the way these little meetings usually go?"
"Usually go?"
"Is this the *usual* pro-cedure for these Group Therapy shindigs? Bunch of chickens at a peckin' party? . . . [A peckin' party is when] the flock gets sight of a spot of blood on some chicken and they all go to *peckin'* at it, see, till they rip the chicken to shreds, blood and bones and feathers. But usually a couple of the *flock* gets spotted in the fracas, then it's their turn. And a few more gets spots and gets pecked to death, and more and more. Oh, a peckin' party can wipe out the whole flock in a matter of a few hours, buddy, I seen it. A mighty awesome sight. The only way to prevent it—with chickens —is to clip blinders on them. So's they can't see."

                                                                KEN KESEY

There are many who argue that a bureaucracy is, basically, little more than the sum of its roles which are "linked psychologically." [20] In other words, one can understand an organiza-

---

[20] For example, see Daniel Katz and Robert Kahn, *The Social Psychology of Organizations* (New York: John Wiley & Sons, 1966).

tion simply by studying the roles of those in that organization. What is important for us is to try to get to the real meaning of such a view—the costs of role-playing to those within the organization. In a sense, the heart of the question revolves around the problem of defining the individual.

Let me state the problem in a personal way. It is possible that a person could relate to me in terms of the roles he or she ascribes to me. I could be seen as playing the role of family member, tennis player, teacher, and television watcher. Those would be my roles. The sum of them would be me. If I were to die suddenly, couldn't there be another person who would fill my roles? A tennis player, a part of the family of Barbara, Tamara, and Amy, a teacher of classes, a watcher of television. In bestowing roles, society can both give identity and take it away. By relating to roles instead of to people, we are continually in danger of being no one knowing nobody.

The sociologist Ralf Dahrendorf describes the tension in the following way: "[An individual's] roles are conferred on him, and he is shaped by them; but when he dies, the impersonal force of society takes his roles away from him and confers them on somebody else in new combinations . . . man has turned . . . from the individual into the member, from a free and autonomous creature into the sum of his alien characters." [21]

Roles depersonalize. They provide an easy means whereby people can ignore other people; they are an excellent device through which an individual can hide from the facts of his or her job. In consciously playing a role, one is doing exactly what the bureaucracy demands. One no longer acts as a human being, but instead as a functioning, rule-following, member in good standing of an impersonal organization.

In part, role-playing means that we are replaceable, interchangeable. To be a good vice-president is to be a good vice-president. It matters little why, or where, or for whom one might be vice-president. A secretary here and a secretary there are simply the same parts in different machines. It is critical for an individual to play a prescribed role correctly so that the

---

[21] Ralf Dahrendorf, *Essays in the Theory of Society* (Stanford, Calif.: Stanford University Press, 1968), p. 75.

bureaucracy can guarantee its own survival, no matter what happens to any particular person.

Elliot Richardson seems to be a good top executive. He can run this agency or that department or be a lawyer or be a diplomat. He floats from one bureaucracy to another, replacing and being replaced. To put it a little differently: In a large class, all you students look alike.

There seems to be a real desire among many to play more than a role; a longing to relate in more personal ways; a reaction to the system. So we go to extremes, we go to the super-personal, we go to encounter groups. Lonely role-playing people pay their money to be tyrannized by a group of lonely role-playing people. One wonders if in an artificial environment, instant intimacy will solve any long-range problems. There is little doubt but that encounters are beneficial, but very possibly they provide only temporary relief.

Some organizations set up encounter sessions once a week for a whole office. Can you imagine the incredible emotional relief in that one hour, after emotions have been stored up for thirty-nine hours? But organizations are wise to do it. People are able to react to the inhumanity of their roles in an equally foolish way, by overcompensating and being inhumanly personal. The beauty of it is that it all takes place in an institutional setting. It is all harmless to the organization. People yell and scream and cry and kiss and then go back to work, emotionally spent, able to endure until the next session.

Now that's depressing. We know the "truth" of how our surroundings affect us: The warning is that we can always be right but miss certain truths.

To act on the intellectual framework we know is accurate may be both wrong *and* destructive.

Not all that long ago I was called an *intruder* by another person. My first reaction was "of course." It was like being a stranger or an outsider, which is a fairly normal American condition.

But that impression was a little off the mark. I was *felt* to be an intruder, which was exactly right. When you know—or want to know another person—you should and do intrude into that person's life.

It is not at all a corporate/capitalist/liberal/legalistic idea of separation.

In the real world of family and friends, loves and hates, we should suspend some of our correct knowledge and figure out what may really be happening. What may be possible.

What I want to argue is that much of your identity—the who-you-are-in-the-world—is contained and cemented in close relationships. In a tangible way, other people carry around a great deal of who you are. I believe it's true that a person's death diminishes absolutely all those people who have surrounded that person.

How we treat the people around us—and how they treat us —forms an arena of unlimited opportunities for acts of integrity. It is the primary location of good and evil. From it, we *should be able* to generalize and enter into the broader world of actions and politics.

What we get is at the same time something fragile and dramatic. It certainly won't guarantee wealth or fame or even happiness. Those all seem to be the wrong words and really belong to different scales of measurement.

What intrusions may do is turn the world upside down, and allow each of us—in interesting combinations—to become creators.

Beats being a bureaucrat.

An After Word

To take this chapter seriously is to begin to understand the world in a different, depressing way. To take large organizations as life-styles which convey a very definite ideology is to limit the use of certain kinds of analyses.

For example, much of the economic interpretation of society—an analysis which depends heavily upon the class conflicts inherent in capitalist, but not Communist, societies —makes little sense. There is no doubt that wealth is concentrated in our society, that there are the rich and the poor, and that there are "managers" and "workers." But the whole dynamic of organized society—the impersonality and role-playing and ever-increasing institutional growth—affects everyone.

What I am arguing is that the ideology of organizations will not change, whether they be in Communist or capitalist countries, in America or England, Russia or Japan.[22] The bureaucrat recognizes the bureaucrat, inter-office or inter-nationstate. Regrettably, class analyses are too optimistic. To eliminate the "ruling class," the upper class, would be in effect to trade one set of highly placed bureaucrats for another. To make a class analysis in a bureaucratic world leaves too many essential problems well hidden.

Essentially, it seems obvious that in an organizational society potentially everyone might get hurt. People at the bottom —the poor, the minorities—are forced to deal with powerless organizational employees who represent an impersonal set of rules. For those in the organization the pay may be higher, but so perhaps are the costs. Organizations do more than buy peoples' time; they represent an impressive way of purchasing an individual's individuality.

The world is safe for bureaucracy only when everyone is a bureaucrat.

It would be a real relief if I could honestly write that all we had to do was to destroy all bureaucracies and all large complex organizations in order to solve our problems. Of course, I can't. That our organizational structure is helping to drive us mad is, I hope, now more obvious. We are surely becoming divided, and are in the process destroying ourselves. The less together we are, the more potentially successful we become. But we can split ourselves just so much.

The problem of how much organization is complex. We seem to be social as well as political animals. There are things we can do in groups—things that are beneficial both physically and psychologically—that we cannot do alone. So we must find new modes of organization and different ways of perceiving each other.

As long as we are simply unimportant, replaceable parts in an impersonal social machine, the best we can hope for is that some day we will go sane and become irreplaceable.

---

[22] For the classic statement of bureaucracy, see Hans Gerth and C. Wright Mills, *From Max Weber* (New York: Oxford University Press, 1958). There are, of course, alternatives. For some examples you might begin with some of the selections in Terrence Cook and Patrick Morgan, eds., *Participatory Democracy* (San Francisco: Canfield Press, 1971).

Politics as Tacky: or, What Do I Do on My Day off?

4

I'm usually at the desk by eight o'clock, half an hour before work starts. Getting set for the day, writing programs, assigning different jobs to different people. When they come in we take a head count. You see who's late and who's not. You check around and make sure they start at eight thirty. . . . You make sure when they go for breaks they take fifteen minutes not twenty. You check for lunch hours, making sure they take forty-five minutes and not an hour. . . . All you're doing is checking on people. This goes on all day.

The job is boring. It's a real repetitious thing. . . .

It's just this constant supervision of people. It's more or less like you have a factory full of robots working the machinery. . . .

Just like Big Brother's watching you. Everybody's watching somebody. . . .

A man should be treated as a human, not as a million-dollar piece of machinery. People aren't treated as good as an IBM machine is. . . .

STUDS TERKEL

The prean is a sea monster with the body of a crab and the head of a certified public accountant.

WOODY ALLEN

Yuck

So, in a book about politics, we have finally reduced ourselves to looking at "dirty pictures." We are forced to face what many people just won't discuss in "polite" society—we have come to the time to talk about economics. We are at a topic that somehow appeals to the very lowest and least noble instincts in most of us. Probably the only thing worse than talking about the effect of economics on ourselves and our society, is not to talk about it.

Because I do not like the subject/practice of economics does not mean I believe it is unimportant—or that being poor is fun—or that cut-throat competition is a lamb in wolf's clothing. I am not saying that.

In part, what is at stake is a matter of vision: If one's vision is no more noble than higher wages or lower prices, then that person may be in some psychological trouble. To put economics at the center of any important argument reduces you to a world of dollars, and I think casts real doubts on your sense.[1]

But this is not to say economics is not important.

It is a real and live outrage that there are some *so* rich and many *so* poor. It is an outrage that there are whole groups of people who take their identity from their financial inheritance, dividend checks, or savings bonds, while others starve because they were not "smart" enough to be born rich, or of the "right" color.

But that is just the obvious bad; there is much worse.

We hide real issues with false ones; we hide moral problems with material ones. We reduce everything to our pocket-book, then we shoot from the hip. We have the capacity to convert every potential political discussion into the vocabu-

---

[1] As a courtesy to the reader, I have taken out most of the puns in this chapter, but the material does lend itself to low humor.

lary of currency, and then cannot figure out why our souls are so poor. We play their games.

Just how many things does one person or one family need? Why do we keep looking out for our financial interests when more often than not they will not solve our real problems? There is no guarantee that being rich will help us be ourselves, or that by gathering money we will avoid being destroyed by that very process.

The urge to acquire, more exactly the proportion and magnitude of that urge, is a sign of something cancerous in our ideology. There can never be enough things—there will never be enough "thing-security." When we put the problem of economics at the center of the universe, we guarantee that our problems will not be solved.

Here we are in college so that we can earn more money than a high-school graduate. I think it appropriate for some honest institution of "higher" education to change its motto from a noble Latin phrase to the American truism: Learn to Earn.

When it gets right down to it, people seem willing to do almost anything for a salary. Being bureaucrats with split work/leisure lives is the destiny for many of us. In an important sense our vision is limited to what is called the root of all evil—we cannot get past our very own economic interest.

Money is the visual sign of the elect, of the elite, and of some of the very worst behavior we can imagine.

It operates on the quicksand of false equality, or in the gray boredom of Soviet Marxism.

There is a classic American definition of politics—who gets what, when, and how—that is a half-step away from economic considerations. We know that the rich get richer, but is that really what politics is/should be about? What about action and behavior and public space?

In the end I'm not entirely satisfied that economics is a topic, but rather an amazingly useful symptom to study. That, in essence, is the way it will be dealt with here. In the following pages, we will look at the world, at industry as religion, and work and leisure. What is important to remember is that much of our everyday, run-of-the-mill, common sense concepts and myths are remarkably value laden and exact much from us. Ideas of economics certainly fall into that category.

Eating the Hand That Feeds Us

For at least another hundred years we must pretend to ourselves and to everyone that fair is foul and foul is fair; for foul is useful and fair is not. Avarice and usury and precaution must be our gods for a little longer still. For only they can lead us out of the economic necessity into daylight.

JOHN MAYNARD KEYNES

In a couple of chapters we will go through materialism in America. It will be tied to freedom, but with a minimum of imagination it should not be too difficult to see how the discussion would fit just as easily here. Our incredible pseudo-capitalism works best when we are all out for ourselves, just producing and consuming as fast as we can. Later, we will see that one of the things we consume is our self. Here, we can start with the obvious: because of the way we do economics, one of the stakes of our times seems the earth itself.

No need for scare tactics, it is simply a fact that we are going about killing the world in very effective ways. Even in economic terms—the economics of numbers and the curious kinds of facts produced by numbers—we are doing a super job of being stupid.

Put in a very simple form, we have had huge successes using technical skills to increase productivity. Nature, seen by many as a friend, has come to be understood as something to conquer. Nature is a resource, a fantastic hunting ground where living things can be converted to spendable cash. Literally the whole world becomes one big technical problem of production. To understand that as shortsighted is to miss the point rather badly.

There is simply some stuff that is irreplacable. And (guess what?) we're using it up. As winters get cold, we remember that fossil fuels keep getting used up and there is no reason to believe we will find an adequate replacement. The amount that we burn is staggering enough, but the way it is distributed is even more amazing.[2]

---

[2] E. M. Schumacher, *Small Is Beautiful,* p. 23.

The richest nations, according to the United Nations, have 31 percent of the people in the world, and those nations use 87 percent of the fuel currently consumed. If the basic question which concerns you is equality, what about this: "If the 'poor' suddenly used as much fuel as the 'rich,' world fuel consumption would treble right away." [3]

But the question, of course, is not equality. The question is how to stop consuming irreplaceable resources. There are two quick, "practical" responses. The first is the extension of the logic: Let's use it all up as fast as we can. Wonderful. What we get with this is a long pipe threatening the natural ecological balance of Alaska. With the pipeline, we can rest comfortably knowing that another generation of oil companies will make lots of money, that another generation can at least marginally forget about the problem, and at some point part of Alaska will be ruined.

The other "practical" response is nuclear power. While it is unclear that we have yet to dominate the world, it is clear that there are limits beyond which our friendly earth will not be pushed. Maybe one can get a bit of perspective from a former Presidential Science Advisor. He said, about radioactive wastes: "One has a queasy feeling about something that has to stay underground and be pretty well sealed off for 25,000 years before it is harmless." [4]

One secret, of course, is to shoot all that stuff into space so we can pollute the heavens themselves.

The basic point, one so elementary, is that our industry is now in the process of systematically using those materials upon which it is based. Eating, if you will, the hand that feeds it.

If eating is the metaphor, then digestion is a real problem. There is little use to go into the details of pollution. To be as free as the air you breathe is now only a sick joke. As part of our summer weather reports we are told if it is safe to go outside, not because of the heat, exactly, but because of the digestion problems of our industry. In Alaska, now that there are so many pollution producing cars, there is an opposite

---

[3] Ibid., p. 24.
[4] Ibid., p. 18.

problem: When it gets too cold, the exhaust freezes and it is unsafe to go outside.

All those facts are true: no single person has a cruel enough imagination to dream them up.

In truth, I haven't the heart (or stomach) for the details of the argument: The children or old folks or trees or whales which just don't have a chance given the physical facts of our productive society. Most of you know the tensions that exist between those who want ecological purity and those who want employment.

It is, if we pretend sanity for just a moment, a monument to off-the-point arguments. What kind of society is it that gives us a choice of jobs which will kill us, or ecological purity which will starve us? I have read that drowning in a few inches of water is, ultimately, the same as drowning in the deepest part of the ocean.

Generally, discussions of economics, especially "political" discussions, are centered around injustice. There are too few making too much and too many getting too little. Those arguments are correct. Further, unequal distribution of economic resources leads directly to an unequal distribution of power. We all know that, too, is true. But, lurking just beyond these important facts are a whole set of myths which (regrettably) we seem to share. Wanting to be rich is as strong a desire as wanting to stay rich. We are killing ourselves, equally in some ways, unequally in others. Some of us sniff pollution from our Mercedes, others from public transportation. Some of us kill our bodies with expensive medication, others by eating food manufactured for animals.

It is both right and wrong to argue we are—in a true collective effort—killing ourselves. To stop there would be wrong. We are all vulnerable to our industrial/capitalist/consumptive excesses; that's right. There is no good excuse for people to starve, or have no medical care, or no dignity. That the rich are exposed to bad air, water, and food has nothing to do with the injustice of the distribution of wealth.

Instead of going through the statistics that prove wealth and equality have no obvious relationship in our country, it makes more sense to begin to play with economics, and see it in different ways.

Industry as Religion

Thus spoke the Devil to me once: "God too has his hell: That is his love of man."
And most recently I heard him say this: "God is dead. . . ."
FRIEDRICH NIETZSCHE

Let's back up and repeat some of the things we know. We are myth-based creatures. Our myths form the way we see, order, and understand our facts and existence. It can be set up like this: We respond emotionally to a wide range of things. We respond, in part, to what is comfortable. We are capable of creating myths in order to *fill* our feelings. There is another half of this whole.

There are social myths—constructions of reality—which help shape and supply us with myths. When there is a connection between a self-sense and a social construction of reality, it is possible to get an extraordinarily powerful myth: a religion.

At the turn of the century, our industry was pretty "uneconomical" according to almost any standard—animal, vegetable, or mineral. There were amazingly bloody labor disputes, a great deal of which can only be understood as human torture, and a man named Frederick Winslow Taylor who set out to right wrongs.[5] In a very serious way, Taylor wanted to make a social revolution by bringing rationality and bureaucracy (*that* kind of science) to industry.

He was outraged by inefficiency, and decided that each worker should be as machine-like as possible. He believed in —and worked out—a system to measure each movement with a stop watch so no motion would be wasted. The calculation was that output would be greater, wages would be higher, people would be forced to get along better, and a peaceful revolution could be a by-product of industrial reordering.

It was (and still is) an interesting idea. We need not dwell on some obvious points (for example, his whole scheme is built on the twin notions that everyone is primarily motivated by economic consideration and that there really *is* one-best-way to do a job) as they are frequently dealt with. Instead, we

---

[5] See his *Principles of Scientific Management*. The following was suggested, in part, by the work of Chuck Gleason.

must understand that Taylor tapped a set of basic values in us, and put them together in a brilliant (and probably wrong and destructive) way.

In a real sense, Taylor's set of assumptions led to a dynamic which might best be understood using the categories of religion. Think about it:

SIN =	Loafing
REWARD =	Higher wages
RITUAL =	Very elaborate, involving stop watches and a whole bureaucracy of specialists performing exotic acts of neatness and cleanliness
SYMBOLISM =	A well-ordered, right-running machine
AN ETHIC =	Corporate, "cooperative" capitalism
A MESSIAH/LEADER =	Frederick Winslow Taylor, his very own self
REVELATION =	It is replaced by prediction. The mystery is sucked from the magical, and we get something less spectacular but something we can count on.
APOCALYPSE =	In earlier history, there were angry and vengeful gods, plagues, storms, and famine. Now we get class warfare, terrible economic depressions, or the Bomb.
A PERFECT SOCIETY =	Certainty. Everyone cooperates, does the task he or she is best suited for, and gets just compensation. That, in our liberal society which causes splits in our lives, means that people can go home and be happy.
"CHURCH" =	We need a Sunday School, and we get it in the form of the University. In school we are taught to deal well with structure. It is easy to argue that much of the meaning of the University, for most of us, is the Structure of the University. As we learn to oper-

ate in this bureaucratic setting (spring training for a bureaucratic life), as we subconsciously learn the underlying sense of the reality we are placed in, we are being shaped and molded to understand and operate in an after-university life. Grades, graduate/law/medical school: in the end we hum its hymn, whistle its tune.

FAITH ITSELF =

Traditionally, a real belief is what would stir the gods. To stop believing was to stop the effectiveness of those gods. Now, there is an extraordinarily critical difference: We can stop believing and *this* industrial god keeps on producing.

HISTORY =

There is no doubt that we are worshipers. We go to school and learn. We become practitioners, and we strive to fulfill particular kinds of god-like urges from our past. We have come full-circle from the Deists. We become small reflections of the Big God: rational, predictable, productive, well-ordered, right-working machines. We come close to filling the dreams; the personal becomes the impersonal; the I becomes the IT.

> *I give human traits to machines and machine traits to humans.*
> *And it is productive and it is therefore good.*
> *And we all say:*
>
> *Amen.*

Let me try to get at some of the same material in regular paragraph form. Familiarity is sometimes useful. It seems to me that if we are to take economics seriously we must understand how each of us is involved and affected. In the case of economics, as with all "soft" sciences, it is necessary to look at the assumptions upon which exotic theory grows. Poisoned soil, after all, yields poisoned fruit.

We have seen, and we certainly know, we don't do much of a good job in making food, employment, power—and the accompanying dignity—available to enough people. Further, we are killing the earth and ourselves and leaving the prospect of misery for the next generation.

Another way to get at the problem is to see that the way those events are carried out are, in part, reflections of our mind. Yes, we are sickened by the way we organize and produce and consume and destroy. But we somehow see it as an external thing. The truth is all those things *organize our minds*. The myths—even to the partially playful Religion of Industry —do much to tell us how to see, what to look at, where to act.

There is, to my knowledge, no proof that we were meant to be wholly "rational." It is an invention which is interesting, and sometimes useful, but no one can seriously make the argument that traits of rationality are anything close to a full listing of human traits.

The models of economics, the powerful myths of economics, rest firmly on the notions that we are (or at least should be) rational "actors." The myths and their material products are powerful. They are powerful enough to organize our heads, make us ignore our hearts, and generally encourage us to be a fairly uninteresting lot.

Part of this economics lesson is about its products. I am not arguing that we should embrace poverty, starvation, or illness. Much of the material products of our economics is impressive. But the lesson has to do with our mind-set. It is one, I believe, that is faulty at its very core.

To make the last point more clearly, we need to go to another topic.

On Hard Times

What's your first reaction when the phone rings in the morning and it's a job call?
   "Oh, crap."

STUDS TERKEL

Work and leisure, two everyday economic topics, are almost too close to us to figure out. They are givens—facts of life. They are so common and commonplace that we really don't, or maybe even can't, think very clearly about them.

After all, we know that there is work-time and play-time and you do one, and enjoy the other, and that is just the way it is so why hassle about it. What I want to argue is that somehow work and leisure are important, things that we should make an effort to understand.

Following the logic of the topic, the order will be work now, and leisure next.

I thought it would be interesting to see how a textbook defined work. Interesting to see what the scholars had to say. I quote: Work is a "form of activity that has social approval and satisfies a real need of the individual to be more active. To produce, to create, to gain respect, to acquire prestige, and incidently, to earn money . . . the paycheck must mean different things to different people." [6]

So that is what work is in serious language. One of the truly fantastic things about textbooks is that they often hide, divert, or obscure meaning. Sometimes they just lie—and teach us a great deal by what they systematically miss. We still have our problem: What does work mean to a person? In a most serious way, maybe it means this: To many people, most of the time, a job is a job is a job.

Work is what you do eight hours a day for money to get things. If you do not work, society will shun you. You will not be able to participate, you will not be able to do or make or buy. Let's face it: work is one way society has to keep you off the streets.

Cheaper than jail and very effective.

But that is a little off the point. I think the point is that work does not really have to be as brutalizing as it is.

People, naturally, have some kind of normal tempo. Each of us, before we learn any better, has a natural rhythm of producing and consuming which is in harmony with our surroundings.

---

[6] Milton L. Blum, *Industrial Psychology: Its Theoretical and Social Foundations* (Harper & Row), 1968.

That relationship—our labor—should keep up until we die. But we are denied labor and instead have something we call work—and with work we use such words as "hard," and "make," and "boring." [7]

The tempo is no longer ours. It is not of people, but it is made by people. Ours is an environment genuinely not human. We serve the rhythm of mechanical movement. Labor might have been noble, for it was our own relationship with ourselves —but what we get instead is work, and the brutal logic of the time clock.

In our crazy, complex, capitalist, consuming setting—in our work and leisure life—the individual comes unglued.

Think about it. There is no clear relationship between a job and a finished product. That just no longer exists. One person does one small thing: We are a nation of experts, full of sound and fury, separately signifying nothing.[8] Certainly we know that raw materials are transformed—dead trees or high school graduates are turned into the finished products of paper or consumers. What is magical is that no person involved in that organized work process ever seems either involved or responsible.

We get separated from our very own work. And we get separated from people around us. And we get separated from our own imaginations.

So here we are. Work fills time and space; it displaces our self-worth for money; it divides us from others for material reward; it speeds us up in order to satisfy the logic of machinery.

That is hard work. Enough. Enough. It's time to relax, take a break, get into leisure.

On Easy Times

An evening of violence and brutality on the television screen is deemed a morality play because the culprits are punished in the last

---

[7] Alas, even "shit."

[8] The incredible part is that in the beginning science was exciting and helpful and—sadly—restricted. Listen to this mid-nineteenth century story: "The Royal Institute, which existed in England to further the progress of science and its application to industry was forced, when it became a fashionable place to visit and wished to preserve its exclusivity, to brick up its back door to keep out the mechanics who stole into the gallery." In Harry Braverman, *Labor and Monopoly Capital: The Degradation of Work in the Twentieth Century* (New York: Monthly Review Press, 1974), p. 134.

moments of the last act. But Satan dominates the play . . . When the devil is denied, he manifests himself nonetheless. . . .

KENNETH KENISTON

Some years ago there was a movie called *Easy Rider*. Not a great movie, not a bad one. It was about two bike riders who sold dope, made a lot of money, and were on their way to Florida to live happily ever after. One biker, Dennis Hopper, was really excited: "We made it; man—we made it. All the bread we need and on the road."

"No," was the answer. "We blew it."

In a real sense, that may be a key issue to leisure: "We blew it."

What do we do when we are free from work? One thing, of course, is we fill our social and economic obligations. We spend to fill time, to fulfill our ego, to try and fool our frustrations. We spend and consume, spend and are consumed.

Then we're broke—spent, if you will—and we go back to the highly structured situation of work. So we repeat ourselves.

It is more involved than that. We watch television, see a movie, get drunk, chase men or women. Essentially, just escape. Get our minds off things, off school or work or whatever. Dull ourselves. Become mindless and meaningless in our "off" hours. Leisure, to be sure.

What the hell good is it, is leisure, if it does not somehow relate to work? We work so we can escape it, but our escape is all too often uninterestingly blah. Our work and leisure should be extensions of each other; put differently, without meaningful labor we cannot expect meaningful leisure. To isolate the two leads directly to all kinds of alienation.

We should feel cheated. We need work and play in order to feel good about our selves, in order to feel needed. Easy times, it seems, aren't necessarily easy in the long run, and not necessarily a blessing if you use time poorly.

To talk about economics, to get right down to it, we might want to begin with saving our lives—socially and spiritually. A reasonable economic question would be: How do we make the world safe for itself and for its people? A reasonable way to begin to answer is to do what we can to ignore corporate capitalist/socialist/Marxist economics. While it is clear that they do not go out of their way to abuse common sense, it certainly *seems* that way. Some kinds of capitalism can be good and some kinds of Marxism bad, and it works just as easily the other way around. To get into the details is not worth our time just now.

In an essay entitled "Buddhist Economics," E. F. Schumacher writes that work should fill these three functions:[9] "to give a man a chance to utilize and develop his faculties; to enable him to overcome his ego-centeredness by joining with other people in a common task; and to bring forth the goods and services for a becoming existence."

More gets built into that kind of work. It makes sense to continue to use Schumacher's words.

> Wisdom demands a new orientation of science and technology towards the organic, the gentle, the non-violent, the elegant and beautiful . . . We must look for a revolution in technology to give us inventions and machines which reverse the destructive trends now threatening us all.
>
> . . . . We need methods and equipment which are
> —cheap enough so that they are accessible to virtually everyone;
> —suitable for small-scale application; and
> —compatible with man's need for creativity.[10]

It is not difficult to see what is left out of these calculations. No talk of manager elites and of the masses. They simply have no place when economics becomes a serious affair for individuals. Nor is there the false calculation that large size is more "economical" than small, or the desire to try to quantify the concepts of gentleness, elegance, and beauty.

The way we choose to operate our material relationships, our economics, is a basic question of how we live our lives and how we do our politics. The important value questions we ask for ourselves should be asked of our economics.

If we try tying labor with leisure, of producing in a non-destructive way, of making work compatible with creativity, of making goods and services accessible in a more equitable way central—if we decide on these kinds of values we can only expect a world radically different (and probably much more wonderful) than we have now.

---

[9] Schumacher, *Small Is Beautiful*, p. 51.
[10] Ibid., pp. 31–32.

It seems safe to assume that there will be no one best way to answer the new set of questions, no one set of people, no single class or council or committee or board of directors who will give us folks the word. The way we choose to organize and to create should take its directions from our self, our physical surroundings, and our social setting. As each gets mixed in different amounts for different reasons, and as we relearn the uses of our imaginations, our economic dealings and our politics and our lives will line up in ways to make all of those things more interesting.

I can think of no way to make the notion clear and understandable. When there are no single answers, but only sets of multiple answers, one is forced to sacrifice the clarity of dogma.

Let me try it this way: Imagine that instead of General Motors, America had a number of independent, small, beautiful, organic peaceful places making different kinds of transportation vehicles. Instead of General Motors, America would be full of Specific Motors.

Politics as Fraud: Liberalism and Voting in America

5

While studying liberalism, I came across the following quote which does much to sum up the problem: "The way this business is run," said the lady, "we would have failed long ago if we did not make so much money."

[People] have to make themselves predictable, otherwise the machines get angry and kill them.

GREGORY BATESON

Murray Edleman tells the story of the election-day interview of a Little Old Lady in England.
"Who are you going to vote for?" she was asked.
"Oh, I never vote," she said. "It encourages them so."

I am a good friend of a fellow whose family never tells jokes. All they say are the punch lines of jokes they told years before. Sometimes one of them will offer a new punch line, and generally the rest of the family will be able to construct an appropriate story around it. In many ways, that is how Americans are about voting. The punch line is always "vote"; only the story changes to make the punch line seem appropriate.

It would be unreasonable to begin with the idea that voting in America is a positive virtue and then continue our study from there. Indeed, given the biases of society—Madisonian people, in an objective world, organized bureaucratically—we cannot understand voting out of its context. It would seem reasonable to argue that considering the way we have set up voting in America, voting is only a trivial distraction to keep the masses happy, to keep them occupied, to keep them powerless.

But that is getting ahead of ourselves. To get to the view of voting that makes it seem worse than irrelevant, there are certain historical and social science things we should know. We should know what our ideology has to do with government, and our attitudes toward it. We should know how political scientists, and the general mythology of society, view voting. Finally, we must begin to develop a different way of questioning what voting is all about.

Liberalism

The United States is a self-consciously liberal country. All our scholars agree, and surely our common sense tells us, that for a long time we citizens of America have held (pretty much) the same view of the world. We believe the same general truths, have the same general kind of ideology; in sum, we are all liberals in a liberal state.[1]

It is important to make clear that when I use the term "liberal," I mean something more by it than "Democrats" are somehow "liberal" and "Republicans" are somehow "conservative." Beneath the common liberal/conservative language of our newspapers lie the classic liberal and conservative political

---

[1] The following discussion of liberalism is based on Louis Hartz, *The Liberal Tradition in America* (New York: Harcourt, Brace & World, 1955).

theories. It would be wrong to say that the liberal tradition was the only one in America, that it was the only ideology. We are now in the process of rediscovering the Puritans and the Populists, the Southern bourbon aristocracy and the Wobblies, the Native Americans, the blacks, and the Chicanos. But, as we shall see, it would be equally wrong to argue that America was anything other than a liberal state—in the classic sense—or that the vast majority of her citizens were not liberals.[2]

> He nodded heavily and called for another scotch & soda. "It's a goddamn shame," he muttered. "But what can you really expect? You lie down with pigs and they'll call you a swine every time. . . ."
> As for politics, I think Art Buchwald said it all last month. . . .
> "I always wanted to get into politics, but I was never light enough to make the team." [3]
>
> H.S.T.

A Lock(e) on Us

Liberalism, at least in its American manifestation is in large part the intellectual formulation of the Englishman John Locke.[4] The writers of the American Constitution had read Locke, and his influence on them is obvious. At the time Locke wrote, the medieval world was ending. The guilds and the fiefs and the manors of western Europe were crumbling, and the nation-states were being built. This change led to a tension in Locke's liberalism, and ultimately to a tension in American liberalism.

---

[2] Indeed, one of the first—and most important—problems for any minority is to avoid being coopted by the liberal ideology.

[3] It is always a problem to decide who to include and who to exclude in written work. There are always questions of *who* does *what* and *how* for *whom*. Finally, it came down to taste and what seemed right. Who better to explain the true meaning of voting than a science fiction writer and speed freak doctor of journalism? The writers are Kurt Vonnegut and Hunter S. Thompson: "In A Manner That Must Shame God Himself" excerpted from *Wampeters Foma & Granfalloons* by Kurt Vonnegut Jr. Copyright © 1973 by Kurt Vonnegut Jr. Originally published in *Harper's Magazine*. Reprinted by permission of DELACORTE PRESS/SEYMOUR LAWRENCE. Hunter S. Thompson, *Fear and Loathing in Las Vegas* (Random House, 1972).

[4] It is very instructive to read John Locke, *The Second Treatise of Government* (Indianapolis: Bobbs-Merrill, 1952).

There are several ways in which one can view what people were like in a mythical state of nature. Maybe people were noble savages, maybe just savages. John Locke believed that if left alone, most people, most of the time, would get along all right. There would be harmony, but not total peace. This was not to say that government was unnecessary. In fact, Locke wrote that government was important, especially as a counter-weight to the tyranny of the Church, the guilds, and the manors of medieval times. Locke thought that the state should have control over all of them. But Locke was more complex than that. He also believed that, potentially, government could do evil.

So, in his liberal state, government was to act only as a referee, as a judge for the people. This would allow the people to do just about what they wanted to do (privately), while being assured that their property—something tied closely to their lives and happiness—would be protected. But it also did one other thing. It divided the public and the private; the crease that divided the one from the other was to become a huge split, with the important half of the split being the private.

There is not much difference in basic temperament between a good tight end and a successful politician. They both go down in the pit and do whatever has to be done—then come up smiling, and occasionally licking blood off their teeth.

H.S.T.

We Americans both added to and misunderstood Lockean liberalism. Certainly our heritage seems to include the idea that a citizen should be afforded rights. We assume life and liberty and the pursuit of happiness/property. We also think we are guaranteed any religion, a fast trial, and the right to assemble. All these seem to be for the good.

But what we do not assume, what we do not seem to have, is the space in which to act like citizens. While we are given rights, we are not given the responsibility for acting on those rights.

This, in many important ways, is a major flaw in our liberalism. The citizen is granted rights, but is given no place to exercise them; each person has potential power, but no place to actualize it. The individual is given political tools, but no area in which he or she may act politically.[5] Surely we have tried to turn things on their heads.

Part of the problem is due to the fact that the American experience was not the European one. Locke was well aware that institutions unchecked by government could be repressive. That was the lesson of feudalism. But America had never experienced feudalism, had never known the tyranny of the private realms. So, only half of Locke was accepted. We liberals assume that government might be evil, that it might be repressive. What we forget is that government was to be set up to protect us. Because of our fear of government, we set it up to protect us from itself. Further, we have a belief in a "private realm" that we think is best left unregulated.

> Sterns: *"When it really came down to it, they had less guts than we had. We were willing to sell out the women. . . ."*
>
> Sterns: *"There were perhaps 250 people on the floor who had a good idea of what was going on. There were another 50 or 60 who had a pretty complete idea of what was going on. And then there were about 20 who knew what was going on."*
>
> H.S.T.

In essence, we have managed to make liberalism a double curse. We are continually getting raped by the private. We get polluted and paved and built around and torn down in the name of free enterprise. On the other hand, we fear government in part because we have no control over it. Both realms are uncontrolled by the people. We will not control the private because of our faith; nor can we control our government because of our fear.

So we are caught between the terror of anarchy and the tyranny of the state. We become immobilized by our beliefs.

> *As it turned out, the Lindsay campaign was totally flawed from the start. It was all tip and no iceberg. . . .*
>
> *The main problem with any democracy is that crowd-pleasers are generally brainless swine who can go out on a stage & whup their supporters into an orgiastic frenzy—then go back to the office & sell every one of the poor bastards down the tube for a nickel apiece.*
>
> H.S.T.

---

[5] This point is made most clearly in Hannah Arendt, *On Revolution* (New York: Viking Press, 1963).

Locke wrote that the state was formed by a contract between the people and the government. Each had a duty, each had much responsibility. Locke carefully explained that when the government failed to carry out its responsibilities, then it was the duty of each citizen to break the contract.

That is a serious thought: to break the contract. Regrettably, it is a thought with which we all must conjure. When we do, when we think about breaking the contract, we find a problem. A real one. We find that our liberalism gives us no hint of an alternative, no idea of anything different. We seem stuck, afraid of more government or of less government, of more freedom or of less freedom. We are waxed statues who melt under the pressure of trying to create.

> The "mood of the nation," in 1972, was . . . overwhelmingly vengeful, greedy, bigoted, and blindly reactionary . . . the Silent Majority was so deep in a behavioral sink that . . . all they wanted in the White House was a man who would leave them alone and do anything necessary to bring calmness back into their lives—even if it meant turning the whole state of Nevada into a concentration camp for hippies, niggers, dope fiends, do-gooders, and anyone else who might threaten the status quo.
>
> H.S.T.

We seem to be unable to think of change, so we cop out, and go to the polls periodically to vote. Once every two years or four years or more, we fool ourselves into thinking we are saving freedom, protecting democracy, by pulling a lever of a machine. We are so proud, so self-righteous.

But as we vote, we never think that voting does nothing but condemn us to the status quo. To vote is the ultimate act of futility; it is to pretend change while prolonging stability. Our only act of citizenship, our only public act, turns out to be a private farce. As we vote, we simply endorse our own immobility.

> The two real political parties in America are the Winners and the Losers. The people do not acknowledge this. They claim membership in two imaginary parties, the Republicans and the Democrats, instead . . . losers can join imaginary parties. Losers can vote.
>
> K.V.

Wrong you say? Imagination you say? What about Salvador Dali? Salvador Dali is a hero of mine. A man of genius and imagination who has been an artistic creator in our century. He is now an old man and lives in a castle. Nearby, in a neighboring castle, lives his wife who was a Russian princess. They are growing old together, in a very stylized way. When Dali has a picture, or some such thing to show his wife, he sends her a message to that effect.

In return, Dali receives a formal, written invitation for tea the next day at his wife's castle. He goes and, one imagines, they enjoy themselves. It seems to be a very workable and satisfactory arrangement.

The point is that as liberal Americans, we understand *neither* part of Dali. He outflanks us on *both* sides. Not only is he more creative than we, he is also more formal, stylized, "conservative" than we. He sees the beauty of the artistic frontier as well as the richness of social form. I am not arguing we should do both, or either for that matter. What seems so striking is that we can't do much of one or the other; even our imagination cuts us off from feeling why Dali can love and do both.

We are dead-center liberals, missing the best of both worlds.

The Voting Fetish

To begin to truly understand voting in America, we must put the whole discussion in context. We have got to know just how it fits into our view of the world. It may be best to discuss it by "pretending." Pretend that we are constructing a state. This state is to be inhabited by evil people; the population is to be motivated by self-interest. The world view is to be scientific. That is to say, reality and value are to be attributed only to those things that are physical and material, to those things that are countable and quantifiable. Finally, the population is to organize itself bureaucratically.

As good political scientists, as good creators, we would have to deal with a very fundamental problem: How do we keep citizens within the system? How can we give them an illusion of power so as to keep them content? How can we distract them from important questions—and possibly answers—while making trivial behavior seem important? The answer is deceivingly simple: Make voting a meaningless gesture (both to the individual and to the society), but also make voting a myth of important proportions.

Discussions of voting, and the questions asked about it, almost always miss the point. To look at how voting is discussed is an exercise in understanding how questions can predetermine answers. To understand the voting fetish, we must familiarize ourselves not only with the common questions and answers but also begin to ask questions not ordinarily asked.

The idea of voting is important in America, very important. The public schools pump our heads full of the importance of elections, the TV networks spend millions on their coverage, and we social scientists study and restudy elections and electors and the electorate. Even bars are closed on election day to insure that we become heady from voting and not drunk from liquor. Before one election has begun, people are making plans for the following one. There seems little doubt that elections—and voting—are the biggest games in town; but do they really mean anything? To put it differently, what does it mean to vote? How does it count? [6]

Political scientists have worked hard studying elections. In part, elections are perfect to study if one believes in objective reality. Voting is an objective fact. A vote is something real, something that can be counted, computed, and "played with" in a variety of ways. Further, about the time one batch of votes is used up, there is another election and another batch. So we know a great deal about voting and we are told much about elections. For example, the distinguished political scientist Austin Ranney writes:

> ". . . political scientists study the behavior of individual voters in order to understand the behavior of electorates, for their object is to comprehend the forces affecting the outcome of elections,

---

[6] The argument has been made that the importance of the process lies in its folly. For instance, Herbert McClosky has written, "It is not clear . . . that either the parties or voters want the conventions reformed. Like the circus to which they are sometimes compared, they are among the greatest shows on the earth." The *New York Times Magazine*, August 4, 1968.

which, as we shall see, are the principal democratic devices for holding government responsible to the people." [7]

It is all there—the myth of voting, that is. Let us examine the findings of those who study voting and elections, and see if we can understand the myth more clearly. More importantly, we could understand what they don't ask.

> *Losers have thousands of religions . . . The single religion of the Winners is a harsh interpretation of Darwinism, which argues that it is the will of the universe that only the fittest should survive . . .*
>
> *Winners . . . learn how to be pitiless. They understand that the material resources of the planet are almost exhausted, and that pity will soon be a form of suicide.*
>
> *The Winners are rehearsing for* Things to Come.
>
> K.V.

The argument about voting often centers around the idea of democracy. In a simpleminded way, we are taught that to vote is democratic and that those who vote will have a say in determining policy. Political scientists are interested in who votes, in part to see which groups choose those who govern. Who votes? The more education a person has, the more likely the individual is to vote. The higher an individual's income, the greater the chances of his or her voting. More white people than black vote, and more white-collar than blue-collar workers vote. Finally, more men than women vote. ("One woman respondent told an interviewer, 'Woman is a flower for men to look after'; another said, 'I have never voted, I never will. . . . A woman's place is in the home'; and a third declared, 'Voting is for the men.' ")[8]

The suggestion has been made that the nonvoters—the black, the blue-collar, the "uneducated"—may not vote because they believe that elections make no difference.[9] Simply stated, these individuals hold that whoever—Democrat or Republican—holds power does not hold it for their benefit. On the other hand, the voter—the white, the "well-educated,"

---

[7] Austin Ranney, *Governing* (New York: Holt, Rinehart & Winston, 1971), p. 141.

[8] Ibid., p. 147. It is just such statements that point out how difficult the task of liberation will be.

[9] Ibid., p. 148.

the white-collar worker—may really believe that his or her
vote makes a difference and that voting in national elections
could change the world.[10]

To understand the nature of elections and the nature of
our party system is to begin to understand that the "uneducated" black who failed to vote may well be right.

> But you must know in your heart what every Winner knows:
> that one must behave heartlessly toward losers, if one hopes to
> survive. . . .
> All the rest was hokum.

                                                                    K.V.

One basic criticism of elections is that they are not democratic. There is more than some truth in this contention. It is
important to understand this point of view, and then to understand why it does not get us far enough.[11] To be democratic,
elections should fulfill the following four requirements: First,
either the parties or the candidates should offer clear-cut
choices to the voters. Not a choice of hair color or of speaking style, but of politics and programs. Second, the voters must
be concerned with and aware of the choices. Third, voting
should somehow indicate how the majority feels about the
issues. Finally, when a candidate is elected, he or she should
somehow be bound by his or her promises. What we know
about elections indicates that none of these conditions are
met, or that they are even in very much danger of being met.

First things first: Are these policy alternatives? The answer
is no. People do not run on issues; they run to be elected.
Political parties are interested in winning the greatest number
of votes, so they try to avoid taking stands which might offend
or bringing up issues which seem to deviate too far from the

---

[10] What about advertising people? Those modern moralists of Madison Avenue? ". . . many [ad] agencies reject [selling candidates] as unethical or de-
meaning . . . a stand which infuriates George Lois. 'Some idiots say it's morally
wrong to do political ads,' he fumes. 'They're proud of selling some goddam
deodorant, but not a person who can do things for the country.' To which
Jerry Della Femina, another ad agency chief who refuses political ads, re-
plies: 'No deodorant ever bombed Cambodia.' " (*Newsweek*, April 12, 1976,
p. 88. Copyright 1976 by Newsweek, Inc. All rights reserved. Reprinted by
permission.)

[11] Thomas Dye and Harmon Zeigler, *The Irony of Democracy* (Belmont,
Calif.: Wadsworth Publishing Co., 1970), p. 174.

center of things. When two parties equally intent on winning the election clash, the party that is the most vague may well triumph. Making clear the difficult issues is simply risky electoral politics. Our parties, our candidates, almost always play follow the leader; the funny part is that the leader never gets off dead center.

> *The convention had left me speechless. It was so heavily guarded, spiritually and physically, that I hadn't been able to see or hear anything that wasn't already available in an official press release. "It's Disneyland under martial law," I said.*
>
> K.V.

Because the major parties deliberately try not to articulate the choices, the answer to our second condition is easy: The voters cannot be aware of policy alternatives when there are none. I blush at the redundance of the statement.

If people do not vote on issues, why do they vote? Generally speaking, people join the same party their parents joined. When elections come, most people, most of the time, vote for the candidate of their party. If people vote according to party, then what do the parties do, what functions do they serve?

Robert Dahl argues that political parties are of great help to the voter because they "present to voters a very small number of alternatives out of the total number theoretically available." [12] So that is what parties do! They help us to make rational choices by limiting those choices to two. They ease our anxiety over right and wrong—or, at least over who or what to vote for—by limiting our selection to an identical set of alternatives. Parties make it possible for us to choose between two representatives of the system—and they make the choice relatively unencumbered by numbers.

> *A lot of naturally funny people who want to help losers aren't going to clown anymore. They have caught on that clowning doesn't throw off the timing or slow down cruel social machinery. In fact, it usually serves as a lubricant. . . .*
>
> *The idea, of course, was to make the victim comical rather than pitiful. Pity is like rust to a cruel social machine.*
>
> K.V.

---

[12] Robert Dahl, *Pluralist Democracy in the United States* (Chicago: Rand McNally & Co., 1967), p. 250.

Is it possible somehow for voting to indicate how the majority feels about the issues? The answer, of course, is no. With two—or three—candidates hedging on the issues, and each taking weak stands on many issues, it is simply naive to believe that a vote can be translated into support for a particular policy or set of policies. Our elections are not organized so that the voter can help decide what the major policies of the country will be. When an individual is elected, all that means is that he or she gets to hold office. Because the campaign promises were vague or silly or both, and because we do not really expect such promises to be kept, policies are not the result of elections.

So maybe that poor, black person is right not to vote. In 1968, 40 percent of the people who were eligible did not vote; in 1972, 44.6 percent didn't; by 1974 the percentage was up to 63.8. There just are not that many blacks in the country.

In the future the definition of an exciting election may change. Instead of being excited about who might win, we might be excited to see if anyone votes.

> We don't covet anybody's territory. We would just like to buy or rent some of it, if we can. . . .
>
> If I were a visitor from another plant, radioing home about Earth, I wouldn't call Americans Americans. I would give them a name that told a lot about them immediately: I would call them realtors . . . They had sent some Republicans up there [to the Moon] to have a look around, to cancel some stamps, to pray and hit a few golf balls, and they knew better now. Not even losers, with all their lazy resourcefulness, could survive on the moon.
>
> K.V.

Surely voting must do something, help someone. Oddly enough, it is not entirely clear just who does gain from elections. The voter may gain psychic satisfaction in knowing that he or she has "protected democracy" or whatever other symbol that citizen was serving. Someone gets elected, so certainly that someone is helped. In honesty, I believe the best we can do, the most we can say, is that voting contributes to the system. It symbolically hooks people to the process, at little or no risk to that process. Systems seek stability, and for us voting has uniquely served the status quo.

There are too many ways to make the ties between our-selves and our myths and our voting. One way to do it is to review some fairly recent history.

Daytime TV

"For make no mistake about it, if our way of life derives from Amer-ica's 'givenness,' Nixon is what will be given us."

GARY WILLS

A couple of summers ago—the summer of such good TV—we changed Presidents; horses in mid-stream or some such trite phrase. It was interesting and oddly traumatic and regrettably necessary. Regrettable because we might learn things we don't want to know, for in the end, Richard Nixon is one of us. Think about: He was the one who Made It.

That summer, people would ask questions of each other about Watergate, and impeachment, and the weather, and normal things. It finally made sense to me to try and work out some kind of Watergate Answer. After all, I taught at a Big State University and was being paid to do that. More than that, it is my country and it was important for me to know what the hell was going on.

I composed an answer to the question: What do you say when someone asks you about Watergate? Depending on my mood, the kind of day it had been, who I was talking with, how long we had to talk, and the like, I would do all or part of the following in whatever manner seemed appropriate.

It seemed that I always got to this point: we all had a com-mon stake in what was going on. The stake was a strange one, as almost all the *real* effect of Watergate was *mood*. Some-how, Watergate is a reflection of ourselves as a funny-shaped Sixty-Year-Old-Man. To see that more clearly is to go through levels of American myths; through levels of thoughts in our own heads until we get to the parent myths. It is, in part, to catch a glimpse of how political myths work in ourselves.

Henry [Kissinger] has the best deal Faust ever made with Mephistopheles. . . .

The Super-Realtors, with Dr. Kissinger as their representative, have worked out crude agreements with the few other truly ter-

rifying powers of the planet as to what can be done and what must not be done with the real estate of the meek.

                                                                    K.V.

There were all kinds of preresignation explanations we all heard, maybe said, possibly even believed. For example:

Conservatives: To save the country, we must save the presidency. We cannot afford to mess around with our hallowed national institutions. If the irresponsible (crummy) liberal Eastern Establishment Press would just stop all of its idle chatter and destructive work, everything would be fine, et cetera, et cetera, BLAH, BLAH, BLAH.

American Civil Liberty Union Liberals: America is really an all right place, there are just some bad people. So, the Constitution and the courts and the country will be vindicated when the legal system gets finished. We all know that no matter how painfully and slowly it works, the letter of the law always gets the wrongdoer. [Macho, in legal language and Latin phrases.]

Radical: It would be "wrong" to impeach him. Keep him. Neuter Nixon. Let things gently fall apart. Let the corruption and rot show through so that space will be opened up for radicals. Then, something constructive could go on. [My nose always keeps running, I think I'll cut it off to spite my face.]

Essentially, the first range of response is as much style as anything. While we can learn something about the person who answers in one of these ways, that fairly narrow range of newspaper-type reasoning won't get us as far as we need to go.

Another way to go about it is to talk about what the "best" impeachment case might be, and what the "best" legal case might be. Those wise people among us would say, and rightly so, that if it had ever come to trial—The United States of America vs. Richard M. Nixon—the charges would be decided on "political" considerations.

For example, a very good legal case might have been made against Nixon because of his bombing of Cambodia. It was, after all, secret, unauthorized by Congress, and illegal. Fairly impressive causes for a legal case. Evidence? Sure. There were memos, military people who knew, the press who saw it, and on and on. But, to bring charges would be politically risky. Why?

Why? In part because of the games of our elected officials. There is, as a case in point, a congressional committee which is supposed to watch the military. To bring charges over Cambodia is to make those on the committee look like fools, or worse. If they admit they knew about the bombings, they acted illegally; if they didn't know, they weren't doing their jobs. Either way, it was pretty clear Nixon would escape this outrage.

There could have been charges stemming from the Milk Fund mess. It was only a fair case and, anyway, almost everyone took milk money. Even Congressman Rodino took $100, and there are remarkably few cows in his part of Brooklyn.

> *So a Pavlovian connection has been made in the minds of people who are really awfully nice: when more than two people show up with a humanitarian idea, the police should be called.*
>
> *If the police don't act immediately, and if the humanitarians behave in a manner that is dignified or beautiful or heartbreaking, there is still something nice people can do.*
>
> *They can ignore the humanitarians.*
>
> K.V.

So, it was sensible to believe that the issue would be Watergate—not because it was the worst crime, the most damaging or destructive, but because no one else had done exactly that same one. It is a kind of fun analysis to make, but, like the first set of answers, it ignores most of the interesting and important theoretical points.

Dummies and Card Games

If part of the purpose of our learning about politics is to see the ties which bind myths, and actions, and our life then we should study the relationship of Richard Nixon to the way our heads work. We can talk about Nixon as the ideal American: The Horatio Alger Hero of Our Times.

There are a couple of questions to keep in mind: Is there a Richard Nixon and, if so, do we want to see his face if we look into a mirror?

There are a couple of keys to remember: Playing the game, and proving and reproving yourself is part of our liberal upbringing.

Gary Wills, in his fine book *Nixon Agonistes,* tells of young Dick as a footballer at Whittier College. There were almost no funds for the football team, and there were few players. Nixon was both small and clumsy, but determined even then. For three seasons he and one other man were literally tackling dummies for the first team to practice on.

Nixon finally lettered his senior year.

The important thing is that we have some empathy, if not respect, for that continuing effort—that trying so hard to succeed. There is an American myth which, in part, assures us that if you try hard enough, you *deserve* to win . . . and you will.

> *Several hundred American gunfighters, killers from the war in Vietnam, formed themselves into platoons. . . . Many wore the raffish, spooky rags of modern jungle warfare. They marched silently, in the slope-shouldered route step of tired, hungry veterans—which they were. Their hair was often long, which gave them the cavalier beauty of Indian killers from another time.*
>
> *Some were in wheelchairs. Many had wounds. John Wayne, the gunfighter's gunfighter, was in Miami Beach somewhere. But he was nowhere to be seen when these real gunfighters came to town . . . .*
>
> *They sat down silently, which was a crime. They were blocking a public thoroughfare. Some sighed. Some scratched themselves.*
>
> *Their message was this: "Let the killing stop."*
>
> *They went home again.*
>
> *How many nice people came out of the hotel or came to hotel windows to watch them? None—almost none. It was a police affair.*
>
> K.V.

An obvious question is: What does the world look like in the myth? The world, for the Richard Nixon in us, is one of a series of starting lines—or of card games—in which you are continually made to prove yourself. The world is seen as countless opportunities to start and restart. High school, college, jobs, sports—the American vision of competition. Every so often you line up and race to beat your mates.

Politically, the metaphor is closer to a card game than a race. We get the New Deal and the Fair Deal. Somehow, we find ourselves in this amazing game of You Bet Your Life; every once in a while we throw in our cards which are reshuffled and dealt. We continually try to win "pots."

Of course this particular myth lacks substantial evidence in reality. In lots of senses, the rich stay rich or get richer, and the rest of us are always playing for penny-ante pots. But that's what is so fascinating about Nixon: He kept trying. He earned his letter and became President. So, he becomes a kind of perfect/ideal model. He is the modern Horatio Alger.

Who is Horatio Alger? What was this dimestore-novel novelist into?

For Alger, there was a sacredness in the running; in showing that, by effort, you *deserve* to win. The important part was on rising. On showing how hard work can mold character; listen to the book titles: *Making His Way, Helping Himself, Struggling Upward, Bound to Rise.* The poisonous thing wasn't that Alger's heroes aimed at wealth or success; the hero didn't aim at those things.

The tricky part is that the hero aimed not at success, but at succeeding.

Wills writes that this person becomes "a martyr to duty." The self-made man or woman is the true American monster. If you *make something* outside of yourself—build a chair, write a paper, grow a garden—that *thing* comes from the self, but is apart from the self.

But the *self* maker, the self improver, is never finished; cannot stand alone; isn't apart from or severed from the self. The person must always tinker, improve, adjust, start over. There is always the fear your product—your self—will be out of date, or it will rot from non-use.

You always have to go back and begin again.

You have to have the heat of decisions—of crises in Nixon language—to know yourself. The whole stress, in '71, was not to be a good President but to be re-elected. The sickness of always competing and of never completing your project—of never really having a self—was eating away at Nixon.

There may not be a Richard Nixon. If there is, and he looks into a mirror, there may be blank spaces; an incompleteness of self which is understood as moral failure.

When you vote for the Presidential-Candidate-of-Your-Choice, I think Nixon's presidency is a good model: One with no vision, or goal, or aims which are really understandable. Because he was up to his neck in his need to keep succeeding; because he was such a self-improver, Watergate wasn't really immoral. Tricky maybe, but everyone was at the starting line— and the aim was to finish first, and to start again.

> *Those Indians seemed to have turned to redwood. They did not talk. They did not swivel their heads around to see who was who.*
>
> *They had a coffee table all to themselves. On it were mimeographed copies of a message they had come great distances to deliver. They were from many tribes . . .*
>
> *The message said this in part: "We come today in such a manner that must shame God himself. For a country which allows a complete body of people to exist in conditions which are at variance with the ideals of this country, conditions which daily commit injustices and inhumanity, must surely be filled with hate, greed, and unconcern."*
>
> K.V.

It is enormously destructive to think that Nixon really is our model, not because he made it, but because he is a vacuum.

It is in that sense that we really do have *Self* government. We are not monsters, nor are we political. But, we're all about the same; all private and always tinkering with our products— which is our very own self.

So Students of Voting, there is/was Richard Nixon receiving an amazing electoral mandate. Vote and save democracy. Indeed.

The most grotesque part of Watergate is that we somehow forgot that America is its people; its shared, collective past; its noble deeds and good examples, as well as the bad and rotten. We know for a fact *it is not* the institution of the Presidency; nor any institution I can think of.

There is no defense for Watergate; maybe a lesson or two for us, but certainly no defense.

It is a moral stain.

Voting and Politics

Up to here, two distinct arguments have been made. First, that our liberalism keeps us from an active involvement in politics. Second, that discussions on voting only show us that voting in

America does not live up to the "requirements" of democracy. We have implied more than that. Certainly it seems possible to understand voting as fulfilling a stabilizing, symbolic function, as a method of keeping people from making important decisions and away from power. Few people ask what voting means if, in a bureaucratic society, most leaders are interchangeable anyway. But even that may not be the most important point.

If this is a book about politics, then it is necessary to ask at least one more question about voting in America. It is important to ask a very obvious question which is almost never asked: Is voting in America a political action?

> *(And I must digress at this point to coin an acronym that can serve me now, which is "JACFU." A similar acronym, "JANFU," was coined during the second world war, along with "SNAFU." It meant "Joint Army-Navy Fuck-Up." I would like "JACFU" to mean "Joint American-Communist Fuck-Up.")* . . . .
>
> *The walking wounded within our own boundaries, our undeserving poor, are not by any stretch of the imagination victims of JACFU. We creamed them ourselves. Money is tight. We can only afford to heal them a little bit; and even that little bit hurts. Winners like bloody murder, in the years to come.*
>
> K.V.

We have already discussed politics. To act politically, one must honestly work toward an eventual outcome. That means —more or less—that one must help frame the issues; one works for those issues; and, finally, one must help carry out the results of those issues. Ideally, this is done openly and with others. The argument, stated most simply, is that we make something legitimate, make something moral, by actively participating in it. By being political, we give meaning to what goes on. It is not a simple process of acquiescing; it is action.

In order to understand politics, we must understand what it means to take action. We can get at this by discussing the differences between behavior and action. Behavior is the normal, the routine, those things that are carefully closed by boundaries. To behave is to do the predictable, to do what has always been done. Pets behave; children "should" behave.

In oddly similar ways, rats behave for scientists as voters behave for the system.

> *The Nixon-Kissinger scheme, the Winners' scheme . . . for lasting world peace is simple. Its basic axiom is to be followed by individuals as well as great nations, by losers and winners alike. We have demonstrated the workability of the axiom in Vietnam, in Bangladesh, in Biafra, in Palestinian refugee camps, in our own ghettos, in our migrant labor camps, on our Indian reservations, in our institutions for the defective and the deformed and the aged.*
> *This is it: ignore agony.*
>
> K.V.

To take action is to cut across traditional boundaries. It is to invent new methods, create new means, make new connections. It is to consciously help define who you are by what you do. It is an individual's way of relating to the whole, but in his or her own, unique, special way. You are what you do, if you act. You are what you are told to be, if you behave.

In order to act, one must have space. There must be political space provided by the state. Space metaphysically and actually. Space in which citizens may come together for creative political action, not simply for normal behavior. The greater the space available, the greater the opportunity for each citizen to act. But people must want and fight for and finally protect their political space. It is as much a human property as a property provided by the state. In other words, one of the reasons we have no political space is that it might endanger the system; another is that we are not actively working to get that space.

> *He [a visitor from another planet] would tell us, I think, that no real Winner fears God or believes in a punitive afterlife. He might say Earthlings put such emphasis on truthfulness in order to be believed when they lie. President Nixon, for instance, was free to lie during his acceptance speech at the convention, if he wanted to, because of his famous love for the truth. And the name of the game was "Survival." Everything else was hokum.*
>
> K.V.

Briefly, a person must have space in order to act creatively, in order to engage publicly in politics. But just what does that really mean?

For the purposes of our discussion, it simply means this: Voting as we practice it is not a political act. We know that we have no real say in who we vote for. All the candidates look the same. It is like being given a choice between identical twins in a beauty contest. We surely cannot feel creative, nor can we feel we are defining ourselves by what we do. There is no sense of participation.

The way voting has been set up, it is neither politics nor action. It is not even public. It is simply a fact that having three minutes alone in a three-foot by three-foot space once every few years neither furthers democracy nor enhances freedom. It is almost all those things we were taught that it was not.

> *THE WINNERS*
> *ARE AT WAR*
> *WITH THE LOSERS,*
> *AND THE FIX IS*
> *ON,*
> *THE PROSPECTS FOR PEACE*
> *ARE AWFUL*
>
> K.V.

In many places, voting has come to mean behavior in the most confining sense. It is only a method of endorsing those who will keep doing the same old thing, in the same old way, according to the same old rules, under the same old system. It is the meaningless raised to important societal myth.

Voting keeps you where you are. It is not action, it is not politics; it is merely reaction, simply endorsement. The rulers keep ruling, the people keep voting. The franchise has widened, eighteen-year-olds now vote. We have spread the novocaine; everyone gets deadened. The numbness of voting merely envelops more of us.

At the end of a creative political act, people should vote; but as it is now carried out, voting is a terrible fraud.

It is best we heed these words of Nietzsche: "I say unto you: a man must have chaos yet within him to be able to give birth to a dancing star."

Politics as Loneliness and Pressure (or, What Holds America Together?)

6

How else do things work always unless by imitation bred of the passion to be liked? All the processes of society are based on it, all individual development. For some reason, it was something that we seemed to have a conspiracy to ignore or not to mention, even while most single-mindedly engaged in it. There was some sort of conspiracy of belief that people—children, adults, everyone—grew by an acquisition of unconnected habits, of isolated bits of knowledge, like choosing things off a counter: "Yes, I'll have that one," or "No, I don't want that one!" But in fact people develop for good or for bad by swallowing whole other people, atmospheres, events, places—develop by admiration. Often enough unconsciously, of course. We are the company we keep.

DORIS LESSING

One of the guarantees of freedom in a planned society will be the maintenance of the individual capacity for adjustment.

KARL MANNHEIM

The theory of infinite human plasticity . . . errs by confusing the ability of man to adapt *successfully* to these pressures: it confuses the ability to survive with the ability to flourish. . . . Psychosis is after all a form of adaptation. . . .

KENNETH KENISTON

We are all here. All together in the same country, products of more or less the same culture. We are mass-produced Americans. The nation in which we live is seemingly vital. Like a huge machine or a giant hungry animal, it continues to produce and grow, grow and produce.

But what does that really mean? What does it mean to be a part of America, to be American? More specifically, what holds the machine together? Why doesn't it fall apart? Why does it cohere; what is the glue which holds us as parts of the system, and in turn holds the system together?

To begin to answer these questions—even to get wrong answers—there are several steps we must take. The punch line of this chapter will be the suggestion that, just possibly, the system is held together at our expense. That by sacrificing some of our rights and powers, the system continues to run. To get to that point, however, it is first necessary to understand more about what a system is and is not, and what that has to do with politics and people.

Systems

The easiest way to outline what a system is is simply to list some of its most salient features. Social science tells us that a system has a boundary, that it has some kind of communications network, that it may be natural or voluntary, legitimate or illegitimate, efficient or effective or both or neither, functional or dysfunctional, accessible or inaccessible, open or closed. Also, it would appear that the bias of most systems is to want to survive and, in most cases, to grow.[1]

---

[1] The classic statement of systems analysis is to be found in David Easton, *The Political System* (New York: Alfred A. Knopf, 1953).

If you consider these traits, sweeping and vague as they are, the conclusion is obvious: We know for sure that we have a "system" in America. To be more exact, we know that segments of our society can be accurately understood in terms that describe a system. It seems equally obvious that what we call the political system cannot be separated from most social and economic goings-on. Social scientists tell us that a political system must have methods of formulating issues, deliberating them, resolving them, and finally finding solutions for them. What they do not tell us is that most issues are political ones and that many are "resolved" in less than open, political ways.

In other words, the system may work well in its own terms. It may stay together, function normally and smoothly, yet never really be a "political" system. The high school as an institution is a political system in which the students are rarely given a political voice. The important questions are decided by the "experts" within the system: the teachers, the principal, even the school board. Students are simply an "input" into the system. At the end of a few years, the students leave school, thereby becoming "outputs" of the system. In systemic terms, nothing has changed basically. The only thing that has really been affected is the student, who has been exposed to what it means to be a "citizen" of the system. It will not come as a big surprise to learn that college is not very different. There *appears* to be more freedom, and maybe there actually is. There should be, because by the time a person has spent thirteen years in public schools, his or her imagination should be sufficiently limited so that he or she can be trusted with a small increment of freedom. In systemic terms, a functional output is one which will continue to support the system. It is clear that our educational system, in spite of signs encouraging to some, continues to produce functional outputs.

While the school system enables us to understand more about systems in general, it does not help enough. One of the critical deficiencies of systems analysis is that it is blind either to change or values; it cannot really tell us about ourselves and can tell us only a very little about our surroundings. A systems analysis seems to assume that whatever is functional is good and that whatever is dysfunctional is bad; but to know that is to remain completely uninformed about either good or bad.

It is simply to know what makes a system stable, to know what might affect the status quo. We must know more than that. What we are most interested in is what the system means to us; how, essentially, the system holds itself together, with us in it.

One way to begin to understand what our system does is by studying what it does not do. More accurately, we can begin by discovering what is not included in the system.

From James Madison, writing in *Federalist* No. 10, we learned that ours was a rational system, one that was set up to run almost in spite of people. Power was separated, balanced, federated, and, some believe, pluralized. But what about the relationship among politics and the people and the state? To get at those questions, we may begin by asking these:

1. Do we have any idea of what it means to have a political community?
2. Do we have any idea of political obligation?

Community

. . . suburbanites who philosophize over their back fence with complete sincerity about their "dog-eat-dog-world," and what-is-it-all-for, and you-can't-take-it-with-you, and success-doesn't-make-you-happy-it-just-gives-you-ulcers-and-a-heart-condition would be enraged should their children pay serious attention to such a viewpoint. . . .

We seek a private house, a private means of transportation, a private garden, a private laundry, self-service stores, and do-it-yourself skills of every kind.

PHILIP SLATER

It is possible to relate to some of the concepts of a "political system" simply because we are surrounded by its words. "Community" is different. The idea of a system and the idea of a community are very different. Different in almost every way, from the way each is set up to the way it feels to live in one.[2] Let us begin with how each is created.

---

[2] For an analysis of the differences between community and what we now have in America, see Robert Nisbet, *Community and Power* (New York: Oxford University Press, 1962). Another approach to the problem can be found in Perry Miller's brilliant book on the Puritans, *Errand into the Wilderness* (New York: Harper & Row, 1958).

There are several theories about how governments, or political entities, are created. For example, there are those who believe that God chooses someone to rule: hence, a divine right provides legitimacy to the leader, to kings and queens and such. Our tradition is not divine right. In a society infatuated with law, it is no mistake that we believe that governments are founded by contracts, by people banding together and agreeing to the conditions under which the state will function.

For our purposes, there are at least two ways in which this contract can be drawn up. The first way is for all of the people individually to give their support to one source, for each person to make his or her own pledge, and to have his or her private compact. This kind of contract leads to a "political system" as we know it. There is no community, for everyone is alone; no politics, for each has his or her own private interests; no power other than that of the state, for everyone is isolated. As we shall see, this is the contract of individualism.

The second kind of contract binds each to the other. Each citizen becomes responsible for every other. The bonds among people are personal ones, visible ones. Identity comes from membership in and participation in the actions of the community. Decisions are reached communally and openly and, hopefully, for the good of those concerned. Power resides in the group, in the many. In theory, power is held by all, in common.

Ours is a political system, not a political community; ours is a society created by 220,000,000 single contracts, pledging support to an impersonal system. As we shall see, the illusion is individualism, the reality political isolation; the hope is equality, the truth much different.

In place of community in America, we have interests. Of course, interests may be greater than any single individual, but interests are not communities. Our interests are private. Further, our interests are either social or economic, and in America these are generally the same.

We serve our interests because we are on the make, not because there is a better vision of the world. The calculus is precise: We are driven into the public realm only to the extent that we must protect our private interests. Our business is predominantly private, very often selfish, and has the long-run effect of leaving us isolated. By substituting the idea of interest politics for political community, we have put business in the place of brotherhood. Of course, we have good friends, and some of us even have an idea of what a nice neighborhood is, but these are difficult to achieve. If they exist, they exist in spite of, surely not because of, our system. These things speak more to the urges of people than to the dynamics of the process.

Interest politics is a popular (and rightfully so) subject in books about American politics. We are well acquainted with the arguments that private interest groups—pressure groups —often exercise a great deal of influence on national, state, and local policy.[3] We also know that the most effective of these groups are generally well-organized, wealthy, and white. What I would like to argue is that the system is set up to reward these groups, while teaching that we are each an individual, each with a contract with the state, each equal in power —or, powerlessness. The reality of most private interests and of politics based on them is privatization.

Privatization is not a bad thing, if one does not care about those major decisions which affect one's life.

Have We Any Idea of Political Obligation?

Do we really have any political obligations? Does the system encourage us to be political? Some things seem clear. It appears that we have a war obligation to the state. We must also assume a tax burden. There is pressure to vote—but little pressure to understand what that means. After all, voting has come to mean that apolitical act we go through from time to time to choose a person already selected by the system to serve the purposes of that system. We seem to have a greater obligation to the system than to the body politic, to the private sphere than to the public, to the anonymous than to the known. In an important sense, the essence of our political obligation is simple: We are taught that one should not talk about income, God, or politics in polite company.

---

[3] For a fine treatment of interest-group politics, see Grant McConnell, *Private Power and American Democracy* (New York: Alfred A. Knopf, 1966). A further discussion of interest groups is found in this book, Chapter 9.

One argument is that the system may be held together by people being political. In its most simple form, the logic is this: If privatization makes us vulnerable by way of power-lessness, then politics—openness and publicness—is the solution. But instinctively we know that a true plurality of interests would be unpredictable. We know that when presented in a public, political way, plurality looks like chaos, and chaos is dysfunctional to a willful, self-protective system. The combinations of isolation and representation, individualism and Madisonian liberalism, seem to pull us further and further away from any positive, healthy sense of the political. It pushes us toward behavior which is best understood as systemically functional.

I am not arguing that the potential for politics has never existed in America. Just the opposite. The sense that politics was a way in which the individual could interact with the many and insure personal freedom and individualism was expressed most clearly during the 1830s by a Frenchman named Alexis de Tocqueville. Tocqueville, an Old World aristocrat, well understood the tensions between liberty and equality, between individualism and isolation, and believed that the best way to guard against the triumph of equality/isolation was through politics. In *Democracy in America*, we can find an analysis of the potential problems and solutions in the then new democratic state of America.

The following passage is from the first volume of his two-volume work. It describes, in Tocqueville's terms, "Political Associations in the United States." [4]

> In no country in the world has the principle of association been more successfully used or applied to a greater multitude of objects than in America. Besides the permanent associations which are established by law under the names of townships, cities, and counties, a vast number of others are formed and maintained by the agency of private individuals.
>
> The citizen of the United States is taught from infancy to rely upon his own exertions in order to resist the evils and the difficulties of life; he looks upon the social authority with an eye of mistrust and anxiety, and he claims its assistance only when he is

---

[4] Alexis de Tocqueville, *Democracy in America*, Vol. 1 (New York: Vintage Books, 1945), pp. 198–206.

unable to do without it. This habit may be traced even in the schools, where the children in their games are wont to submit to rules which they have themselves established, and to punish misdemeanors which they have themselves defined. The same spirit pervades every act of social life. If a stoppage occurs in a thoroughfare and the circulation of vehicles is hindered, the neighbors immediately form themselves into a deliberative body; and this extemporaneous assembly gives rise to an executive power which remedies the inconvenience before anybody has thought of recurring to a pre-existing authority superior to that of the persons immediately concerned. If some public pleasure is concerned, an association is formed to give more splendor and regularity to the entertainment. Societies are formed to resist evils that are exclusively of a moral nature, as to diminish the vice of intemperance. In the United States associations are established to promote the public safety, commerce, industry, morality, and religion. There is no end which the human will despairs of attaining through the combined power of individuals united into a society.

I shall have occasion hereafter to show the effects of association in civil life; I confine myself for the present to the political world. When once the right of association is recognized, the citizens may use it in different ways.

An association consists simply in the public assent which a number of individuals give to certain doctrines and in the engagement which they contract to promote in a certain manner the spread of those doctrines. The right of associating in this fashion almost merges with freedom of the press, but societies thus formed possess more authority than the press. When an opinion is represented by a society, it necessarily assumes a more exact and explicit form. It numbers its partisans and engages them in its cause; they, on the other hand, become acquainted with one another, and their zeal is increased by their number. An association unites into one channel the efforts of divergent minds and urges them vigorously towards the one end which it clearly points out.

The second degree in the exercise of the right of association is the power of meeting. When an association is allowed to establish centers of action at certain important points in the country, its activity is increased and its influence extended. Men have the opportunity of seeing one another; means of execution are combined; and opinions are maintained with a warmth and energy that written language can never attain.

Lastly, in the exercise of the right of political association there is a third degree: the partisans of an opinion may unite in electoral bodies and choose delegates to represent them in a central assembly. This is, properly speaking, the application of the representative system to a party.

Thus, in the first instance, a society is formed between individuals professing the same opinion, and the tie that keeps it together is of a purely intellectual nature. In the second case, small assemblies are formed, which represent only a fraction of the party. Lastly, in the third case, they constitute, as it were, a separate nation in the midst of the nation, a government within the government. Their delegates, like the real delegates of the majority, represent the whole collective force of their party, and like them, also, have an appearance of nationality and all the moral power that results from it. It is true that they have not the right, like the others, of making the laws; but they have the power of attacking those which are in force and of drawing up beforehand those which ought to be enacted.

If, among a people who are imperfectly accustomed to the exercise of freedom, or are exposed to violent political passions, by the side of the majority which makes the laws is placed a minority which only deliberates and gets laws ready for adoption, I cannot but believe that public tranquillity would there incur very great risks. There is doubtless a wide difference between proving that one law is in itself better than another and proving that the former ought to be substituted for the latter. But the imagination of the multitude is very apt to overlook this difference, which is so apparent to the minds of thinking men. It sometimes happens that a nation is divided into two nearly equal parties, each of which affects to represent the majority. If, near the directing power, another power is established which exercises almost as much moral authority as the former, we are not to believe that it will long be content to speak without acting; or that it will always be restrained by the abstract consideration that associations are meant to direct opinions, but not to enforce them, to suggest but not to make the laws.

The more I consider the independence of the press in its principal consequences, the more am I convinced that in the modern world it is the chief and, so to speak, the constitutive element of liberty. A nation that is determined to remain free is therefore right in demanding, at any price, the exercise of this independence. But the *unlimited* liberty of political association cannot be entirely assimilated to the liberty of the press. The one is at the same time less necessary and more dangerous than the other. A nation may confine it within certain limits without forfeiting any part of its self-directing power; and it may sometimes be obliged to do so in order to maintain its own authority.

In America the liberty of association for political purposes is unlimited. An example will show in the clearest light to what an extent this privilege is tolerated. . . .

In 1831, when the tariff dispute was raging with the greatest violence, a private citizen of Massachusetts proposed, by means of the newspapers, to all the enemies of the tariff to send delegates to Philadelphia in order to consult together upon the best means of restoring freedom of trade. This proposal circulated in a few days, by the power of the press, from Maine to New Orleans. The opponents of the tariff adopted it with enthusiasm; meetings were held in all quarters, and delegates were appointed. The majority of these delegates were well known, and some of them had earned a considerable degree of celebrity. South Carolina alone, which afterwards took up arms in the same cause, sent sixty-three delegates. On the 1st of October 1831 this assembly, which, according to the American custom, had taken the name of a Convention, met at Philadelphia; it consisted of more than two hundred members. Its debates were public, and they at once assumed a legislative character; the extent of the powers of Congress, the theories of free trade, and the different provisions of the tariff were discussed. At the end of ten days the Convention broke up, having drawn up an address to the American people in which it declared: (1) that Congress had not the right of making a tariff, and that the existing tariff was unconstitutional; (2) that the prohibition of free trade was prejudicial to the interests of any nation, and to those of the American people especially.

It must be acknowledged that the unrestrained liberty of political association has not hitherto produced in the United States the fatal results that might perhaps be expected from it elsewhere. The right of association was imported from England, and it has always existed in America; the exercise of this privilege is now incorporated with the manners and customs of the people. At the present time the liberty of association has become a necessary guarantee against the tyranny of the majority. In the United States, as soon as a party has become dominant, all public authority passes into its hands; its private supporters occupy all the offices and have all the force of the administration at their disposal. As the most distinguished members of the opposite party cannot surmount the barrier that excludes them from power, they must establish themselves outside of it and oppose the whole moral authority of the minority to the physical power that domineers over it. Thus a dangerous expedient is used to obviate a still more formidable danger.

The omnipotence of the majority appears to me to be so full of peril to the American republics that dangerous means used to bridle it seem to be more advantageous than prejudicial. And here I will express an opinion that may remind the reader of what I said when speaking of the freedom of townships. *There are no countries in which associations are more needed to prevent the despotism of faction or the arbitrary power of a prince than those which are democratically constituted.*[5] In aristocratic

---

[5] Emphasis added.

nations the body of the nobles and the wealthy are in themselves natural associations which check the abuses of power. In countries where such associations do not exist, if private individuals cannot create an artificial and temporary substitute for them I can see no permanent protection against the most galling tyranny; and a great people may be oppressed with impunity by a small faction or by a single individual.

The meeting of a great political convention (for there are conventions of all kinds), which may frequently become a necessary measure, is always a serious occurrence, even in America, and one that judicious patriots cannot regard without alarm. This was very perceptible in the Convention of 1831, at which all the most distinguished members strove to moderate its language and to restrain its objects within certain limits. It is probable that this Convention exercised a great influence on the minds of the malcontents and prepared them for the open revolt against the commercial laws of the Union that took place in 1832.

It cannot be denied that the unrestrained liberty of association for political purposes is the privilege which a people is longest in learning how to exercise. If it does not throw the nation into anarchy, it perpetually augments the chances of that calamity. On one point, however, this perilous liberty offers a security against dangers of another kind; in countries where associations are free, secret societies are unknown. In America there are factions, but no conspiracies.

The most natural privilege of man, next to the right of acting for himself, is that of combining his exertions with those of his fellow creatures and of acting in common with them. The right of association therefore apears to me almost as inalienable in its nature as the right of personal property. No legislator can attack it without impairing the foundations of society. Nevertheless, if the liberty of association is only a source of advantage and prosperity to some nations, it may be perverted or carried to excess by others, and from an element of life may be changed into a cause of destruction. A comparison of the different methods that associations pursue in those countries in which liberty is well understood and in those where liberty degenerates into license may be useful both to governments and to parties.

Most Europeans look upon association as a weapon which is to be hastily fashioned and immediately tried in the conflict. A society is formed for discussion, but the idea of impending action prevails in the minds of all those who constitute it. It is, in fact, an army; and the time given to speech serves to reckon up the strength and to animate the courage of the host, after which they march against the enemy. To the persons who compose it, resources which lie within the bounds of law may suggest themselves as means of success, but never as the only means.

Such, however, is not the manner in which the right of association is understood in the United States. In America the citizens who form the minority associate in order, first, to show their numerical strength and so to diminish the moral power of the majority; and, secondly, to stimulate competition and thus to discover those arguments that are most fitted to act upon the majority; for they always entertain hopes of drawing over the majority to their own side, and then controlling the supreme power in its name. Political associations in the United States are therefore peaceable in their intentions and strictly legal in the means which they employ; and they assert with perfect truth that they aim at success only by lawful expedients.

Tocqueville gives us a vision of what he believes should be an idea of politics, a form of association which would not only protect individuals from tyranny but actively involve them in the making of decisions. It is the poetry of our democracy, it is the image of what we have never become.

To return to one of our central questions: If we are to use Tocqueville as a model, it becomes clear that our system is not being held together by the kinds of creative political activities he describes. This is true, in part, because the ideology of the system encourages neither political community nor political obligation.

Things and Symbolism: What Does Hold Us Together?

To know that politics does not hold us together gets us just so far. It gives us one less thing to worry about—we can check it off our list—and it gives us something to aim for. But the point is we still don't know what holds us together. We might get closer to an answer by trying to understand what seems to be really important, what we seem to believe, and how that affects staying together.

Maybe the system is held together by material objects. It is possible, if one were cynical enough, to argue that in this land of electric can openers and vibrating beds, possessions are far more important than politics. Houses and cars and big bikes and boats really do count. People work very hard to be able to buy and to own. In the end, we may have to conclude that "things" hold us together, tie us to the system, and insure the status quo.

There are other equally important products of the system. There is the violence of television sports or the gooey-ness of the ice cream from the local parlor. Somehow, these things are important. We do identify. Maybe it is ice cream that holds us together. Sweet and sticky, available and fattening: Prisoners of Ice Cream.

But the ice cream image can easily be strained and over-emphasized; its truth is not inclusive enough. There is a greater possibility of learning more about the system and why it holds together by discussing words, by understanding language.

The Use of Words

To know the reality of politics, we have to believe the myth, to be-lieve what we are told as children.

NORMAN O. BROWN

We all know that systems are dependent, in part, upon the use of a common political language. Common language carries common myths. These words, these myths, are terribly impor-tant for any system—for any set of related institutions—as they provide the most subtle, most economic method of self-mainte-nance. It is critical for the government to set societal rules through language, through the words it uses, in order to keep order.[6]

For a simple example, we are taught that we have a repre-sentative democracy. Those are the words used, they frame our ideas of what is. It takes little insight to know that what we have is only marginally related to representation and that it has even less in common with democracy. The words only repre-sent our official institutional myth. They are part of the symbols that work well to keep the system going. What I should like to argue is that much of our symbolic glue works at our personal expense, at the expense of the citizenry.

If we examine two more myth-laden words, perhaps that thought will be clarified. The two words "equality" and "jus-tice" are as familiar as they are misunderstood, as they are

---

[6] Words? George Carlin gives us the clue to "Our Creator." Think about it, Carlin tells us: God had his/her choice of *any* name and took the very best one.

systemically effective. Because they are words that are so common, words that we seem to understand implicitly, it is important to try and figure out their implications.

As we know, the Constitution was written as if all men (to be sure, white Protestant, propertied men—the framers did mean men) were equal. What that was to mean, what we have understood it to mean, is that no individual was entitled to more rights than another. Each person—in the public realm—was to be treated equally by the system of rules to which all were equally subject. It is difficult to fault such a formulation: Equal is equal.

Justice came to mean equality of rights and equality of treatment. Moreover, justice was equated with fairness. A just or a fair decision was one which *had no objective standard of reason or justice, or even passion;* it merely meant a decision lacking bias. Again the formulation is a standard, everyday definition of what we feel/know to be true. What we must do now is to put the two words together.

By merging the myths of justice and equality, the system is able to overlook many kinds of inequalities. In the process, the system helps protect itself. It works in a simple enough manner: In our alikeness, we become alone. A "fair trial" can overlook the money, connections, color, and cultural background of the defendant. We all become bleached white; we all look the same—each alone, each the same, no matter what. Justice comes to mean the equality of everyone, equal or not. When we try to band together to work out our public problems, whether we become Panthers or militant PTAers, we learn that equal rights and equal treatment mean simply this: equal dependence and equal subjection.

Let me put it a little differently: To put equality together with justice, yet ignore such things as politics, community, and culture, results not in interesting kinds of individualism but in mass conformity.[7]

What I have been suggesting is that the system is held together—and this may seem a paradox—by the very fact that

---

[7] In a sense, this is the logical extension of the public-private problem of liberalism which was discussed earlier in connection with bureaucracies. The point here is that private advantage is often overlooked in public alikeness.

each of us is alone. The system coheres—and coerces—because the one has no defense against the mass. Even though it can be demonstrated that some people control much more wealth than others, that some make much more wide-ranging decisions than others, the fact remains that people don't think of America or of themselves in very meaningful class terms. The point is that those who hold "real power" are well limited by the boundaries of the system. (Indeed, one wonders if it is worth the price to get it.) It is the unique, the challenging—in a word, the political—that is mistrusted. The "real power" is the power of the guardian, and the guardian is as limited in creative political terms as those he or she "watches over." The powerful and the powerless are equally susceptible.

Most of us think of ourselves as some variation of middle-class; and it is arguable that our imginations are as limited as our self-definitions. The seeds of our powerlessness lie in the isolation of being the same. We may turn again to the writings of Alexis de Tocqueville to understand the problem he identifies as the "Tyranny of the Majority." [8]

> A distinction must be drawn between tyranny and arbitrary power. Tyranny may be exercised by means of the law itself, and in that case it is not arbitrary; arbitrary power may be exercised for the public good, in which case it is not tyrannical. Tyranny usually employs arbitrary means, but if necessary it can do without them. . . .
>
> In general, the American functionaries are far more independent within the sphere that is prescribed to them than the French civil officers. Sometimes, even, they are allowed by the popular authority to exceed those bounds; and as they are protected by the opinion and backed by the power of the majority, they dare do things that even a European, accustomed as he is to arbitrary power, is astonished at. By this means habits are formed in the heart of a free country which may some day prove fatal to its liberties.
>
> It is in the examination of the exercise of thought in the United States that we clearly perceive how far the power of the majority surpasses all the powers with which we are acquainted in Europe. Thought is an invisible and subtle power that mocks all the efforts of tyranny. At the present time the most absolute monarchs in Europe cannot prevent certain opinions hostile to their authority from circulating in secret through their dominions

---

[8] Tocqueville, *Democracy in America*, Vol. 1, pp. 269–72.

and even in their courts. It is not so in America; as long as the majority is still undecided, discussion is carried on; but as soon as its decision is irrevocably pronounced, everyone is silent, and the friends as well as the opponents of the measure unite in assenting to its propriety. The reason for this is perfectly clear: no monarch is so absolute as to combine all the powers of society in his own hands and to conquer all opposition, as a majority is able to do, which has the right both of making and of executing the laws.

The authority of a king is physical and controls the actions of men without subduing their will. But the majority possesses a power that is physical and moral at the same time, which acts upon the will as much as upon the actions and represses not only all contest, but all controversy.

I know of no country in which there is so little independence of mind and real freedom of discussion as in America.[9] In any constitutional state in Europe every sort of religious and political theory may be freely preached and disseminated; for there is no country in Europe so subdued by any single authority as not to protect the man who raises his voice in the cause of truth from the consequences of his hardihood. If he is unfortunate enough to live under an absolute government, the people are often on his side; if he inhabits a free country, he can, if necessary, find a shelter behind the throne. The aristocratic part of society supports him in some countries, and the democracy in others. But in a nation where democratic institutions exist, organized like those of the United States, there is but one authority, one element of strength and success, with nothing beyond it.

In America the majority raises formidable barriers around the liberty of opinion; within these barriers an author may write what he pleases, but woe to him if he goes beyond them. Not that he is in danger of an auto-da-fé, but he is exposed to continued obloquy and persecution. His political career is closed forever, since he has offended the only authority that is able to open it. Every sort of compensation, even that of celebrity, is refused to him. Before making public his opinions he thought he had sympathizers; now it seems to him that he has none any more since he has revealed himself to everyone; then those who blame him criticize loudly and those who think as he does keep quiet and move away without courage. He yields at length, overcome by the daily effort which he has to make, and subsides into silence, as if he felt remorse for having spoken the truth.

Fetters and headsmen were the course instruments that tyranny formerly employed; but the civilization of our age has perfected despotism itself, though it seemed to have nothing to learn. Monarchs had, so to speak, materialized oppression; the

---

[9] Emphasis added.

democratic republics of the present day have rendered it as entirely an affair of the mind as the will which it is intended to coerce. Under the absolute sway of one man the body was attacked in order to subdue the soul; but the soul escaped the blows which were directed against it and rose proudly superior. Such is not the course adopted by tyranny in democratic republics; there the body is left free, and the soul is enslaved. The master no longer says: 'You shall think as I do or you shall die'; but he says: 'You are free to think differently from me and to retain your life, your property, and all that you possess, but you are henceforth a stranger among your people. You may retain your civil rights, but they will be useless to you, for you will never be chosen by your fellow citizens if you solicit their votes; and they will affect to scorn you if you ask for their esteem. You will remain among men, but you will be deprived of the rights of mankind. Your fellow creatures will shun you like an impure being; and even those who believe in your innocence will abandon you, lest they should be shunned in their turn. Go in peace! I have given you your life, but it is an existence worse than death.'

Uniformity and Individualism: The Politics of Our Very Own Tyranny

Imagine a mass of cancerous tissue, the cells of which enjoyed consciousness. Would they not be full of self-congratulatory sentiments at their independence, their more advanced level of development, their rapid rate of growth? Would they not sneer at their more primitive cousins who were bound into a static and unfree existence, with limited aspirations, subject to heavy group constraint, and obviously "going nowhere"? Would they not rejoice in their control over their own destiny, and cheer the conversion of more and more normal cells as convincing proof of the validity of their own way of life? Would they not, in fact, feel increasingly triumphant right up to the moment the organism on which they fed expired?

PHILIP SLATER

To understand how the system is held together, it may help to think of a huge machine. The machine, when healthy, seems almost organic. Looking inside the machine, one could see the hundreds of thousands of political associations Tocqueville described in the first reading in this chapter. While there could be no single "rational" plan of action for that kind of system, neither could there be an ongoing tyranny of the individual by the many.

Now imagine the same machine sick. Indeed, imagine those political associations gone, the insides of the system rotted. The system is then dependent not upon the politics of the citizens but upon the strength of the state, the oppressiveness of the cover of the machine. As the inside weakens, the outside gets strong. As the population becomes isolated, the force of the state goes unchallenged. As we become less interested in joint action, in politics, we become more susceptible to oppression.

The tyranny of the majority, the terrible conformity and confinement of which Tocqueville warns, is as important as it is obvious. Each of us is, at one and the same time, both the tyrannized and the majority. Our instincts drive us into private life, while the majority determines our choices in that life. It may be instructive to anticipate that discussion here.

When I was growing up, there were four of us in the family. The usual assortment: A mother, father, older sister and myself. One day my sister (I think she was maybe 14 or 15) brought home the fifth member of the family. We took in They Say.

You know They Say. "Why do you *have* to do that?" "Well, They Say," or "Is it really important that you do that?" "Well, They Say." or, "How do you *know* that?" "Well, They Say."

Put differently, we can name—can actually see—the pressure of the faceless majority that comes right into our homes. That majority can walk right in and be a faceless power and force in how we think and act. The tyranny of the majority is as real as They Say, and carries the weight of all those around us.

What is so magical is that everyone seems at the mercy of They Say. Equally true, it always seems that everyone *else* is a member of They. It comes to this: The power of being part of the They does us no good, while being at the mercy of the They all too often hurts.

I'd have probably been happier had They Say stayed away.

As individuals, we like to believe that there are a series of choices—important ones—we will have the opportunity to make. We fret not only over the make of the automobile we are going to buy but also over its color. In weaker, less guarded moments, we realize that these decisions are not really critical ones; indeed, they are not even important. These insights rarely mean that we will stop worrying over such matters of consumption. To review the preceding chapter on voting is to begin to understand that doing things alone does not necessarily lead to individualism, and that doing things in association does not automatically eliminate it.

Symbolically, voting is American democracy at its height, the apex of political participation: The common person, spending a few minutes every two or four years, alone in a small booth, choosing between two individuals who were selected by people he or she does not know, to make decisions that individual should be able to participate in. Behavior is our substitute for action, psychic satisfaction our substitute for power.

Our concerns are those of the majority, those the system prescribes for us. When we make a choice, and then take an action, we generally do it alone. Our choice is the same others make, our behavior the same as theirs too, but somehow we convince ourselves that it is unique and that we are individuals. Philip Slater describes the phenomenon thus:[10]

> When a value is as strongly held as is individualism in America the illnesses it produces tend to be treated by increasing the dosage, in the same way an alcoholic treats a hangover or a drug addict . . . withdrawal symptoms. . . . The desire to be somehow special inaugurates an even more competitive quest for progressively more rare and expensive symbols—a quest that is ultimately futile since it is individualism itself that produces uniformity. This is poorly understood by Americans who tend to confuse uniformity with "conformity," in the sense of compliance with or submission to group demands. Many societies exert far more pressure on the individual to mold himself to fit a particularized segment of a total group pattern, but there is variation among those circumscribed roles. Our society gives far more leeway to the individual to pursue his own ends, but, since *it* defines what is worthy and desirable, everyone tends, independently but monotonously, to pursue the same things in the same way. The first pattern combines cooperation, conformity, and variety; the second, competition, individualism, and uniformity.

One must agree that there is irony in the great traffic jams that occur when hundreds of thousands of vacationers all leave for home early in order to "beat the traffic."

---

[10] Philip E. Slater, *The Pursuit of Loneliness* (Boston: Beacon Press, 1971), pp. 7, 8–9.

Maybe the system is held together—and continues to function in lockstep precision—because of the symbolic value we give to, and what we ironically call, individualism.

The more peaceful a community has become, the more cowardly the citizens become; the less accustomed they are to standing pain, the more will worldly punishments suffice as deterrents, the faster will religious threats become superfluous. . . . In highly civilized peoples, finally, even punishments should become highly superfluous deterrents; the mere fear of shame, the trembling of vanity, is so continually effective that immoral actions are left undone. The refinement of morality increases together with the refinement of fear. Today the fear of disagreeable feelings in other people is almost the strongest of our own disagreeable feelings. One would like ever so much to live in such a way as to do nothing except what causes others *agreeable* feelings, and even to take pleasure in nothing more that does not also fulfill this condition.

FRIEDRICH NIETZSCHE

Politics and Freedom

Albert Camus writes of the myth of Sisyphus.

Sisyphus was a Greek god who was condemned to the earth to push a giant rock to the top of a mountain. Once at the top, the rock would roll back to the valley of its own weight, and Sisyphus would walk down and again begin pushing the rock up. The fate of Sisyphus is the ceaseless rolling of the rock up the mountain.

Camus argues that Sisyphus experiences a kind of silent joy. "His fate belongs to him. His rock is his thing." He experiences joy—but not simply when the rock is at the top, when his task is "completed." Camus writes:

"I leave Sisyphus at the foot of the mountain! One always finds one's burden again. But Sisyphus teaches the higher fidelity that negates the gods and raises rocks. He too concludes that all is well. This universe henceforth without a master seems to him neither sterile nor futile. Each atom of that stone, each mineral flake of that night-filled mountain, in itself forms a world. The struggle itself toward the heights is enough to fill a man's heart.

"One must imagine Sisyphus happy."

If everyone has the right to express his will . . . what does this right mean if their will is merely an echo of the chorus around them?

JOHN SCHAAR

On Freedom

It is a tricky thing to be free, and awfully hard. One would guess that there are a lot of people who want to be free—but surprisingly, there are many who do not. We know that there are many people who think that they are free, and that there are very few people who really are.

In this chapter, we can only begin to understand why there is so much confusion about being free. There will be a short essay, and some explanation, and a few excerpts from literature to help show us how hard it is to arrive at a meaning of freedom. As a topic, it is pretentious. I admit that. But it seems so sloppily defined, so misunderstood, yet so often assumed an important part of life, that it seems reasonable to spend some time thinking about it.

Out of all of our literature, out of all of American letters, it seems natural to begin with Henry David Thoreau. Maybe he wrote about freedom. Maybe we all want to go to Walden Pond to commune with nature, with the ghost of Thoreau. Or to the mountains or to the ocean or to an island to just be away. To just be free. To do our number alone. Do it by ourselves, to ourselves, and for ourselves.

But is that being free, or is it simply being separated from others, experiencing anomie or being alienated? Thoreau might be a part of the American Dream, but is he truly part of the legacy of freedom?

Get away. Now that is a good idea. We Americans are impatient types. There has always been a West, and somehow freedom was always there. So, with covered wagons, or iron horses, or some exotic van or bus or camper or God-knows-what, we all move West to get free and get rich. Americans move and move and move. From New York to New Mexico, from California to Cambodia, we move. From the South to the North, from Memphis to Montana, we restlessly go from one place to another, looking for ourselves, looking to be free.

We run to any place, going nowhere. Nowhere people living

in a Nowhere land. Is it really freedom, to move from but never to?

As we go, we waste one place after another. The pattern now seems to be well established. In our restlessness, we buy and destroy, buy and destroy. Our home is only where our investment is. As soon as the river is polluted, or the land is barren and the winds carve out a dust bowl, or when all the trees are down, and the land will not support even animal life, then we move on. We move West. We move free.

We consume and, in doing so, destroy, then restlessly move to more consumption and destruction. We do this as a free people, yearning to stay free.

But if we have no freedom in our physical "homes," then are we free in our beliefs? Doesn't it seem logical that we all might believe in the same thing; in other words, that in our similar moral beliefs and actions we could find a kind of freedom?

For example, the Puritans believed that they had a covenant with God and that by working together they could build the New Jerusalem in the New World. A model community that would stand out as a beacon against the depravity they perceived in Europe's Christian community. What I would like to suggest is that, in fact, the Puritans had a kind of freedom we no longer possess. That, despite their "Puritanism," they were tied together by a vision of the world they wanted to create.

Can we define our own freedom in any kind of positive terms? Are we truly naive enough to claim that what we call freedom includes the ideas of building or creating? Do we even have any kind of binding belief that might lead us to the freedom which comes from shared visions?

Of course the questions are rhetorical. It seems impossible for us to understand freedom as something truly positive. We have an almost impossible time distinguishing between *freedom from* something and *freedom to* something. What we need is freedom to; what we have is freedom from.

So we move from place to place, looking for Walden Pond, looking to escape. We continually prove our freedom from by running away as fast as we can. We are bound by nothing, tied to no one. And we call the isolation and destruction freedom, and defend it with our very selves.

The Ideology in Our Letters

He slept on the straw with the groom, and memories weighted heavily on his chest; he awakened many times. Scattered and infertile, the scenes of his life stretched out behind him, rich in magnificent images but broken in so many pieces, so poor in value, so poor in love! In the morning, as they rode away, he looked anxiously up to the windows. Perhaps he could catch another glimpse of Julie. A few days ago he had looked just as anxiously up to the windows of the bishop's palace to see if Agnes might not appear. She had not shown herself, and neither did Julie. His whole life had been like that, it seemed to him. Saying farewell, escaping, being forgotten; finding himself alone again, with empty hands and a frozen heart.

HERMANN HESSE

There are, as indicated above, different ways to think about freedom. In the rest of the chapter, I will discuss, in turn, freedom and how it has been interpreted in American letters, freedom and economics, freedom and psychology, and freedom and politics.

To begin with Thoreau is to begin with the classic statement on being free by being alone. He makes one case all too well: What we must do is to get away; discover ourselves by being alone; find freedom by experiencing nature. Thoreau was a poet, a spokesman for that urge in us that tells us to ignore society and relearn primary associations, to learn to commune with nature.

By sketching in Thoreau's experience at Walden, and understanding some of it in his own words, the point of our common past can best be made. He was born in 1817 and did what the bright men in those days did: He went to Harvard College. For a time, after he graduated, he wrote, opened a private school, and was friends with people like Ralph Waldo Emerson. He made a little trouble (he was fired as a school teacher for refusing to administer discipline), had problems deciding on a vocation, but was generally regarded as a promising scholar. On July 4, 1845, Thoreau went to live at Walden Pond. There he kept a journal.[1]

"The real attractions," Thoreau writes of Walden, "were: its

---

[1] Henry David Thoreau, *Walden*, ed. Sherman Paul (Boston: Houghton Mifflin Company, 1960). The following quotations come from the chapter titled "Where I Lived, and What I Lived For."

complete retirement, being about two miles from the village, half a mile from the nearest neighbor, and separated from the highway by a broad field." So he is set. In the wilderness, but by a town. Indeed, only a field away from a highway. But by himself. For what?

"To enjoy these advantages I was ready to carry it on; like Atlas, to take the world on my shoulders—I never heard what compensation he received for that—and do all those things, which had no other motive or excuse but that I might pay for it and be unmolested in my possession of it." That is what he wanted: to enjoy the benefits and to be unmolested. Certainly we understand that. He knew what that meant, and counselled: ". . . to my fellows, once for all, As long as possible live free and uncommitted."

To examine Thoreau's Walden thoroughly is not the object of these paragraphs. But it would be unfair not to glimpse his "day" at the pond; it would be a loss to miss his perceptions.

> Morning is when I awake and there is a dawn in me. . . . The millions are awake enough for physical labor; but only one in a million is awake enough for effective intellectual exertion, only one in a hundred millions to a poetic or divine life. To be awake is to be alive. I have never yet met a man who is quite awake.
>
> I went to the woods because I wished to live deliberately, to front not only the essential facts of life, and see if I could not learn what it had to teach, and not, when I came to die, discover that I had not lived. I did not wish to live what was not life. . . . I wanted to live deep and suck the marrow of life . . . to drive life into a corner, and reduce it to its lowest terms. . . .
>
> Our life is frittered away by detail . . . simplicity, simplicity, simplicity! I say, let your affairs be as two or three, and not a hundred or a thousand; instead of a million count half a dozen, and keep your accounts on your thumb nail. . . . Simplify, simplify . . . the nation itself, with all its so-called internal improvements, which, by the way are all external and superficial. . . . If we do not get out sleepers and forge rails, and devote days and nights to the work, but go to tinkering upon our *lives* to improve *them,* who will build railroads? And if railroads are not built, how shall we get to heaven in season? But if we stay at home and mind our business, who will want railroads? We do not ride on the railroad; it rides upon us.

Of course Henry is right. What American could disagree with *that?* Just to have two problems, to simplify, to be awake. But, of course, to be only half-awake is at least to be aware that the world has some problems. Are we Americans—or anyone who has decided to live in a world with anyone else—are we perhaps too complex simply to be simple? More importantly, at least practically, what do we do if there are not enough ponds to go around?

In other words, Thoreau's powerful experience, and equally powerful prose, is limited in its helpfulness. We are not much farther along in understanding ourselves in a world full of people. We cannot understand who we are in terms of social or cultural interactions. We are no closer to the idea that freedom might be contained in commitment or that being free might include something more than ourselves.

Freedom as a Highway

What remains of the ideology is the quest. The search. The Open Road. What the pioneers helped start and Thoreau romanticized, Walt Whitman described and D. H. Lawrence analyzed. In the American epic poem *Leaves of Grass,* Whitman took seriously Thoreau's longing for freedom on the road. Freedom from found clear expression in Whitman's art. To understand more of ourselves, more of our idea of freedom as fleeing, more of why we vacation by the quantity, by the mile, it is worthwhile reading from a remarkable essay on Whitman by D. H. Lawrence.[2]

> The Open Road. The great home of the Soul is the open road. Not heaven, not paradise. Not "above." Not even "within." The soul is neither "above" nor "within." It is a wayfarer down the open road.
>
> Not by meditating. Not by fasting. Not by exploring heaven after heaven, inwardly, in the manner of the great mystics. Not by exaltation. Not by ecstasy. Not by any of these ways does the soul come into her own.
>
> Only by taking the open road.
>
> Not through charity. Not through sacrifice. Not even through love. Not through good works. Not through these does the soul accomplish herself.
>
> Only through the journey down the open road.

---

[2] D. H. Lawrence, *Studies in Classic American Literature* (New York: Viking Press, 1966). The following comes from the chapter titled "Whitman."

The journey itself, down the open road. Exposed to full contact. On two slow feet. Meeting whatever comes down the open road. In company with those that drift in the same measure along the same way. Towards no goal. Always the open road. Having no direction even.

Or, read these words of Henry Miller's "The Air-Conditioned Nightmare":

America is made up, as we all know, of people who ran away from such ugly situations. America is the land par excellence of expatriates and escapists, *renegades,* to use a strong word. A wonderful world we might have made of this new continent if we had really run out on our fellow-men in Europe, Asia, and Africa. A brave, new world it might have become, had we had the courage to turn our back on the old, to build afresh, to eradicate the poisons which had accumulated through centuries of bitter rivalry, jealousy and strife.

But the desire to keep moving, to be left alone, is just one way to handle freedom. Deep down, it may be the one with which we have most sympathy; it is certainly a most obvious one. It is going to Europe to get away (for one summer); it is traveling cross-country just to count the miles you are away from where you started. At some point, the quest for some thing—for some meaning some where—changes into the simple idea of leaving, of getting away, of movement. Whitman is Thoreau on the road. It seems both legitimate and necessary to ask if either gives adequate advice about freedom.

We have already raised problems connected with this approach. But we are not yet ready for an "answer." It would be premature to present a full-scale retort or even to tentatively offer a different approach. There are other ideas, other circumstances and approaches which must be dealt with before we get to politics and freedom.

Freedom as Material

Instead of being primarily concerned over right and wrong, men would learn, while fighting over these issues, that political arithmetic could be substituted for ethics, that they could live more peaceably by a calculus of forces than by the spirit. At the end of the seventeenth century, the medieval synthesis, in which all activities were gradations within a coherent organization of existence, was broken apart. Into this new world, the world of reason and commerce, Virginia was prepared to enter as early as 1624; it was stripped of its medieval notions and was started on the road which led from teleology to competition and expedience, where the decisive factor would be, not the example from the Apostles, but the price per pound of tobacco.

PERRY MILLER

There is, buried in us—maybe deeply, maybe close to the surface—an idea that somehow freedom is tied to material things. Certainly there are impressive advocates of such a position. The argument is that people who are free from material wants are free from oppression; they are, in fact, free to be themselves. There is little doubt that the advocates of material freedom have a point. It is neither intelligent nor sensible to argue that people are best off when they are hungry, or have no shelter, or are in poor health. That is not what I wish to defend.[3]

I want to argue that we have connected freedom and materialism in extreme ways. That we have probably long since passed the point where we could all be fed and housed and medically treated, and yet we still pursue a material goal. We pursue that goal without realizing its costs.

If the above sections about Thoreau and Whitman—ideas about us—are right, then we should expect to find some evidence of the pursuit of goods somewhere. There should be some evidence in our history that points to a moving towards freedom from the past. Moreover, that moving might have economic overtones.

There is evidence, and it lies right in the middle of one of our nicest, most romantic myths: the myth of the yeoman farmer.

Remember the yeoman farmer? The brave and noble pioneer who moved West to settle the land? To find roots? To be self-sufficient, to be away, to be hard-working, and to be free? Had we just been born *last* century, then we could have known the land. Then we could have communed with the stuff of our primordial past—with nature.[4]

---

[3] For a fine argument that man can be more than his material surroundings, see John Schaar, *Escape from Authority* (New York: Harper & Row, 1961). To quote: "Some part of the mystery and grandeur of human beings lies in the fact that they make paintings on the walls of miserable caves and write poetry and philosophy in the midst of hunger and filth."

[4] For a fine example of the restlessness involved in moving West, see Ken Kesey, *Sometimes a Great Notion*.

There is no doubt that the myth of the yeoman farmer stems from the facts. There *were* those who went West and felt free. There *were* some small towns where a communal spirit existed; where each person took an interest in the other; and where citizens personally got together and personally helped their neighbors. Rural America, with the Noble Farmer, is a part of our collective past worth remembering—at least in that vision.

The facts about the farmers seem much closer to our assumptions than our myths: They moved a great deal, wanted to be "free," and were interested in the land primarily for the money they could make from it. Not much romance in that. Richard Hofstadter, in *The Age of Reform,* tells us:[5]

> The predominance in American agriculture of the isolated farmstead standing in the midst of great acreage, the frequent movements, the absence of village life, deprived the farmer and his family of the advantages of community, the chances of association and cooperation, and encouraged that rampant, suspicious, and almost suicidal individualism for which the American farmer was long noted.... The characteristic product of American rural society was not a yeoman or a villager but a harassed little country businessman who worked very hard, moved all too often, gambled with his land, and made his way alone.

Not very noble, that vision of freedom. The vision of the small isolated farmer continually moving for profits, relating to the land primarily for the economic reward, communing with an investment while thinking about future riches. But that is the past, a part of the past buried almost as deeply as our treatment of the Indians, who really did have a home in the land.

We have not lost the idea that wealth is important, that it is "freeing." We move from our civilization—from our problems, from our cities—to the suburbs. Money or at least mortgages physically remove us from social responsibility. To be free in a tract home. But we know that enough money will also buy us power, will enable us to control. There has been a whole literature in sociology and political science telling us where power is, who possesses it, and why they have it. A nice example of such a book is *Who Rules America,* by G. William Domhoff (Englewood Cliffs, N.J.: Prentice-Hall, 1967).

---

[5] Richard Hofstadter, *The Age of Reform* (New York: Random House, 1955), p. 45.

Domhoff tries to prove what many people suspect:

1. That there is an upper class;
2. That it owns a disproportionate amount of the country's wealth and receives a disproportionate amount of its yearly income;
3. That it—along with its high-level executives—controls the nation's major banks, corporations, elite universities, and l˜rgest mass media;
4. That its control extends to the executive branch of the federal government;
5. That it merely influences the Congress, most state governments, and most city governments.

That is a big job for any group of people. I suppose one could conclude that this is no mere idle rich. But there are more important implications. If power and freedom are tied together (whoever heard of powerlessness being freedom in America?), then the message is clear: Get rich. Money is power, power is freedom. We work out a perversion of this every day. Instead of being rich, we can at least appear rich. So we earn small and buy big. We give ourselves the illusion of power, through the magic of plastic.

I am not happy to leave the analysis at that. Too many things are forgotten, too many things are assumed. We forget that people really do need food and shelter and medicine, and that we are skilled enough to provide everyone with all these things. We are, if nothing else, a productive people. We also assume that to have money is to have control, is to be free. I am unconvinced, I am simply unsure. Henry Kariel hints at the problems: [6]

> But freedom from want and for leisure is not enough .... Abundant resources may themselves be produced by means utterly indifferent to the values of political freedom. In point of fact, abundance is made possible by large-scale technology and a sweeping division of human labor, which have already entailed the subordination of personal interests. ... Men must be free, therefore, not only from the necessity of finding the means

---

[6] Henry Kariel, *The Promise of Politics* (Englewood Cliffs, N.J.: Prentice-Hall, 1966), p. 39.

for sustenance but also from the presumed imperatives of technology. . . .

In short, it matters *how* material abundance and the amenities of life are provided.

What Kariel implies is that there are hidden costs to our over-abundance, real prices we must pay in order to buy our way to freedom or power or both. Let us list some of the costs. In our search for freedom we have lost our home. While developing the skills of speculation, buying, and then selling for profit—in other words, developing the skills of a "developer" who does not stay on his or her development—we have lost touch with the land. We have sacrificed any meaningful relationship with our surroundings by thinking of it in terms of debits and credits. It is simply a ledgerbook relationship where wheat and grass have come to mean money and possible independence. Maybe even freedom.

As we are beginning to find out, this kind of dynamic can go on until we have destroyed our surroundings. There are just so many trees to be cut, deer to be shot, lands to ruin, oceans to muck up, and lakes to kill. We produce things by destroying other things. The price of material freedom is paid, in part, by breathing our own air. Taxes seem cheaper.

That, of course, is the common argument, the easy one. Part of what I would like to suggest is that even if we had cleaned up everything—air and water and minds—we might not be much better off. The problems of "clean" are certainly soluble. Ralph Nader knows that.[7] What is at stake is our freedom. Do we really have power? Can money give us the control to make us free? As argued earlier, I think not.

There are at least two ways to get at the problem of money and power leading to freedom. The first way is to look at those at the "top"—the rich, the executives. The whole idea of deal-ing with this group is obvious. These are the envied, the ones who have won, the ones, we suspect, who might be free. But

---

[7] The whole Ralph Nader/ecology problem is in itself a problem. Nader promises cleanliness but not really reform. If he is successful, it will merely mean that we can live in the same system—which will have been made stronger—without the pollution. We will soon find out that there is much money to be made from ecology and that lawyers have found yet another way to funnel public problems through the courts.

the point is painful for the belief. These people, as much as or more than any others, are in many ways the prisoners of bureaucracies.

They are where they are because they have best learned and acted out the money/production/freedom ethic. That is their morality, the defining limitations of their imaginations and actions. They are different only because they push bigger buttons from more comfortable offices. Given a choice between comfort or discomfort, money or poverty, big buttons or no buttons, most of us would choose comfort, money, and buttons. But that set of choices may mask the real issue of freedom: the freedom to act together, the freedom to define oneself by one's actions.

The second way to get at the problem is by looking at those who have not "made it," at those who are outside the ethic. It seems clear that things other than money can lead to freedom, if money is not the principal value. Minorities who have not been allowed to participate equally in the pursuit of materialism may be more free than those at the top. The militant minority may have understood more about freedom than the executive.

All I want to suggest is that materialism as an ideology may not lead us to freedom. Further, that those we consider "economically disadvantaged" may be able to teach us valuable lessons about the costs of financial success—and the power of ideology.

Freedom and Psychology (With a Word About Dope)

Electrical stimulation of the brain produced pleasurable sensations in three epilepsy patients. One patient, a bright and attractive thirty-year-old-woman, experienced a pleasant feeling of relaxation when stimulated. . . . Her enjoyment must have been intense . . . the patient . . . openly expressed her fondness for the therapist (who was new to her), kissed his hands, and talked about her immense gratitude for what was being done for her.

A second female patient was not to be outdone. Reporting that she liked the stimulation "very much" and that it caused an "enjoyable tingling sensation" in the left side of her body "from my face down to the bottom of my legs" the patient became increasingly talkative and flirtatious as stimulation continued; finally expressing her desire to marry the therapist."

Even a young male patient seemed emotionally attached to the doctor.

LEWIS M. ANDREWS AND
MARVIN KARLINS

There are times—all too frequent—when it occurs to me that freedom is a used up, unrealistic problem. Most people do not consider it for long enough to count; they are able to "common-sense" it out, to come to terms with it, and then to let it go. Essentially, Who Cares? There are other times—almost as frequent—when it occurs to me that *that* is part of the problem. We act as if we know what freedom is, without working on it. We accept what we are told, or what we observe, and leave it unquestioned.

If freedom is an important concept which ought to be acted upon, then it makes sense to try to figure out what it means. Further, if freedom has something to do with other people, then it should be properly studied as a topic of politics.

It is possible that we—"we" being an ill-defined group of people who are either young or "hip," or modern, or "liberal," or simply identify with Now—are beyond some of the above American definitions of freedom. While the Open Road may still be attractive, materialism may not be quite so alluring. While nature may be attractive, maybe obvious destruction has lost some of its appeal. But while some science seems to have lost its appeal, other science has taken its place. It is this latter science, the science of people's behavior and people's minds, which now purports to have insight into a new freedom.

The new scientists—the behavioral psychologists, for example —are serious people who make serious claims about our lives and our freedom. It is only fair to take them seriously.

Behavioral scientists are capable of formidable magic. They can train animals to run the right way or to salivate on cue; pigeons can learn to play ping-pong. These scientists are even able to make human beings feel good or bad, angry or happy, by running electric currents to certain parts of the brain. No sense in being frightened or outraged or anything else, it is simply a scientific fact: Scientists can make us feel and do certain things they want us to. They put their faith in determinism: the belief that each act is caused by something, or a series of somethings, and that if one can only determine the stimulus, then one can predict the response.

That, of course, is science and determinism reduced to simplest terms. But the kernel of the belief is there: that it is theoretically possible to understand every action by discovering all the things that have gone into determining the action. Given this assumption, freedom—standing by itself—is a nonsense concept. If we learn what to do, how we act and react, then the behavioral sciences are surely right. In the book quoted at the beginning of this section, *Requiem for Democracy?*, arguments for "freedom" are presented and then discussed.

For example, we are told that it is foolish to believe that people can be free in the absence of "scientific behavior control." The authors write: "We cannot deal rationally with the behavioral sciences until we realize that control *per se* is not even an issue. From the scientist's viewpoint, all human actions follow laws and patterns, just as physical events do, and are, in that sense, controlled.... The real question is not 'Should [people] be controlled?' but 'How should [they] be controlled'?" [8]

The words used seem so reasonable, so value-free, so ... scientific. It is as if rationality really were the basis of the world, and that we know what that rationality is. It is as if physical events are controlled by laws and patterns which we know— and so too human actions. There is no hint of Einstein's descriptions of the relativity of perception; there is no recognition of the phenomenologist Hussurl's idea that rationality has its roots in subjective thought. What we get is "value-free reason" run amuck, a belief system in behavioral science clothes.

Back to the argument. Andrews and Karlins continue by assuring us that the scientific control of behavior is not evil ("An atomic reaction can light a city or burn it") and that it does not appear, at this time, as if an elite corps of scientists or a tyrannical government could use behavioral control technology to regulate human conduct. There are, of course, some potential

---

[8] Lewis M. Andrews and Marvin Karlins, *Requiem for Democracy?* (New York: Holt, Rinehart & Winston, 1971), p. 39.

problems seen by Andrews and Karlins which they formulate as follows:

Effective behavior control technology	$+$	Alienated individuals	$=$	Conditions conducive to formation of a psytocracy

To put it another way, we may be more easily controlled by the technology of the behavioral sciences if we persist in being alienated from our fellow citizens. In part, a good insight. But the avoidance of a psytocracy does not mean that we are not determined, does not mean that we are "free."

According to the behavioral scientists, "If man's sense of freedom is to be restored, it must be expressed within the framework of science." [9] It is as simple as that. Freedom is determinism. Science makes us free. Not only is it science which frees us, but it is, more particularly, the mind. The process people (those who accept determinism but think it is complicated, those who think the key lies in the "highly elaborate information-processing organ," the brain) believe that we are determined. But determined in a special way. That way involves our thought: *"the quality of thought is not a given; it is a product of training and experience."* [10]

So this is where behavioral science takes us, to where we can be free, to where we can determine our own quality of thought. Some scientists assume that is freedom. The utimate freedom. Certainly the ultimate if one accepts that freedom is bound by the rules of science. The human condition is pretty easy to understand if we just believe. The struggle to be free (they mean within boundaries, of course) is as easily done as this:

> When conflict arises, the man with simple information-processing skills will fall back on ethical systems, serial sets of priorities, and other external criteria. His behavior is determined in the rigid, classical sense of the word. The free man, on the other hand, *has been determined* to resolve his conflicts by generating new ideas and concepts.[11]

---

[9] Ibid., p. 103.

[10] Ibid., p. 116.

[11] Ibid., p. 115. Much of the following discussion is similar to that in Theodore Roszak, *The Making of a Counter Culture* (Garden City, N.Y.: Anchor Books, 1969).

We can be free if we enter the world of these scientists. We have a chance if we can stop being old-fashioned, if we just drop those old "serial sets of priorities" and "ethical systems." Indeed, many of those "external criteria" should no longer be considered if we *really* want to be free. But why be cynical? The points are fairly obvious: Everything has an ideology, nothing is value-free. The question is, why accept the ideology of science? Aren't there worlds we cannot predict, actions we cannot determine? Why should there be total emphasis on our minds, our brains, our "elaborate information-processing organ"? Is there any reason to abandon "ethics" for the ethics of a process? Is science really the highest freedom, and have we finally reached our destiny?

Have we lost serendipity?

The problems raised for freedom by the behavioral scientists are not easily answered. What we cannot do is to accept their pronouncements without understanding their biases, their beliefs. We must examine what they do not say, as well as what they do; we must try to understand what their words would mean if they constituted a valid vision of our lives; we must ask if their offer of good is accompainied by unarticulated "bads."

Dope

"Better Things for Better Living Through Chemistry." So reads one of the prominent hippy buttons, quoting E. I. DuPont. But the slogan is not being used satirically. The wearers mean it the way DuPont means it.

THEODORE ROSZAK

It may be helpful if we examine a small part of our behavior-changing science, a real-life, everyday offering of our new "freedom." Like most offerings, it is a very mixed blessing. Like most, it has a distinguishable idea of freedom. The example is of dope, of drugs.[12] Of course it would be foolish to condemn scientists for the tremendous abuse of drugs. I do not mean to and have no intention of suggesting it. What I would like to suggest is that, if understood in a certain way, the drug head

---

[12] Doug Amy reports the classic Monday morning conversation: "What did you do over the weekend?" "Mushrooms."

and the scientific mind have something in common—and something to teach us.

Certainly drugs are not new. They have a distinguished history—from Indians of this continent to the great religions of the East. They have religious meaning, hold the key to certain kinds of magic, and can help cure the sick. There are those in our time—people like Aldous Huxley—who have combined science and intellect and knowledge with drugs, and have increased our shared knowledge. They have broadened our worlds; helped increase both our understanding and our perception of the things around us. Moreover, we have medical drugs—for every ill from headaches to ulcers—that will help us to live longer and with less pain. Drugs are simply not all bad, unless one likes pain. Even the stuff we call "dope" (marijuana, mescaline, and so forth) is not all bad; but we will get to that later.

What is important for this discussion is the dope user, the individual who is seeking something and finds drugs. Part of the seeking, of the pursuit, is for freedom. It is that part which is in the tradition we have been discussing. Philip Slater writes that drugs "promise a return to pure experience, to unencumbered sensation." [13] Not only that, it is just the way the behavioral scientists would want it: through the mind. Drugs extend freedom, in that particular sense. We find our new solutions by willingly changing our minds. We determine our own response by our own artificial stimulus.

The body simply becomes a kind of machine. It becomes our "property," our "asset." We can use it; we can direct it through drugs. Freedom to be ourselves, so long as it does not harm anyone else. That is apple-pie American. But what I want to argue is that it has become self-destructive. There seem too many of us to have visions of Walden Pond, to think of freedom as physically escaping, to believe that science has our social answers. As the businessman farmer used the land, so the drug abuser uses himself or herself. The doper is used up, then destroyed. It is solitary and mental and "freely" done.

The politics of dope is more complex than that. In fact, many people seem to have learned something from dope. Indeed,

---

[13] Philip E. Slater, *The Pursuit of Loneliness* (Boston: Beacon Press, 1970), p. 93.

just taking an illegal drug and finding out that one does not become some kind of mad-dog-drug-freak makes one wonder about the value of the "official" pronouncements. But there is the question of the end of the experience. If we all took dope, would we all become better people and revolutionize the world and live in love forever after? There is no reason to venture an answer to that until we ask just why we do dope, and what it means.

Isn't it possible that freedom is the issue, that freedom is the value, but that instead of freedom we get drugs? Maybe we have created a world in which we just cannot live; so we escape, or, at least, we learn to regulate ourselves according to a new pace, a different drummer. We can make ourselves speed up, slow down, go to sleep, be mellow, or wake up. Could it be possible that the union of people and science has become an unhappy one? That we are not suited—in any kind of natural way—for the "freedom" of science or the society it has built? In that case, we need to rethink society and science and ourselves.

But what if, on drugs, Theodore Roszak asks, we

> suddenly find ourselves blessed with a society of love, gen-
> tlemen, innocence, and freedom? If that were so, what should
> we have to say about ourselves regarding the integrity of our
> organism? Should we not have to admit that the behavioral tech-
> nicians have been right from the start? That we are, indeed, the
> bundle of electrochemical circuitry they tell us we are—and not
> persons at all who have it in our nature to achieve enlighten-
> ment by native ingenuity and a good deal of hard growing.[14]

To seek freedom through drugs is, at once, to misunder-stand freedom and to give in to the very dynamic that is causing many of the problems. Drugs—dope—can provide extraordinary experiences. They can lead one to startling flashes of insight, to moments of heightened perception. But there are at least two important points that should be made.

First the visions, the flashes, the moments must be prepared for to be fully understood. It's only another Open Road if you are not ready to look for something. Read Aldous Huxley's

---

[14] Roszak, *The Making of a Counter Culture* (Garden City, N.Y.: Anchor Books, 1969), p. 177.

The Doors of Perception or, better yet, Carlos Castaneda's writings to begin to understand elaborate preparations, intelligent perceptions, and potential dangers.

Second, momentary insight changes nothing unless one works at what the insight means. To rely on drugs to keep you in a more or less constant state of "insight" is to be little more than what Roszak suggests: a "bundle of electrochemical circuitry." Dope can be fine. It can point you in the direction of the hard work—but little more.

What I want to argue is that freedom is a positive concept that involves people's relationships with one another. And that Thoreau and Whitman, materialism, behavioralism, and drugs only help show us why we think as we do. They do not give us clues to politics, hints to how we might make freedom a part of our world. To change our ideas of freedom is hard; to explain such a concept may be impossible. The best we can do is to explore one possibility of freedom. To stay as we are is to leave power—and powerlessness—and the possibility of real change untouched. Freedom is safely out of our reach if we continue on our current ideological path. We will remain unfree, busily involved in the politics of self-deception.

Freedom To

He breathed deeply the moist, bitter-scented air of the park and at every step it seemed to him that he was pushing away the past as one who has reached the shore pushes away a skiff, now useless. His probing and his insight were without resignation; full of defiance and venturesome passion, he looked to the new life, which, he was resolved, would no longer be a groping or dim-sighted wandering but rather a bold, steep climb. Later and more painfully perhaps than most men, he had taken leave of the sweet twilight of youth. Now he stood, poor and belated in the broad daylight, and of that he meant never again to lose a precious hour.

HERMANN HESSE

The heading "Freedom To" is full of promise. Freedom to what? To the Revolution, or to The Movement? Freedom to have a fixed income, or freedom not to go to school? Freedom to grow up, or to continue as we are now—freedom to hurry from the cradle to perpetual adolescence? There is no doubt that there are many things I did not mean to suggest when I wrote the words "Freedom To." What I propose to do is to make some suggestions about a place where we might be free and to explain the thoughts behind it. The discussion is taken, in part, from Hannah Arendt's *The Human Condition.* The book deserves much thought.

Instead of beginning with the assumptions of the behavioral sciences, with the belief that we are determined to be, it seems sensible to start again. In the final analysis, it seems impossible to "explain" human nature. Certainly the words of our surroundings do not explain us. We know that words like *life* or *mortality, love* or *home,* can never fully answer our questions about who we are. This is not to deny that we may be in part determined, nor is this to argue that there is a God who created the heavens and the earth. It is simply to say that the problem of human nature seems unanswerable.[15]

That we have no final answers does not mean that we cannot solve at least parts of ourselves, especially those parts which have to do with being free. A possibly helpful model offered by Hannah Arendt has to do with the Greeks. In particular, it has to do with the Greek idea of what was involved in freedom.

For the Greeks, political life was important. A particular kind of politics and organization. For them, it was the *polis,* a place where people—as equals—could get together, make common decisions, and take actions. It is important to understand that the political realm was not the household, that the *polis* was not private. The household dealt with those things necessary for survival. The household, in Arendt's words, "was born of necessity, and necessity ruled over all activities performed in it."[16]

But the *polis* was the realm of freedom. It was a public realm, where individuals met as equals. In one sense, freedom meant neither to rule nor to be ruled. It ignored the kind of material and "power" differences which so characterize contemporary

---

[15] I think it is important to recall the earlier discussion on phenomenology. We do seem to be social, and we can understand consciousness as a form of reaching out to the world. This carries with it the importance of understanding the relationship between the individual and the world he or she lives in.

[16] Hannah Arendt, *The Human Condition* (Garden City, N.Y.: Doubleday & Co., 1958), p. 159.

"politics." What freedom—and, hence, politics—formerly included was a common world of thought and action. In this
commonality existed a kind of freedom that is hard for us to
understand. Everyone became involved with the same object,
with the same cause, with trying to figure out how to define
the same thing.

It was this sharing, this tugging at the same object in order
to give it meaning, that helped limit the chances of being tyrannized. When people are isolated, when they are alone, when
they have no common vision, then no one can agree with anyone else. But by ignoring everyone else—all other seeing and
hearing and insights—each becomes dependent upon some
central source to define a common world for everyone. To put
it differently, without deciding on common things, we become
terribly susceptible to the tyranny of conforming to the perceptions of some other force. We accept another's vision; we accept it as a chorus of strangers, unable to communicate felt differences.

In this public world, this political world, people were defined
by their acting and their speaking. To act is to do the unex-
pected: to begin, to initiate, to lead. It is through speaking
and acting that one becomes distinctive, one begins to define
self. In the *polis,* people publicly, in sight of their peers, answered the question of who they were by taking positions and
taking actions. To quote Arendt, "In acting and speaking,
men show who they are, reveal actively their unique personal identities and thus make their appearance in the human
world, while their physical identities appear without any activity of their own in the unique shape of the body and sound of
the voice. This disclosure of 'who' in contradiction to 'what'
somebody is—his qualities, gifts, talents, and shortcomings,
which he may display or hide—is implicit in everything somebody says or does." [17]

In creating and revealing, an individual experiences freedom.
It is far from an easy thing; there are surely costs one must pay.
The future becomes uncertain, unseeable and an undividual is
no longer the unique master of what he or she does. But that is

---

[17] Ibid., p. 159.

the price of freedom, the price of citizens being equals, and of reality being a shared experience. Certainly the struggle of creation, of action, the possibility of understanding one's self, and of helping to make important decisions in a public way are rewards in themselves. They are, indeed, the stuff of freedom.

The people who are not bigoted are the people who have no convictions at all.

Justice: Free Last Meals Next Door?

8

Trout's favorite formula was to describe a perfectly hideous society, not unlike his own, and then, toward the end, to suggest ways it could be improved. In 2BR02B he hypothecated an America in which almost all of the work was done by machines, and the only people who could get work had three or more Ph.D.'s. There was a serious overpopulation problem, too.

All serious diseases had been conquered. So death was voluntary, and the government, to encourage volunteers for death, set up a purple-roofed Ethical Suicide Parlor at every major intersection, right next door to an orange-roofed Howard Johnson's. There were pretty hostesses in the parlor, and Barca-Loungers, and Muzak, and a choice of fourteen painless ways to die. The suicide parlors were busy places, because so many people felt silly and pointless, and because it was supposed to be an unselfish, patriotic thing to do, to die. The suicides also got free meals next door.

KURT VONNEGUT, JR.

For in the land of the free, the greatest delight of every man is getting the better of the other man.

D. H. LAWRENCE

The Problem of Justice

Law n' order, law 'n order. Ya can't have no culture without order —no order without law. Do you hear/is that clear?

Rules and regulations/regularity/judges and Judgements. Trial by jury/Trial by peers. Trial to justice by the weight of evidence. Objective. Be Objective. Weigh the facts, know the law.

The Truth—is the rule—is the law—is the order. Let us have a trial; let us go to court.

The question is obvious: Does all this have anything to do with justice, or is it simply the ideology of our leaders, the beliefs of those in power?

The "title" of this section is "The Problem of Justice." A simple, misleading set of words. The word "problem" suggests that there is a solution. I am firmly convinced that there will be no clear solutions to the problems we discuss. The word "justice" is just as misleading. To write about it is to assume a definition of it. Not necessarily the truth in this case. This chapter will consist of thoughts in search of a definition, of ideas and phrases which try to capture an illusion. Maybe justice is simply an illusion. Maybe this should be titled: "The Unsolvable Problem of an Illusion."

So much for accuracy. What about justice? What about law?

Most of us have a great respect for the law. At least, a respect for the *idea* of Law. We are taught to think that our system of law is only natural and normal, well and good. What we do not question is the respect. Moreover, we rarely ask about the law itself. We seldom seem to think about the basis of the law, and we think even less about justice. Let us begin by trying to understand what we might assume about the law.

I think that most of us assume that there is a kind of perfect order which exists somewhere. A world where all forms are perfect. A realm, possibly, of thought which is uncorrupted by anything material. We seem to believe that from the perfection of such a world, we might get an idea of some ultimate order, an idea of the perfect working of things. It is also from this world that we seek our definitions of justice.

The world of thought is untouched and perfect. In our heads, there might be an idea of justice. From our heads, we get our laws. From our laws, we assume we are just.

The idea that law and justice are mental, that they are an ideal, is neither new nor unique to the United States. Plato, of course, presented the argument most clearly. He thought, silly ancient that he was, that a world of perfect forms really did exist. That, because we were but imperfect reflections of that world, we must spend our lives striving to think perfect thoughts, to be perfect.

His arguments were—and still are for many—compelling for the mind, for the world of the perfection of thought. We can conceive of a perfect circle; we cannot make one. Plato wrote an allegory about a cave. It is helpful to understand it.

Imagine a huge cave. In the cave sit many people facing a wall. They are chained, and can neither move nor turn away from that wall. There is light coming in from behind them. There are people constantly moving between that light and those chained, and shadows are cast upon the wall. Those casting the shadows carry puppets and other objects, which make interesting and bizarre images on the wall.

The prisoners, having been exposed to nothing else, soon understand the shadows on the wall to be real. It becomes their shared life: They know and recognize the images; they converse and argue about the shadows.

What Plato argues and what we often believe is that our reality is simply a reflection. That there is a true order of things and that we must strive for this order intellectually. The Republic of Plato is nothing more than a society striving to find that order, and by doing so have that society be in accord with the justice of the universe.

There are powerful social implications in the neat arrangement of Plato's Republic. The divine order included, indeed depended on, a rigid social scheme. Plato tells us of the intelligent and the less intelligent, of the warriors and the farmers, of the bureaucrats and the merchants. There was to be a right place for everyone, and everyone was to be in his or her place.

From the world of perfect forms came the idea of perfect order. With a great deal of schooling and training, the intellectuals of the Republic were to understand better the world of perfect forms. We are asked to assume that their rule would be just; that it would lead to harmony in the society.

Find the right order; get the right law; the result would be justice.

Of course, that formulation of justice has its shortcomings. We shall involve ourselves with different views of justice later on and, in doing so, reply to the Republic. But it may be helpful to anticipate some of the obvious problems. To believe that, ideally, there is a universal definition of justice is to avoid something important. It is to avoid much of reality. To put it simply, intellectual abstraction can be a way of by-passing unpleasant forms of reality. To base a legal system on a particular form of mental process means that the enforcement of that law will be but an attempt to force unwanted reality out of existence.

A perfect order, a mental realm of universally "right" ways of acting, may be to deny our essentially confused, chaotic selves. I do not intend to argue that there is no room for idealism, but I hope to avoid the mistake of making an individual a slave to his or her mind.

Let us shift the discussion a bit, make it a little more personal. What do we feel about justice? What does it seem like when we are involved in it? What are our thoughts when we think about justice? We *might* think about justice in this way: We will try to make people do what we think is best for them. To put it another way, we judge other people by imposing on them our standards and desires, and then decide what is best for them.

This approach to justice is many-sided. It might be the basis of a system in which all people would be given food, or it could support something quite the opposite. Let us now worry about only two of the possibilities implied by this approach to justice.

The first part of the formulation would go something like this: "If we were they, this is probably what we would do." But what does it mean if justice is to judge matters that way? Doesn't this approach mean that we assume a great deal? Aren't we saying that we can be objective and, moreover, that other people will want what we want?

It strikes me that at heart this is a very pompous attitude. Can we know? Should others want what we want? There may well be a place in justice for the mingling of people's ideas, for a sharing of and deciding on wants. But to truly know one another takes a kind of intimacy, a kind of knowledge that one must spend a great deal of time and effort developing. Even then, we rarely know for sure, and what we do know may not be the basis of justice.

The point is simply that it is both necessary and important that we have an idea of what is right and that we try to make others understand that idea. But we must also understand that to translate our ideas into the world of real people with real ideas and feelings is difficult. The problem of how this can be done is the other matter we must discuss.

The second part of the formulation ("We will try to make people do what we think is best for them") assumes that justice has something to do with judging from above. It is to impose. To regulate. To set ourselves over others, and to demand that they do what is right. But is this justice, or is it the rule of the strong parading under a different label, under a nicer name?

To sit in judgment of another may be many things, but it is not necessarily an essential element of justice.

What I should like to argue is that there are dynamics at work in our conceptions of law that may have nothing to do with justice. It seems clear that we rarely get too far from the idea of perfect images, from the enticing pictures of the mind. We link justice with ideas that are drawn from an independent, unearthly existence. We try hard to suck from justice a vital, human element. We try to make it the reflection of something we are not—perfect. Or we believe that if we can impose something on those less powerful, we are just.

With these elements at work, it is not surprising that some

consider us a nation of law and order which lacks the soul of justice.

D. H. Lawrence writes: "Anger is just, and pity is just, but judgment is never just."

The Normal View

In earlier chapters, we have described and discussed liberalism and, in appropriate cases, dismissed it as harmful or unhelpful. We must return to liberalism, for it is almost impossible to write about justice and law in America without coming to terms with its liberal framework. Liberalism represents the rules of debate for most of what we consider justice.

It seems reasonable to begin once again with the writings of John Locke, as they were very influential in the drawing up of our Constitution. Locke believed that the natural state of human beings was peaceful and reasonable enough. He thought that most people, most of the time, could be counted on to cause little or no trouble. In fact, there was almost no reason for government to exist—almost, but not quite.

According to Locke, sometimes there were disputes; some people did break the rules. Therefore, there was a need for impartial magistrates, a need for fair judges who would settle arguments and punish wrongdoers. In a sense, it was government as referee, an idea that should not sound entirely strange to us. In many ways, we have simply taken this formula of Locke's and turned it into an elaborate belief system.

The rules of our debate about justice (sic—law) have become the rules of intricate processes and definitions of "impartial" judgments.

The liberals want to make the debate on justice easy: All we must know is how fair and impartial judicial decisions seem to be; then we can measure justice. If we can spot trends in court rulings, then we can determine whether we are becoming a more or less just nation. It is the way judgments are made, the process, that is important. Because we always debate within the framework set by these rules and assumptions, it is necessary to understand more fully what the liberals are talking about so that we can at least know what we are missing.

The liberal argument as written by a liberal: "In essence, the distinction between civilization and savagery is the willingness to settle disputes by other means than force. We say that we are governed by the rule of law, which means that we accept decisions by impartial courts rather than by force of arms. If we are going to remain civilized, we must continue to accept the decisions of our courts, whether we agree with them or not."[1]

The liberal continues by offering proof that those impartial courts are deciding cases justly. During the last twenty years, for instance, the Supreme Court has made decisions which, seemingly, widen our freedom. Since 1954, it has been illegal to have segregated school systems, bathrooms, drinking fountains, motels, or lunch counters. Further, people accused of crimes must now be told of their rights (they cannot be forced to incriminate themselves), and individuals brought to trial must be represented by an attorney. The Court has also held that wire-tapping—except in certain circumstances—is illegal, and that "one-person, one-vote" means that every citizen's vote should count about the same.

Who could argue with these decisions? Who would challenge them? The system seems so reasonable. Laws are made and then impartial justices decide if they are constitutional or unconstitutional, good or bad.

In the liberal framework, given the basic premise of what people are supposed to be like and what governments should do, it is hard to fault recent decisions. It is not comfortable to advocate wire-tapping, self-incrimination, or segregation. No, it is foolish to challenge a recent set of decisions. What we need to do is to understand the biases of the framework itself and to understand that we have more of a choice than that between "civilization and savagery" if we give up the rule of law.

---

[1] The quote is from Erwin Griswold, and was found in James Clayton, *The Making of Justice* (New York: Cornerstone Library, 1964), p. 7.

Doing Justice

You can't get away from this.
Blood-consciousness overwhelms, obliterates, annuls mind-consciousness.
Mind-consciousness extinguishes blood-consciousness, and consumes the blood.
We are all of us conscious in both ways. And the two ways are antagonistic in us.
They will always remain so.
That is our cross.

D. H. LAWRENCE

It should be obvious that laws and trials mean something. They carry with them a way of looking at the world, a way that permits some people to control the actions of others. What has been argued is that the law, as Americans conceive of it, leaves out some important elements. Our law and "justice" seem an attempt to impose our mind over our other reality. In a sense, it means that justice is something thought, not something actively done; something imposed, not something shared.

The Bible admonishes us to "do justice, and love mercy." Part of justice, it seems to me, is to be done; it is something a person does. Justice is not necessarily created in a void and then imposed on others. Maybe it is more an action than a judgment, more an activity than an idea. In a sense, I mean to suggest that justice may include more than a proper judicial process; it may include, but go well beyond, the world of equality of procedure.

I am not saying that process and procedure are necessarily evil in and of themselves. I am suggesting that justice is much more complex than that, and although one might have a sense of security in knowing that a lot of money can buy a good attorney who will assure a "fair" hearing according to our laws, there is no reason to equate security with justice. Indeed, there is a real question about "fair" to whom and "impartial" to what. There are weaknesses in our liberal idea of justice; there are built-in biases.

First, property is protected. More precisely, private ownership is protected. That makes sense to us, but we rarely think of it in terms of justice. Sometimes private property—a lot of it—is defended as having been "earned" by a hard-working, intelligent person. We know that this means, more precisely, that the person has a marketable skill and that he or she is willing to sell. We also know that people can acquire property by having a relative die. But all this is obvious. The point is that built into our legal system is the idea that private property is sacred; yet relevant to justice may be the fact that some people go without food or clothing.

Back to John Locke. He believed that many problems in a pre-governmental society arose out of disputes over property. One reason for instituting government was to protect that property, to protect the fruits of an individual's labor. When our Constitution was written, and the public and private realms were split, it became the duty of the public to protect the property of the private. The business of government was to protect private business. Contracts bound the relationships.

The case is easily documented. It was the Supreme Court, in the Dred Scott case of 1857, which ruled that slaves were property and that property was protected by the Constitution. Indeed, in its history the Court has struck down laws which attempted to regulate the hours per week worked by children and the age at which they were permitted to begin. There was a long series of rulings during the early 1930s which held, essentially, that government could not regulate the wages or prices of industry. It was, primarily, the *principle* of the thing that mattered: the principle being that property was to be protected; the social costs seemed to be an entirely different matter.

Second, our system is built on the premise that in every case there is an innocent and a guilty party. It is an adversary method; one against the other. Neighbor versus neighbor doing battle in the court of law. One must be right, the other must be wrong; one is praised, the other blamed. In the end, one often gets a cash reward. We never consider the possibility that a problem might extend way beyond the two who are actually engaged in the proceedings.

This particularized, personalized liberal justice makes almost no attempt to incorporate the principle of collective rights, or the idea that a people might collectively be wronged.

The law is blind to groups of people: Everyone looks alike; single and alone.[2]

Third, the system leaves us at the mercy of those who know the law. Our instincts for justice are exchanged for the expertise of the attorney. Lawyers are simply an elite. Their backgrounds are generally upper-middle class, their educations particular and expensive, and they possess the power to shape real events into a form unrecognized by us, but recognized by our system. They are the agents of the Process, no matter which side they take. Theirs is a profession that is almost exclusively involved in adherence to rules. We, in turn, are dependent upon them.[3]

To stay within the liberal structure of the debate is too limiting. We will forever be forced to talk about Process. Think back to the "advances" made by the Court. Most had to do with the process itself. To understand the Court as a biased, elite-oriented part of the system is to understand that *even if* the process were to become "perfect," we might still be no closer to justice than we are now.

If justice is nine people (appointed and approved for life by an elite) whose decisions generally favor what white, upper-middle-class people favor, then ours is a system of justice. There is a less complicated way of saying the same thing: American "justice" sings the song of the upper-middle class. A brief history should be helpful. According to the account given by Thomas Dye and Harmon Zeigler:

> Before the Civil War, the Supreme Court was spokesman first for the Federalists under John Marshall and later for Southern planters and slave holders under Roger Taney . . . . Following the emergence of industrial capitalism in the second half of the nineteenth century, the Supreme Court became the spokesman for the prevailing elite philosophy of social Darwinism. The Court struck down the federal income tax; prevented prosecutions of corporations under the Sherman Antitrust Act, while applying this Act against labor unions; and struck down child labor laws and laws limiting the work week. The Court gave such a restrictive interpretation of the interstate commerce clause

---

[2] This is too important to be left unexamined, so we shall return to it at the end of this chapter.

[3] For a beautiful account of this, see Alexis de Tocqueville, *Democracy in America* (New York: Vintage Books, 1945).

that it prevented federal regulation of the economy. It interpreted the "due process" clause of the Fifth and Fourteenth Amendments and the contract clause of Article II, Section 10, in such a way as to protect business enterprise from almost any form of government regulation." [4]

The time the Court was in greatest trouble was when it "failed to respond swiftly to changes in elite philosophy . . . . In a four-year period, 1933–37, the Court made the most active use of the power of judicial review over congressional legislation in its history, in a vain attempt to curtail the economic recovery programs of the New Deal. It invalidated the National Industrial Recovery Administration, nullified the Railroad Retirement Act, invalidated the National Farm Mortgage Act, and threw out the Agricultural Adjustment Act. Having denied the federal government the power to regulate manufacturing, petroleum, mining, agriculture, and labor conditions, the Court reaffirmed the notion that the states could not regulate hours and wages." [5]

During the 1960s, the Court seemed to be most interested in civil liberties. Certainly "progress" was made. But the fact seems to be this: Essentially, nothing has changed. The Court is still a group of individuals with the biases of stability and security. Even as liberals work hard to purify the process, justice in America is still only judging. Rhetoric aside, justice's proverbial "blindness" to differences, the "majesty" and "sacredness" of the law, and the "equalness" of due process remain confining and biased concepts.

Justice is greater than any sum of judgments, generally more inclusive than two arguing individuals, and should be accessible to more people than the few who know the "secret" language. In a sense, justice is too important and too immediate an activity to be left in the hands of only a few. It is too far-reaching to be limited to laws as interpreted by a minority.

The history of the Supreme Court comprehends more than its rulings. It is the history of a people openly able to avoid justice under the label of law; the history of a few judging for

---

[4] Thomas Dye and Harmon Zeigler, *The Irony of Democracy* (Belmont, Calif.: Wadsworth Publishing Co., 1970), pp. 458–59.
[5] Ibid., p. 259.

the many; the history of the law following the times, with only a passing nod at the doing of justice. The liberalism of Locke called for the government to be a referee when the private affairs of individuals came into conflict. It did not offer many useful guidelines as to what it means to practice politics or to do justice. It is possible to understand our reliance on the Supreme Court as a justification for the individual to be uninvolved in justice. Our judicial system has inherited the weaknesses of Lockean liberalism.

But to know that biases exist doesn't necessarily mean that we will change. Indeed, most people still think that this system is the best we can do. There is the taught fear that if we had a system of men, it would simply become a tyranny. One person's whim controlling other people's activities. Certainly an unhappy situation. Another possibility would be that a system of men would turn into chaos, into anarchy. It would mean that the worst of us would be unchecked. It would mean that we could not walk the streets after dark.

But does it?

A Head Job

It is said that to every generation ten just people are born. No one knows who those people are.

There is more than a little reason to believe that many of the people who read this book will want to become lawyers. Some for fairly standard, greedy reasons: money and power. Others will study law because of pressure from parents, still others in order to do "good" work. You know about "good" work: work within the system to change it . . . and who knows more about the system than lawyers? (Rhetorical questions are wonderful. While the *answers* are always clear, the *implications* of the answers are seldom considered and are often very strange.)

I want to spend some time with the do-good-lawyers-to-be among you. Anybody may read this section, as it has to do with all of us; but the people who might want to take notes are the future do-gooders. They are often blind to the fact that law cuts at least two ways: 1) it is the aggressive carrier of our particular brand of liberalism and, 2) its first victim is the law student/lawyer. The lawyer becomes the law, the state becomes the person, the person becomes the lawyer becomes the state.

Law changes you. It does a head job.

You don't have a chance. Not only is it silly to assume *you*, as a lawyer, are going to change the system, it is especially wrong-headed to believe you will escape being changed. They'll get you. Count on it.

Law is something which is done and, in the twentieth century, the fact seems to be you are what you do. More than that, what you do, you're responsible for. In the end, law—that "neutral" arbiter of our society—is built on a whole set of attitudes and results in a prescription for how each of us is *supposed* to relate to the world. Law goes to our heads, and our heads have a lot to say about our doing.

One way to get a view of the law (get a view of ourselves) is to look at how lawyers structure and do their work. The case in point deals with some ideas which seem so common-sensical as to be almost foolish to discuss. It may well be that it is with those most common sense ideas we will have the best mirror to see ourselves. Our mirror image, I must warn you, may not be our self-image.

The case has to do with how "radical" lawyers understand the problems of native Americans, and how they try to solve those problems. It is important not to get too far from the fact that answers are built into questions and we have about as much to learn from the answers the lawyers give as the questions they ask. The following comes from a thoughtful and powerful manuscript written by Linda Medcalf. The details of the lawyer/Indian interactions are not fully explored here, but one hopes Linda's manuscript will be published soon. The *Preface* is not the place for the full lesson, but it is a lesson which should be learned.

The Case: Ongoing Shame

Almost since the time of Columbus, the native Americans have suffered cruelly at the whim of the invaders. That is simply a very terrible, shameful fact. There has been everything from early germ warfare (Lord Jeffrey Amherst gave Indians disease-infested blankets which killed them and made old Lord Jeff even more wealthy) to broken treaties and promises to forced marches from swamps to dust bowls, to simply murder.

To understate, Liberal America has not done itself proud in its dealings with the natives of this land.

Before we started mucking around and moving and murdering the Indians, they seemed to live as they wished. Their tribes were strong communities, their relationship to the environment was not one of control but of respect; they were, mostly, peaceful people. To fast-paced, alienated, bureaucratized, controlling, standard Americans, the Indian—both in fact and myth—seemed to be more whole and together than we are.

They were, in odd combination, a good example and because of that a threat.[6] We have gotten rid of almost everything but the myth.

In an effort to "make things right," there has been a move to provide tribes with aid. Regrettably, it has generally been legal aid. Well-intentioned attorneys have done their best with native Americans; made real attempts to do what they understood as necessary for a group of people who have been systematically abused.

As a group, the Indians are a little different from other minorities: (1) they own about 2 percent of the land in America, and the land is in large enough blocks so that they need not integrate into mainstream city or suburban living; (2) the land they occupy is rich in natural resources—water, timber, oil—to be used if and how they wish, and (3) they have done things in accord with our law, and the courts of the United States regularly uphold their claims.

For attorneys, they are often "difficult" to relate to, but are certainly "good" clients.

The attorneys believe the problems of the Indians they represent can, in a rough way, be understood as: (1) the poverty of the individuals, (2) the lack of power—both personally and tribally, and (3) the lack of education and skills of the people.

---

[6] Michael Rogin has done a first-rate job on this theme. See his *Fathers and Children: Andrew Jackson and the Subjugation of the American Indian* (New York: Vintage Books, 1976).

Those are all problems we can relate to; after all, we sort out much of the world with those very categories. Lawyers are trained to solve those problems in very specific ways, and we know that their training doesn't stop at the Reservation Door.

The problems—poverty, power, and education—are so inter-related as to be inseparable in any real way. When a lawyer makes an attempt to solve one of the problems, he or she is also working on the other ones. The changes, the solving, go on in the context of an ongoing tribal life which the attorneys are committed to keep. Keep, and make better. Those are the words they use.

In an attempt to keep the form of the tribe, the lawyer makes it over into a corporation. The tribal member becomes a shareholder. Of course the corporate style—the *needs* and *aims*—of a corporation are a little different than those of a tribe. The reorganization is built, in part, on the premise that to be strong and to avoid poverty, all those natural resources on the reservations must become economic assets. They must be well-managed to bring in more money.

That means, naturally enough, some different qualities in the Chief (Chairperson of the Board?) and his or her legal advisors. Instead of carrying and refining the traditions and wisdom of the tribe, the Chief has to have the skills of a corporate manager.[7] There's more. In order for the shareholders (i.e., native Americans) to be good citizen/capitalists, they must become educated in the ways of liberal America. The America we learn in school. The one which demands people see the world and make arguments in the form and language of a liberal/individual/competitive style we know as normal.

No more "passive" Red People. No more "submissive" aboriginal tribes. If the lawyers have their way, strong tribal leadership, and a powerful tribe will be the result of a vigorous, intratribal politics based an economic self-interest.

Right(s)?

Once you get to that point in the logic, it seems sensible that people need some protection. It becomes necessary and logi-

---

[7] The language being used is of my choosing and not that of Ms. Medcalf.

cal and seemingly normal to make certain that every person in the tribe be granted *rights*. After all, the individual has certain duties and responsibilities as well as some "freedom" from repression. Rights form a basis of much of our political thinking and it *seems* good that everyone has them. I mean, *what could possibly be wrong with rights?*

The answer, if I understand correctly, is plenty.

The concept of rights is a cultural one. Nothing universal about it. Rights as done by the lawyers for and to native Americans is wholly culturally based. The rights which seem so natural to us are built on the assumptions of individualism which require certain kinds of aggressive actions. To quote Medcalf: "A human being is not a bundle of legal rights; it is a much richer complex of emotions and mind and interaction with others and the environment which has very little resemblance to the bare contractual outline individual rights gives. To reduce human relationships to one of rights and responsibilities, one against the other, is to render the human relationship possibilities barren, to make of human relationships an 'irreducible minimum' before they become nothing at all."

Rights divide and liberalism/legalism conquers.

Let's go back and judge the lawyers. Judge those who have power to ask the questions, define the problems, then solve those very problems. In fact, many tribes have more money. They are becoming (in the most mainstream way) more viable economic actors. The lawyers "did" the law and were successful at it.

The real question is: Successful at What?

Think about the triad of Economics, Education, and Power. Sound familiar? Strike a cord you've heard before? Once those things take on our definitions, and once they become the central issues, the rest simply flows. Corporations, competition, individualism, efficiency, rationality, rights.

We've *Americanized* native Americans.

And the do-gooders? The lawyers? What they do *is* the law. Of course there are well-intentioned, nice, good lawyers. It just seems a crime that we are forced to live in a world which they help create and perpetuate because of the very structure of *their* thought and activity.

It seems more of an indignity that we are trying to "save"

the native Americans by introducing our "neutral" legal system into their lives.

Why are we forcing them to trade even the possibility of a whole life for one of pieces?

Enough is enough.

"Justice" Without Process: Left and Right

So far, two specific arguments have been made: 1) that justice is something to be done, and 2) that our legal system helps protect and perpetuate a rather clear set of beliefs. Normally, these two arguments are not well received. Indeed, it may sound a little like "taking the law into your own hands," which is a formulation feared by all. Defenders of the status quo argue that to "do" justice outside our established legal system can lead only to tyranny, tyranny of either the Right or the Left, of fascism or anarchy. Their arguments follow.

The Right

The far Right certainly "does" its vision of justice. It may be instructive to understand some of the things it does and how it goes about doing them. The most obvious of the far Right groups (at least in the sense of "doing") are those which model themselves after the military. They are people who have an idea of what should be, of the way it can be attained, and an organization to promote both. They are American Nazis, American Minutemen.

What they believe in, specifically, is of only marginal importance for this argument. They are masters of anti: anti-Communist, anti-hippy, anti-black, anti-Jew. These groups favor a strong state that will provide order and stability. They are obviously elitists, being firmly convinced that American white is best. Finally, they believe in social class as well as social order. There is a security, as well as a kind of strength, in highly structured organizations. Both these qualities seem to appeal to the Right.

To achieve their aims, to get justice through order, the paramilitary right has organized and armed itself. They are soldiers in a cause, military-type people who organize by rank. They are ready to "do" justice. When the Minutemen were raided in the mid-sixties, their weapons of justice included:

> 1,000,000 rounds of rifle and small-arms ammunition, chemicals for preparing bomb detonators, considerable radio equipment —including 30 walkie-talkies and shortwave sets tuned to police bands—125 single-shot and automatic rifles, 10 dynamite bombs, 5 mortars, 12 .30 caliber machine guns, 25 pistols, 240 knives (hunting, throwing, cleaver, and machete), 1 bazooka, 3 grenade launchers, 6 hand grenades and 50 80-millimeter mortar shells. For good measure, there was even a cross bow complete with curare-tipped arrows . . . ."[8]

When contrasted with this, the idea of legal process begins to look more pleasing. If one happened to be a black or a Jew or some other kind of "unfortunate," the legal process might even begin to seem acceptable.

The Left

In the case of America, there is very little action. Indeed, a truthful turning of a phrase would pretty much sum up a great deal of our experience: For every *reaction, there is a reaction.* For the violent Right, there is a violent Left. In the Left, too, we find a certain sense of elitism, a penchant for violence, and a sense of tightly knit organizations geared for action. Lenin and his comrades helped capture power out of chaos this very way.

However, the ideology of the Left and Right are not at all the same. The "new" Left is mostly anti-capitalist, anti-big state, anti-centralist, anti-middle class. Like the Right, they do justice. They do it, if we take the Weathermen, with bombs and disruptions. They are after the established patterns, the normal activities, and disrupt whenever possible.[9]

What some see as humor in the Left, others see as anarchy.

---

[8] Eric Norden, "The Paramilitary Right," in Robert Golembiewsky, Charles Bullock, and Harrell Rodger, Jr., eds., *The New Politics: Polarization or Utopia?* (New York: McGraw-Hill, 1970), p. 377. Originally appeared in *Playboy* Magazine; Copyright © 1969 by Playboy.

[9] Since this is a "new" edition, it seems necessary to find more recent numbers. But weapons are out and bombings are in. Violent bombings are what's going on in the 70s. In the first quarter of 1975, 16 people were killed, 106 injured, and $17.6 million done in damage due to bombings.

What some simply ignore as bad taste, others accept as treasonable. Yippie Abbie Hoffman counsels us to discuss and understand the foolish restrictions concerning property rights, human rights, and sexual freedom. He writes, "Our message is always: Do what you want. Take chances. Extend your boundaries. Break the rules. Protest anything you can get away with. Don't get paranoid. Don't get uptight." [10]

When put in these terms, one can understand why those who have a stake in the system might be happier with the current legal setup than in supposed anarchy.

All this makes sense. It corresponds with what we were taught: The Right is fascist, the "new" Left anarchist. Both guarantee little, neither offer justice. So we generally stop here and conclude that although our system of laws isn't perfect, it is better than what could happen. Of course, we know that these laws are not necessarily the same as justice, but we stop thinking anyway. We were taught to.

Justice and Politics

Thus far, we have struggled with justice but have not really gotten much closer to it; we have worked through some of the problems without getting much closer to the solutions. We have done something. We no longer need trouble ourselves with the idea that law (our "justice") is impartial. No law is impartial; probably justice is not either.

Laws are set up to help and protect certain people and certain things. Police make sure that some of the violators are caught, and our judicial system enforces the laws. Now, if one is white and middle-class, that may sound a great deal like justice. Police protect "us" against "them." Laws are designed to help "us," not "them." It may be with that us-them formulation, in that space between security and terror, where we might begin to understand justice.

While it is not terribly successful to argue that there are social classes in America (almost everyone considers himself or herself part of the middle class), it is undeniable that there

---

[10] Abbie Hoffman, "The Raising of the Pentagon," in Laurence Veysey, ed., *Law and Resistance* (New York: Harper & Row Torchbooks, 1970), p. 285.

are those without power, status, or wealth. If not a lower class, at least a class apart, a class outside the benefits of society. This group of people includes, roughly, the blacks, Chicanos, native Americans, white poor, and those who "drop out." Possibly most dropouts don't count; after all, they can drop back in. The white poor, the white dropout, may, "miraculously" reach the middle class. But the others are outside, subject to a "justice" that does not seem to include them.

The police are ultimately thought of by the white middle classes as friends. Indeed, they are. Police catch criminals, control traffic, and in many ways help people. More exactly, white people. The police are the "thin blue line of protection," so the saying goes. And certainly they are. But they are much more than that. An example of ghetto justice may help show why.

James Baldwin writes of a black salesman in Harlem. One day, after leaving a customer, there seemed to be a great deal of activity in the street. People

> were running from the police. Other people, in windows, left their windows, in terror of the police because the police had their guns out and were aiming their guns at the roofs. Then the salesman noticed that two of the policemen were beating up a kid: "So I spoke up and asked them, 'why are you beating him up like that?' Police jump up and start swinging on me. He put the gun on me and said, '*get over there*.' I said, 'What for?' "
>
> An unwise question. Three of the policemen beat up the salesman in the streets. . . .
>
> As of my last information, the salesman is on the streets again, with his attache case, trying to feed his family. He is more visible now because he wears an eye patch. . . . His tone is simply the tone of one who has miraculously survived—he might have died; as it is, he is merely half-blind. . . . It is a dishonorable wound, not earned in a foreign jungle but in the domestic one —not that this would make any difference at all to the nevertheless insuperably patriotic policeman—and it proves that he is a "bad nigger." [11]

It is not easy to find justice in this example. Whites expect the police to protect them—and this generally happens. The

---

[11] James Baldwin, "A Report from Occupied Territory," in Laurence Veysey, ed., *Law and Resistance* (Harper & Row, 1970), pp. 318–19. Originally appeared in *The Nation*, 203 (July 11, 1966), pp. 39–43.

person in business expects to carry out his or her white-collar crime, or illegal gambling, uninterrupted—and this generally happens. Anything beyond that is of little concern; beyond that is someone else's problem. So the police are left to deal with the problems of poverty and race hatred and decaying cities. Somehow whites expect social injustice to be solved by force, stopped by violence. Between the "us" and the "them," the white middle-class and the black ghetto, justice does not seem to exist. There is security for the whites, injustice for the blacks, and in the impossible middle—unrestrained and powerful—stand the police.

The black is colonized in white America. The black is trapped. How can he or she act "justly?" Maybe justice is treating a person the way he or she deserves to be treated. If that is the case, one can understand the logic of Frantz Fanon. Fanon writes of the colonized black in Africa. He writes of violence, and the justice of it.

> For the native, this violence represents the absolute line of action . . . . The group requires that each individual perform an irrevocable action. In Algeria, for example, where almost all the men who called on the people to join in the national struggle were condemned to death or searched for by the French police, confidence was proportional to the hopelessness of each case. You could be sure of a new recruit when he [or she] could no longer go back into the colonial system . . . . To work means to work for the death of the settler. This assumption of responsibility for violence allows both strayed and outlawed members of the group to come back again and to find their place once more, to become integrated. Violence is thus seen comparable to a royal pardon. *The colonized man finds his freedom in and through justice.*[12]

Perhaps violence is not only necessary but may even be justice in the case of the American black. But possibly justice is more than treating a person the way he "deserves" to be treated. Justice may involve more than that, it may be a reflection not only of the action of the one, but also the action of the other. What I am suggesting is that a "punishment" may reflect the one doing the punishing. One does justice, but

---

[12] Frantz Fanon, *The Wretched of the Earth* (New York: Grove Press, 1965), pp. 85–86.

also loves mercy. It is possible that forgiveness is as much a part of justice as violence. Both may be doing justice, and both may involve freedom for the individual.

Political Trials and People

Part of what I am suggesting is that there are many elements to justice, which at their core have little to do with laws. These elements have to do with people trying to live together in some sensible manner. I am not saying that there should no longer be judges or juries or laws. What I am suggesting is that we examine these things and try to figure out a better method of getting at justice.

We Americans seem hesitant to believe that any—much less many—trials are political ones. In fact, scholars in this field are trying hard to reach agreement on just what a political trial is. Let us stay on the fringes of scholarship and seek some common sense understanding of what political trials are and what they might mean.

In the most obvious sense, a political trial involves people who have been charged with treason against the state, or some such crime. We have very few of these. We can understand the desire of a state to protect itself. There is a history of political trials as old as the history of trials. Both Socrates and Jesus were perceived as enough of a threat to the state to be brought to trial. In a sense, political trials have a noble past.

Yet we deny political motivation. When one is arrested for antiwar or antipoverty activity—and those things are surely political—the likelihood is that the charge will involve something like marching without a permit or disrupting traffic. In other words, we require trials that never get to the issues involved. People intensely involved in acting on what they believe to be right are denied their validity as moral beings. They are denied any chance of having their principles dealt with justly.

There are, of course, even less appealing kinds of political trials. In some cases, police, prosecutors, and judges can conspire to frame—arrest—and try a politically "dangerous" person. The case of Eldridge Cleaver seems to indicate that this can happen.[13]

Being Blind

By the time Patty Hearst walked into the courtroom, we Americans knew a whole lot about her. Even a *Tommy*—deaf, dumb, and blind—would have had a hard time ignoring personal and private details about the woman. Not only was every outrage reported, at least three experts told us what they meant.

We all got caught: At one level the trial was of myths; a symbolic public display of our most recent past. Politics *vs.* Law; Patty *vs.* the Public Prosecutor. What the hell does "equal justice" have to do with a Symbol of the Rich being Kidnapped and Terrorized and her, very likely, Getting Into It and Seemingly Liking It?

At another level, Patty Hearst is a person. You know. Hands and eyes and feet and skin. A person. Feeling. Imagine yourself and you have a sense of, essentially, what/who Patty Hearst is.

So we got caught: Both the myth and the person are real. What to do? Can a law—a rule—give us the answer, show us the way?

It never made sense to me that she was guilty or innocent. Those are the categories that were forced on her, and wrong ones as far as I can tell. What the blindfolded Mother Justice couldn't see was that P. Hearst was probably *both* guilty and innocent.

In a strange way, all of us were.

But the law doesn't allow for the examination of that kind of truth.

Finally, there are trials which on the surface seem to have nothing to do with politics. The prostitutes who periodically get arrested, the tenant who refuses to pay his or her rent until something is repaired, or the long-hair—motivations aside— are automatically guilty. The law is the law. What I want to suggest is that these cases could be handled differently, in

---

[13] For an example of the problems involved, see Kenneth Dolbeare and Joel Grossman, "LeRoy Jones in Newark: A Political Trial?," in Theodore Becker, ed., *Political Trials* (Indianapolis: Bobbs-Merrill, 1971).

such a way that they would take on a political meaning. If this were done, there might even be a chance that justice would emerge.

The People's Courts in Cuba seem to me closer to a just method than what we have been discussing. An idealized description may help. Essentially, these courts are neighborhood-centered. The people in the area choose the judge. The judge is a respected, well-known member of the neighborhood, though not necessarily a lawyer. The judge must simply be a fair, just person who understands the aims of society, the aims of a revolutionary people.

The cases that come before the judge are local ones. They are heard in public; in essence, it means that those neighbors who know of the case, or the defendants, or those who were close to what happened attend. Often, many attend and are part of a case. The catch is this: The audience may be somehow guilty of the crime of the defendant. Guilty for not stopping an argument, guilty for not helping right a wrong, guilty for not helping someone who needed help.[14]

Maybe that is what justice is about. Midway between "an eye for an eye" and "turning the other cheek," we are groping for justice. But the point might be that we should not necessarily wander alone. The People's Courts are one way to begin to understand that to be part of society is to assume some responsibility for what goes on, and that this responsibility reaches into the realm of justice. Not a justice of lawyers and complex legal procedures, but of somehow the doing of justice.

---

[14] The analysis of the Cuban system is meant to be more suggestive than exhaustive. It might be helpful to understand one of the things I am outlining. Not too many years ago, a man stabbed a woman in New York City. That wasn't news. That he stabbed her repeatedly with several scores of people watching *was* news. Under the system now being discussed, those people who watched—or who shut their windows and pretended nothing was happening—would be guilty of doing injustice.

About Groups

It was my destiny to join in a great experience. Having had the good fortune to belong to the League, I was permitted to be a participant in a unique journey. What wonder it had at the time.

... we League brothers traveled throughout the world without motorcars or ships; as we conquered the war-shattered world by our faith and transformed it into Paradise, we creatively brought the past, the future and the fictitious into the present moment.

HERMANN HESSE

"There are going to be times," says Kesey, "when we can't wait for somebody. Now, you're either on the bus or off the bus. If you're on the bus, and you get left behind, then you'll find it again. If you're off the bus in the first place—then it won't make a damn." And nobody had to have it spelled out for them. Everything was becoming allegorical, understood by the group mind, and especially this: you're either on the bus ... or off the bus.

TOM WOLFE

Groups, and Social Science Past

There are times when we want to settle back, when we want to be surrounded by a kind of primordial ooze of companionship. We want the ease of wine or religion or dope. Sometimes we want the womb-like comfort of a group.

Groups have a long—if not noble—history in American politics. From the time James Madison wrote of factions, group theory has tried to mirror the group action in America. We know, too, that Alexis de Tocqueville wrote of groups, of "voluntary associations," which to him seemed the backbone of the republic. Because groups seem to have something to do with our reality, we should try to understand them both as a social science discovery and for what they mean in the real world.

At one time or another, small groups have been seen as the basis of just about everything. The king had his advisors, the pope his inner councils of close friends, the president a kitchen cabinet, and, most recently—but for rather different reasons—the heavy rock people have had their groupies.

But even with all those groups around, even knowing that they have had something to do with why things happened as they did, it is hard for us to truly understand the nature of groups. It is difficult mostly because we do not really want to hear about them. As students, we seem to shy away from an understanding of groups because it might be painful. In the end, it may turn out that we are all "groupies" of one kind or another; yet we do not know a thing about groups.

It seems reasonable to approach this section historically so as to better understand ourselves as an extension of what was. Around the turn of the century, groups were rediscovered in American society, this time by an academic named Arthur Bentley. A seductive theory, his. The idea, in a somewhat bastardized form, was that small groups were the oil which kept society running smoothly. One could look around—casually or carefully—and see that neighbors and corporate executives, army generals and important senators all formed themselves into groups. It was thought all that was needed was to understand how people were brought together, what they did when they were together, and how the different bunches of them interacted—then we could understand all the important things about society.

Just think group, think small, and all answers would be clear.

The understanding of groups did not stop there; indeed, it has been continued, updated, revised, and revitalized by those people who study large organizations. What the investigators found, while a bit of a surprise to them, should be no surprise to us. They found that people who worked in organizations tended to gather in groups. That people in these little groups did things pretty much alike. That they worked at about the same speed, thought about the same thoughts, said about the same things. In sum, members of groups became almost indistinguishable to those outside the group.[1]

In terms of historical importance we can shift from the 1930s to the 1950s, from groups in organizations to groups in society, from the Hawthorne studies to the studies of David Truman.[2] It is through Truman that we can begin to understand some of the basic issues of groupist ideology.

Ideology and Groups

It is clear that when any "reality" is described, when any theory is presented, it carries with it a bias. Sometimes more pronounced than others; sometimes involving a whole world view, other times simple prejudices. Those who write about groups are certainly carriers of bias; they surely have a particular view of society to present.

The point is not that group theorists have biases—that is quite normal; the point is to understand what those biases are. We need to examine the implications of their views to know whether we can share them. We must compare what the roles of groups in society are said to be with what they really are; we must know who groups help, and how; finally,

---

[1] These were the Hawthorne studies. One major finding resulting from these studies was that people being studied were more productive than people not being studied. For a first-rate article on modern working groups, see Elinor Langer, "The Women of the Telephone Company," *The New York Review of Books*, March 26, 1970.

[2] See David Truman, *The Governmental Process* (New York: Alfred A. Knopf, 1951).

we must try to figure out where group theory might be lead-ing us. Maybe then we can begin to make sense out of our group selves.

Groups, according to the writings of David Truman, repre-sent the multiple interests in a society. Our diversity is re-flected—indeed, represented—by the groups to which we belong. Further, if there is a "national interest" it is only the sum of the interests of these groups. In other words, an in-dividual belongs to a group, the group represents the interests of the individual in the public sector, and the sum of the in-terests of these groups is the "national interest."

Now certainly that makes sense. Indeed, it is wholly reason-able until one begins to think about it and question it. What I want to argue is that Truman fails us in very basic ways, and to understand his failure is to begin to understand one of the meanings of groups.[3]

The "sin" of Truman is simply this: He assumes unquestion-ingly that leaders do in fact represent the group interest. He does not ask how they do, or to what extent they do; he just assumes leaders represent their groups. If Truman is correct, then the system of groups seems fair enough. It means that we can join a group and have a voice in what goes on. Re-grettably, however, Truman does not appear to be right.

Theoretically, the internal workings of groups, and therefore the interests they come to represent, are complicated. Groups (for example, labor unions) inevitably come under the leader-ship of people who are insulated from the rest of the mem-bers. Worse, leaders begin developing interests of their own: the desire to stay in power, the desire to form friendships with other group leaders or with powerful, prestigious persons. Much behavior can be understood in bureaucratic terms.

In other words, the desires of the leader are often different from, or even in conflict with, the desires of the membership he or she represents. The leader has aims and goals which, in the last analysis, are conservative. His or her vision becomes limited to a particular position in the system, so that the key to

---

[3] This is similar to the analysis in Mike Rogin's "Nonpartisanship and the Group Interest," in Philip Green and Sanford Levinson, eds., *Power and Com-munity* (New York: Vintage Books, 1970). To get a clearer view of the tradi-tional arguments, one should see Rogin's article.

policy must be to keep the system stable. There is no reason to believe that stability is the goal of the membership of the organization; there is little evidence to show that the interests of the group are represented by the leadership.[4]

Group theory in the 1950s, then, was interesting but certainly not democratic. What Truman described was a system run by an elite of group leaders. The elite was responsible for the safety of the system, for its stability, but did not really concern itself with the democratic workings of the group. By definition, the interests of the leadership were thought to be the interests of the group, but that assumption was only partially correct. As defined by the leadership—by the elite—group interests were represented only if they did not endanger the smooth workings of the system, only if they did not endanger the security of the elite.

When viewed in this light, two things become more understandable. First, at the level of the example itself, it is clear that business and labor *can* agree on many things, because business leaders and labor leaders perceive that they have much in common. The dynamic that pushes the one pushes the other.

Second, it becomes obvious that Truman's theory of groups contains a particular view of the individual. The view is impersonal and material. The individual is to be materially taken care of by the group. That is in the person's interest and the public interest. Yet, in an important sense, a political sense, the individual is not much better off than he or she was before joining the group. The individual is not really represented by anyone; is not a member of a group which democratically decides the interests of that group; is not in control; is powerless.

Such are the individual costs of this group theory, of this "public interest." They represent, in part, the social and political costs of our system of groups.

New Groups for Contact

David Truman was the 1950s; these are the 1970s. Life has become faster. We have to take speed to stay even. Organiza-

---

[4] Ibid , pp. 132–33.

tions have become bigger. We have become smaller cogs in bigger machines. Much smaller. And much, much bigger.

Somehow society has tried to push us apart organically— and togther mechanically. By that I mean that we are less and less able to understand ourselves as human beings, but more able to define ourselves as pieces of social machinery. We are more tool-like; we are more machine-like; we are more pieces of production than ever before.

Where does that leave us? Surely our social science theories would not consciously deny us our own humanity.

Of course they don't. No, social science would not do that. What it does do is what it has tried to do for years—tie us neatly together in little groups of powerless people. It happens at two levels: personally and organizationally. In one sense, this theory of small groups makes the world very recognizable. The United States is made up of millions of little groups. These groups—in car pools, at work, at school, in the neighborhood, while hunting or playing bridge—give humanity and, finally, a kind of self-definition to an individual.

In a sense, the theory might be right. We seem to yearn for our own close groups. Yet even these groups have been changing and so too has our involvement in them. Groups in the brave new now seem to have two distinct qualities: temporariness and great intimacy. Together these traits can be tyrannizing.

We are now pressured together in groups that we know will last only a limited amount of time, so we use them (or they use us) for gratification. America has become an odd sideshow of Hollywood: We "love" everyone, are friendly to all because we know that pretty soon we won't see them again. We pledge allegiance to the group, which demands great conformity and intimacy, and in a month or a year we move on to be tyrannized again.

Groups seem to have reached their logical conclusion in becoming plastic, wholly artificial, and temporary. For $15, or a little more or less, one can buy instant identity, constant attention. One can join an encounter group. As therapy, encounters may be helpful. As for contributing to any political change, to any substantive action, they seem to influence nothing. The groups provide human contact, which is an important neglected need of our times.

New Groups for Speed

It is important to develop in greater detail some of the themes we have mentioned before. This and the following sections will deal with the coerciveness of groups, with leadership and participation in groups, and finally with "magic" groups. Coerciveness seems to be the most reasonable place to begin.

In the above there is the suggestion that there are at least two ways in which groups can limit one's power. By studying the setting of groups—how they are arranged and managed —and group dynamics, we will get closer to understanding how an individual group member may become powerless. First, the setting.

If I understand the trend correctly, we are moving toward a society in which work groups, and hence, all others, are becoming temporary. There is a recent book, *The Temporary Society*, with just such a focus.[5] The argument of the future is roughly this. Society, especially the technical one, is experiencing more and more problems. To get to these problems quickly, to solve them fast, we must change our living patterns. We must be able to move around quickly—move to the problems—meet new sets of coworkers, and form together to solve the problem.

Then, move again to the next problem.

This is more than just a way to organize (or to reorganize); it is a whole ethic, a whole way of understanding ourselves and society. We become without a home, without permanence. We become a permanent part of an ever-changing environment, a perpetual stranger in a group of strangers. To meet the new requirements, we must continually change homes, towns, work groups, and friends. Above and beyond what was discussed in connection with the Open Road, the implications of this style are enormous.

---

[5] Warren Bennis and Philip Slater, *The Temporary Society* (New York: Harper & Row, 1968).

First, and most obviously, power under such a system lies in the ability to move people around. In other words, there is somebody at the center finding problems and replacing people. Those who move become wholly dependent upon their bosses. They have no other stable reference point. It is possible that the military is the forerunner of temporary America. Every year or two the military family moves. From city to city, from base to base. They are thrown into new work groups and a new social life. Only if they are lucky do they see old friends, that is, people from other one-year stays at other bases. The military person is loyal to—and dependent upon— the United States Government (whoever that is). Loyalties are rarely to the location from which he or she is about to move.

The point is clear: In a world of temporary groups, power flows to those who control the moves.

The second point of temporariness involves the kind of person who will fit. The question is this: Who will people the Temporary Society? Who will survive? We can speculate.

The young will survive the moving and adjusting. They are healthy enough for all the hassles. But the survivors must be more than young; they must be technical experts, too. A young person with technical expertise might not merely adjust to such a regimen; he or she could possibly thrive on moving from place to place, continually solving problems of a technical nature. The young could somehow handle the ever-changing groups of people, as long as there was work to do.[6]

They will survive, but for how long? "Young" is not a permanent condition; neither is technical expertise. In these days of new knowledge, an engineer of thirty may be out of date, may be an old-fashioned toolbox with old-fashioned tools.

There are some odd and horrible losses in this temporary world. We both grow "old" too quickly and stay "young" too long. We can't really *be* young and adventuresome. Got to get going—moving and dealing and making it, right out of college. The cream of the crop: have the *new techniques;* the *stamina* to survive; and are *unformed* enough to continually adapt.

---

[6] One particularly vivid and depressing forecast of the future is that it will be like Fort Lauderdale when students are there over spring vacation. See Alvin Toffler, *Future Shock* (New York: Bantam Books, 1970).

So there is the constant fear of being old. Being out of technological date. Being too slow to move and too much of a person to adapt to every silly change.

The temporary world robs both the rush of being young and the true pleasure of aging.

There is an amazing curse put on the young; a curse which goes with our age. It's called potential, and young people almost always have it. One could easily call it a social disease. I'm pleased not to be in college, or even in my twenties. I'm just beginning to glimpse the horrors we put on the young. The weight of the word potential.

There is a denial of personal power, a taking away (a not granting) of a sense of self. Sure you're whole, but empty. Young and hollow. *What does it mean?*

At least two things.

All age seems to have been corrupted. Everyone wants to be young and young people are denied the essences of life.

Second, in our temporary world, emotions get *democratized* and *discounted*.

Let's go back to groups, encounter-type groups, and look at them in a little different way. The real trap in our pop-psychological-instant-intimacy groups is something like this: to be "healthy," one must "express your own personal feeling." To apply a good social science concept to that, a lot of it is just bullshit.

There are many things which are really unimportant . . . even some of your very own emotions. To make all emotions equal means you will never be able to see what's important and what's unimportant.

When another person or an event really *is* an intrusion into your life—really does affect the who-you-are in the world—what do you do if you've just been to an encounter group and have let it "all hang out?" Been "up front." Been "honest" and are "emotionally spent?" What do you do for something important?

We've made love/hate/anger/joy all silly and meaningless by elevating petty moods into important events of our personal lives. We seem all too willing to throw away empathy and care and probably a great deal of our politics and humanity for a cheap version of self-indulgent, childish whimpering.

We *democrats go to encounter groups and vote on emotions.*

What a place we've gotten to.

The temporary society makes no allowance for the very young, for the old, for those not involved in technology. Part of the glue it uses—groups—seems systematically to take us away from our emotional self by flooding us with "emotion." What does it mean? To quote Kurt Vonnegut:

> The problem is this: How to love people who have no use?
> In time, almost all men and women will become worthless as producers of goods, food, services and more machines, as sources of practical ideas in the areas of economics, engineering, and probably medicine, too. So—if we cannot find reasons and methods for treasuring human beings because they are human beings, then we might as well, as has so often been suggested, rub them out.[7]

Rub them out? Is *that* the ultimate solution of the temporary society? Probably not, but it is an idea.

Coercion

Enough about the setting of groups. What about the workings of the group itself, the interactions of those who comprise the group? For several reasons—not the least of which being that they are manageable—many empirical studies have been done on the behavior of small groups. The conclusions of the studies are not surprising. In a small group setting, the pressure to conform to group norms is great. In a simple, now classic study, S. E. Asch demonstrated how powerful group pressure could be.[8]

The experiment involved eight persons seated in a room. They were shown lines of various lengths and were asked obvious questions about the lines. The whole "test" was very easy and monotonous.

---

[7] Kurt Vonnegut, Jr., *God Bless You, Mr. Rosewater* (New York: Dell Publishing Co., 1965), p. 183. It should be noted that "doing away" with people is not Vonnegut's message.

[8] S. E. Asch, "Effects of Group Pressure upon the Modification and Distortion of Judgements," in Bernard Hinton and H. Joseph Reitz, eds., *Groups and Organizations* (Belmont, Calif.: Wadsworth Publishing Co., 1971), pp. 215–23.

As the "test" progressed, one individual began to find himself being contradicted by the rest of the group. His "right" answer did not correspond with the answers given by the other seven. What had happened, of course, was that seven members of the group had been coached to give incorrect answers.

In this very simple exercise involving the judging of lengths of lines, the results were "clear and unambiguous. There was marked movement toward the majority. One third of all the estimates in the critical group were errors identical with or in the direction of the distorted estimates of the majority." [9] The reasons why a person would contradict what he had visually perceived are instructive. When each subject was asked why he had responded to the "test" the way he or she did, the most common explanation was that the group had answered that way. The majority of the group seemed to be acting without hesitation, indeed, with confidence, so the outsider assumed they were right.

Being in a minority seemed to make things hard on the individual. Asch writes that the "principal impression" of the subject was that he was "so caught up by immediate difficulties that he lost clear reasons for his actions, and could make no reasonable decisions." [10]

If the Asch experiment is any indication, it is not difficult to conclude that small groups are potentially very coercive. But it would be wrong to stop with that obvious insight. It would be equally wrong to suggest that all groups are evil or that all groups are bad for their members. In order to begin to understand groups as something other than coercive, we must try to envision changes in our attitudes.

Groups Reconsidered: Passive and Active

This may sound like a paradox, but I do not think that it is: For groups to be less coercive, we must become more involved in them. Briefly, let me try to explain.

Small groups are potentially very important to the way we

---

[9] Ibid., p. 216.
[10] Ibid., p. 217.

act and the things we do. We know that. Further, we know that we are constantly involved, to a greater or lesser degree, in groups. Whether it is a sorority or fraternity, a bridge club or basketball team, or just some snobby little social group, we are involved. The problem is that we are not *consciously* involved. Too often we passively accept membership while never actively taking part in the direction of the group. We accept coercion without accepting participation, we are acted upon without acting.

To put it a little differently, to be a part of a group is to be subject to its rules. This is true whether we accept it or not; it is true whether we actively engage in the group decision-making, or feel we are different from the group, or not really a part of it at all. In part, our identities stem from these small groups. What is necessary to understand is that it is part of you no matter how you feel about that group. To belong to a group and not take it seriously is to limit the power you have over who you are.

What I am arguing is that groups are important to one's self and, as such, should be treated importantly.

Leadership and Power: An Introduction

To get at the problem of living in groups—the problem of participation—is a complicated task. It involves leading and following and membership. Also involved are ideas about democracy and authority and all those themes political scientists should be concerned with. But a discussion that considered all these ideas would be misplaced here. We are, after all, trying to make sense of groups. We are trying to figure out how we can make groups—an everyday fact of life —a more meaningful, everyday fact of life. We are trying to understand how to free ourselves from current group practice by becoming conscious of the benefits groups have to offer.

It is important to realize that people being together—in groups, or politically, or whatever—must come to some kind of understanding of how they will behave. I am not talking about a strict code of rules, or law and order, or even order; I am just suggesting that we make an effort to shape the group toward common interests and goals. We should be aware that power and leadership exist whether we acknowledge them or not.

If that is so, if leadership and power do exist in groups, then their forms should be understood and agreed upon by the members of that group, if they are not to be tyrannized by them. An example may be useful. It is the example of the group living of the people in the Haight Ashbury during 1966 and 1967. It was an interesting time; a good one to learn from for a couple of reasons. First, there was a great deal of energy for change. Second, even with that energy there was failure. Given history, it is only appropriate that we learn from failure. The hippies accepted, a different life-style during this period, and by example tried to change society. Their dealings with groups point up questions with which we must deal. John Howard explains: [11]

> Stated simply, the argument is as follows. The hippies assumed that voluntarism (every man doing his own thing) was compatible with satisfying essential group and individual needs and with the maintenance of a social system in which there was an absence of power differentials and invidious distinctions based on, for example, wealth, sex, or race. That assumption is open to question. Voluntarism can work only where the participants in the social system have a sufficient understanding of the needs of the system to be willing to do things which they do not want to do in order for the system to persist. . . .

Howard asked one of the Diggers why they were no longer distributing food in the park and received this answer:

> "Well, man, it took a lot of organization to get that done. We had to scuffle to get the food. Then the chicks or somebody had to prepare it. Then we got to serve it. A lot of people got to do a lot of things at the right time or it doesn't come off. Well, it got so that people weren't doing it. I mean a cat wouldn't let us have a truck when we needed it or some chick was grooving somewhere and can't help out. Now you hate to get into the power bag and start telling people what to do . . . but without that, man, well. . . ."

---

[11] John Robert Howard, "The Flowering of the Hippie Movement," in Terrence Cook and Patrick Morgan, eds., *Participatory Democracy* (San Francisco: Canfield Press, 1971), p. 209. Reprinted from Vol. 382 (March 1969), p. 47 of *The Annals* of The American Academy of Political and Social Science.

The point that is important to make is that the "power trip" is not, by definition, a bad thing. What is essential is that power be understood and then used when and how the group wants it used. Back to the hippies:

> We had all kinds of people there at first and anybody could stay if there was room. Anybody could crash out there. Some of the motorcyle types began to congregate in the kitchen. That became *their* room, and if you wanted something to eat or a beer you had to step over them. Pretty soon, in a way, people were cut off from the food. I don't mean that they wouldn't give it to you, but you had to go on their "turf" to get it. It was like they had begun, in some very quiet and subtle way, to run things.[12]

In sum, for a group to fulfill the intentions of each individual, elements of the relationships among the members—like power and leadership—must be understood and agreed upon. If that is the case, the chances of the group's becoming a good or even an extraordinary experience are greatly increased.

Oh My God . . .

They are playing a game. They are playing not playing a game. If I show them I see they are, I shall break the rules and they will punish me. I must play their game, of not seeing I see the game.

R. D. LAING

Because there is no public place to be political, no space in which we may be citizens, we are forced to make each of our actions a political statement of one sort or another. From our diet to our dress we make ideological choices. There are lots of serious folks who really do live their politics.

To be fair (not a terribly noble aim, but adequate enough in this case) at least something should be said about religion. In an important way, believers are taking their actions almost ponderously heavily, their day is a reflection of His Day or Her Day, and theirs is a "politics" of True Belief.[13]

---

[12] Ibid., p. 207.

[13] If it makes any difference, I can remember fairly accurately my last "encounter" with God. When I was nineteen my mother and I were talking. We were discussing religion and she said: "It's too bad we don't believe in God. I suppose it would be a comfort." I said something like: "Yea, it's too bad." Enough of True Confessions.

I don't want to push this "fair" thing too far. There is much more about religion that I will not discuss than I will. If your God is real and not mentioned and vengeful, you don't have to worry. I'll get what's coming to me for the oversight.

We are, when we get down to it, Americans. That rates pretty high on a Simple-Minded-Scale, but it is a fact that is fairly helpful to remember. Some of us, and I mean a *very, very few*, are able to un-Americanize ourselves. The rest of us are Americans and it gets into and influences just about everything we do. From hamburgers to god, we are red, white, and blue.

Ain't a bad thing; in fact, there's something good and noble about it.

The problems really don't appear while being yourself; the real trouble starts when you start being one or another kind of an unself.

But, this is about religion. We know, in our very beings, about lip-service religion. A Sunday morning in church if you happen to be with your parents, or two days a year in temple, or catching up on a busy week of sinning in a confessional. Check in *as if* there was a god for an After-Life Insurance policy. Not all that pure of motive, but it's good just to be sure.

A comfortable eternity is worth a few boring sermons.

For some years now, there have been people who were willing *not only to say* that's silly, but actually to do something about it. There are chanters and freaks and preemies and an amazing variety of orthodox Christians and Jews and believers in the Buddha and different kinds of Zen.

Many of these people are making serious and impressive efforts at making sense of the world they didn't ask to be born into; they are trying to live a good life. A life which takes into account the problems of our society and compels them to do something different. I'm not really concerned if they are right- or wrong-headed; I am much more concerned in the statement they make and what we have to learn from them.

There is some sense in starting with what we (mostly) are, and ending up with what we are not. The biggest turn-on, the fastest growing and most popular new non-religion religion is TM. The transcendental meditationists. TM'ers. Ommmm. Hummmm.[14]

If we—a committee of us—were to invent a business for our fellow Americans, there are some obvious sorts of things we would want. In order to make lots of money, we could offer a product easy to make and use, promise it would help all sorts of things (reduce crime in the streets, improve sexual performance, make dull work happier, help you get better grades, help you make more money, and bring about world peace), make it religious/non-religious pop-culture exotic, and let people still smoke, drink, be junk-food junkies, and sell it with something close to a scientific guarantee.

Why, if we did it right we'd be rich.

We could start a university, sell to 30,000 new people a month, have $12 million a year revenue coming in. Fat City.

We could also be sued by the World Plan Executive Council-US (the TM central office) because they already *do* these things and *make* those claims, and *have* that income. (We can learn a whole lot about ourselves by learning about Transcendental Meditation in America. It may turn out that we are what we hum.)

One might want to argue, probably very rightly, that what I wrote is not true. It is wrong in particular, but not in spirit. What seems most wrong is the fact that no committee could invent such a wonderful business. I apologize.

The TM'ers have an impressive list of "up your" promises.[15] For example: Up Your Recall, or Up Your Productivity, or Up Your IQ.[16] And there are lots more. The point—if it's possible to oversimplify—is that the world is going at an out-of-control pace and we poor people can't cope. Who can argue with that?

In order to make sense and keep up what we need to do is relax (to be precise, it only takes forty minutes a day) and get

---

[14] Of course I have a mantra, but I can't tell you. I'mmm sworn to secrecy. Also, I have no doubts that TM'ers who report fantastic results are telling the truth.

[15] The source of much of the following is Denise Denniston and Peter McWilliams, *The TM Book: How to Enjoy the Rest of Your Life* (New York: Warner Books, Inc., 1975).

[16] Ibid., pp. 79, 93, 74.

in touch (in *direct contact*) with the source of thought. We have to tap into the pure energy in the mind.

Step Right Up. Buy Into Your Own Mind.

Anyone can do it. It is easy to learn, and effortless to do, and it actually takes only hours to learn.[17] The magic mantra gives you a rest deeper than sleep (there is Scientific Proof), and can make you more creative and even give you a faster reaction time (there is Scientific Proof).

With the stress off your nervous system, you can avoid those nagging heart attacks, and your mind can use its full mental potential. You can lick this tense twentieth century and reach Enlightenment.

[Let me interrupt this commercial with some clarification. Upon investigation, we find that enlightenment is a fairly heavy-duty concept which comes from many of the Eastern religions. For TM it means having 100 percent of one's potential available for use. More curious still, it is claimed that enlightenment is *everyone's birthright*. Should we now say "Life, Liberty, and Enlightenment?"

Back to our commercial.]

TM technique is "a great scientific discovery." It "makes suffering in life a thing of the past." Not only that, there is nothing to believe in (even an atheist can do it), no special clothes to wear (not even sandals), no change of life-style, you don't even have to concentrate. But there will be changes: *"Some will find calculus a breeze. Others will have no difficulty writing epic poems before breakfast."* [18]

All that, and you can still eat McDonald's hamburgers.

And, as a footnote, if just 1 percent of you in your community do this, the *whole* community will "suddenly . . . increase its efficiency, orderliness, and productivity." [19]

All this for less than $200.

It Might Be Harder than That

If I don't know I don't know
                    I think I know

---

[17] Most of these words are from the TM book, not from me. These, for example, come from Ibid., p. 51.
[18] Ibid., p. 116.
[19] Ibid., p. 336.

If I don't know I know
>   I think I don't know.

R. D. LAING

Crowned with garlands, the three-year-old child plays the drum;
The eighty-year-old man plays with a balloon.[20]

As a treat to myself, I was reading a skinny book—*Zen and the Art of Archery*—before trying to sleep every night. It was written by a German who went to Japan and tried to learn Zen through a Master who taught archery. I would read a few pages, do some thinking about it, and was enjoying it.

I even flattered myself into thinking I understood some of it.

Somewhere around the middle of the book—somewhere around the second or third year of archery/Zen—the Master introduced the concept of the target and how the arrow and the target should meet at a certain point.

Un-American!

The Zen life is one which we seem to be trained and taught not to understand. To grow up in America is to grow up with a set of instincts which closes us off from the essences and meanings of Zen. If that is true, and I have to admit I believe it is, it would be silly for me to write in an authoritative way about what Zen *really* is.

There are a couple of obvious things which might give us the proper distance on those people—and those groups of people—who study Zen. The fact seems to be that one is not "taught" Zen, nor does one actually "study" Zen. Two quotes may be helpful: [21]

> One would not even be able to talk about teaching it since Zen cannot be taught, that is, taught through symbols; it passes directly from master to student, from "mind to mind." The image employed here is a *seal* imprinted on a mind; not a seal of wood, copper, or ivory, but a "mind seal."

and

> *But Zen is not the study of Zen; Zen is life.* Zen is direct contact with reality . . . Zen can only be lived and experienced. As Master Tue Trung Thuong Si said, "This marvelous piece must be

---

[20] Thich Nhat Hanh, *Zen Keys* (Garden City, New York: Anchor Books, 1974), p. 164.
[21] Ibid., pp. 31, 131. Emphasis in original.

played." What is the good of discussing a musical masterpiece? It is its performance that counts.

Let me try another way of getting at not getting at Zen. There are certain Zen monasteries where, upon entering, the novice is given a book called the *Little Manual*. It is a small book, and a famous one. The instinct of the Western mind would be to think of the book as one of philosophy. After all, it is the first book people trying to learn Zen are supposed to read.

In the *Little Manual* there is no Zen philosophy.

The book, basically, is about how to control your mind and concentration, what the required discipline and behavior of life is in the monastery, and an essay encouraging Zen disciples to "take to heart the fact that their time and life are precious and should not be vainly dissipated." The book is used by all monks no matter what their age or the amount of time they have studied Zen.

The essence of Zen is found in the *Little Manual* in part because it suggests an individual focus on each thing he or she does; this action leads to the "Awareness of Being." As I understand it, one would be ill-advised (unless he or she wants to prove stupidity) to write much more. It takes a full lifetime of considered acts by serious and good people with a different mind-set to truly understand the Awareness of Being.

There are few if any actions taken which are not subject to self-awareness and meaning. From the closing of a door to the washing of one's hands, a student of Zen must be conscious and understanding. There are "acts of majestic behavior" and "subtle gestures."

"It is said that in Buddhism there are ninety thousand 'subtle gestures' the novice must practice." [22]

That's a fairly serious project, a lifetime worth. Certainly not the *only* kind of serious project; in fact, it seems remarkably out of our grasp. But it serves as a fine example of how taking the quality of your life seriously can easily be a full-time job. There is something almost magical about those people, but there are equally magical—if not totally different—

---

[22] Ibid., p. 25.

examples of a more recognizable kind. Before doing them, it seems right to end with a story about enlightenment.

> Little Toyo was only twelve years old. But since he was a pupil at the Kennin Temple, he wanted to be given a *koan* to ponder, just like the more advanced students. So one evening, at the proper time, he went to the room of Makurai, the master, struck the gong softly to announce his presence, bowed, and sat before the master in respectful silence.
>
> Finally the master said: "Toyo, show me the sound of two hands clapping."
>
> Toyo clapped his hands.
>
> "Good," said the master. "Now show me the sound of one hand clapping."
>
> Toyo was silent. Finally he bowed and left to consider this problem.
>
> The next night he returned, and struck the gong with one palm. "That is not right," said the master. The next night Toyo returned and played geisha music with one hand. "That is not right," said the master. The next night Toyo returned, and imitated the dripping of water. "That is not right," said the master. The next night Toyo returned, and imitated the cricket scraping his leg. "That is still not right," said the master.
>
> For ten nights Toyo tried new sounds. At last he stopped coming to the master. For a year he thought of every sound, and discarded them all, until he finally reached enlightenment.
>
> He returned respectfully to the master. Without striking the gong, he sat down and bowed. "I have heard sound without sound," he said.[23]

Magical Groups

It may occur to you, sooner or later, that there is very little "hard," empirical objective information—not much social science data—on magical groups. In my searchings of the literature on small groups, I have encountered none indexed under "magical." That should not disallow my using the designation; all it means is that some kind of definition, or at least explanation, should be given.

Up to now, we have been involved with what we know, with ordinary groups doing those things to individuals that ordinary groups generally do. But it seems to me that there is

---

[23] *Zen Buddhism: Stories, Parables and Koan Riddles of Zen Masters* (Mount Vernon, N.Y.: The Peter Pauper Press, 1959), pp. 24–25.

another kind of group, one in which the members are somehow transformed, somehow special, somehow engaged in an enterprise different from the rest of us. The examples of this come from fiction, and close to it: Hermann Hesse's *The Journey to the East* and Tom Wolfe's *The Electric Kool-Aid Acid Test*.[24]

The point of the books and the point I shall try to make is this: Far from the common uses of groups we are generally taught, far from the "normal politics" view of American groups, some groups may actually point the way to different kinds of relationships and to a different kind of politics.

To begin at a common beginning point of political scientists, let us start with power. There are some bad feelings about power, some honest misgivings about "getting into the power bag." If understood in the conventional way, the misgivings are very understandable. Power is dominance over, it is—to use the common definition—the ability of A to make B do something B would not otherwise have done.

In that sense, power is in part negative. The definition may be both limiting and harmful; it may influence us to act in certain ways. First, as students or as citizens, we can well understand what B feels like. We can understand what it means to be made to do something we otherwise would not have done.

Second, while A has power, he or she is also caged by the relationship. The person holding power is limited to his or her own imagination. There is little chance that A can become different, can qualitatively change, can get beyond his or her own thoughts. Seen from that point of view, from the point of view which has A making B do something not otherwise done, we can understand why power seems limited and abusive.

The definition prescribes "reasonable" ways to behave. Given the definition as a guide to action, we could be expected to "hoard" power, to "spend" it only when necessary. There would be no sharing or spreading of that kind of power, only spending and losing it. But power need not be like that;

---

[24] Hermann Hesse, *The Journey to the East* (New York: Farrar, Straus & Giroux, 1970); Tom Wolfe, *The Electric Kool-Aid Acid Test* (New York: Bantam Books, 1969).

there can be a different view of power, a different definition of it which might alter the way we act. There might be a view of power which would make it creative.

In order to redefine power so that it would apply to a "magical group," we need change only one word: Power is the ability of A to make B do something he or she *could* not have done before. Power then becomes a source of creative energy, an ability or skill that will help induce someone to take an action, to strike out anew, to do something which in the past was impossible. Just as significantly, power becomes a shared commodity, something that *increases* when used, not decreases.

The most obvious place for this to take place is in a small group, but it must be a group that is stable, not temporary, one that understands power, not one which ignores it; finally, it must be a group that is working for something in common, not one in which there is little coincidence of interests.

The idea of leadership must also change. In a bureaucratic world, leadership is pictured as involving a supervisor/subordinate relationship. The leader is at the top, the rest of us at the bottom. That seems natural enough, and it is certainly an adequate description of everyday life. To envision being a leader is to envision being at the top of something and possessing a good deal of power. It is, in a sense, to assume responsibility for all those underneath you. A plantation owner "took care" of his or her slaves, a school principal "takes care" of his or her students.

Of course that view of leadership depends on a repressive view of power. It may be important to understand leadership as being not on an up-and-down scale with followership but rather as on a continuum with it. Leadership and followership are two ends of the same line. One is not "over" the other. One person may have some qualities or traits or skills which makes that advice or those directions more acceptable than the others'. In those areas, that person leads.

What is important to understand is that a leader is also a follower. That it is a relationship in which sometimes one leads, sometimes another. If one has the ability to lead a group of people to do things collectively that they could not do individually, and if the members of a group want that to happen, then one person should "lead." But this important fact remains: The relationship between leader and follower is an essentially equal one. From that relationship, the creative powers of the people individually—and of the group as a whole—are increased.[25]

That has the makings of a magical group.

The essence of this discussion—at least the point *I* am most interested in making—is that we are foolish to take groups and group theories at their face value.

Involved in what we think ordinary and obvious are a whole set of assumptions which need to be examined. Such terms as *power* and *leadership* really do mean something, and the way we define them may have an influence on the way we act. It would be at the far reaches of silliness to suggest that by changing the way we define words, the whole world would automatically change. I am not suggesting that. I am trying to make the point that we are tied to concepts and activities we rarely try to understand, to ones we seldom challenge.

There do seem to be other ways to see the world—and maybe that other vision is a better one.

They had all voluntarily embarked upon a trip and a state of consciousness that was "crazy" by ordinary standards. The trip, in fact the whole deal, was a risk-all balls-out plunge into the unknown. . . . Stark naked had done her thing. She roared off into the void and was picked up by the cops by and by and the doors closed in the county psychiatric ward, and that was that, for the pranksters were long gone.

TOM WOLFE

---

[25] Just as it seems ·harmful always to be private, always alone, so it seems harmful always to be public, always open. The tension comes in being open, yet retaining some sense of privacy, some sense of that part of us which makes us individuals. What is important is that privacy does not make much sense without publicness. One needs the other to set boundaries and to give meaning.

Friendship

9½

Friendship, friendship: Just the perfect blendship
When other friendships have been forgot
Ours will still be hot.

This is not really a whole chapter. It is a part of one, a piece of a whole. The ideas that follow are most closely tied to the preceding discussion of groups. The group chapter is incomplete. There is something basic to, as well as prior to, small groups. Friendship is an ingredient of groups and it is a topic that deserves some attention.

It is important that at least two things be said before we begin to work through the idea of friendship. First, it is a fantastically complicated topic, one which is possibly impossible to fully understand. In order to make our effort more reasonable, more manageable, we will limit the discussion to friendship in America.

Second, the effort is worth making because it might give us insights into our social and political environment. If we *are* the system, if we carry a miniature version of the system in our heads—and act as the system would have us act—then we need to think about how we act.

Friendships: American Myths

Our first myth is somehow true, and somehow not. The kind that we do not want to believe, but for some reason act as if we do. The myth involves women. It seems to me that the first myth we may share is this: Men make better friends than women.

The myth is amazingly degrading. It assures us that two women are rarely true friends; rarely friends who honestly share, who honestly give, friends who are able to stay close for years and years.

But why? Lurking in us is the thought that the essence of women's failure to be friends with other women lies in their jealousy. In a male chauvinist pig sort of way, men seem to believe that each woman is too insecure to be the friend of another woman. The idea is that what women need are strong males, someone to whom they can talk, someone on whom they can lean.

Americans seem to believe that women together are either hens or bitches, but never friends.

What about men and women? Can they truly be friends?

Again, our vision is clouded with doubt. We know that men and women can *like* each other; but is that friendship?

The stereotype thought is obvious to all. They can be lovers, or they can be "just like sister and brother," but the idea of being friends with someone of the opposite sex seems just plain foolish. We are in a strange time; a time when we realize men and women *are not* the same, yet *are* the same. It is a time when we must not assume that women doing "men's jobs" is a sign of liberation, or men doing "women's jobs" is a sign of weakness. In the flux of all of us having an identity crises, friendship is tough to find.

For men, women are okay to sleep with, but it is foolish to try to be too friendly with one.

Friendships between men—so goes our myth—are also limited. The first obvious limitation—obvious indignation—concerns black men and white men. The myth is that for a white, the black man is everything but a friend.

For two hundred years, we were taught to believe that the black was a "boy." A grinning, happy boy. Tough to be best friends with a boy.

Then there was the myth that black men were sexually superior. Tough to be best friends with a rival. A rival who was better.

Finally, in enlightened, liberal circles, the black man became a status symbol. Whitey had to have one at every party. But the black was not there as a friend; he was there to be on display.

So blacks hated whites and whites hated blacks; and friendship was limited in yet another way.

The results of all this are limiting. White men end up being friends with white men. Given that one is not too much richer than the other, two white men seem to be able to be friends in America. They can drink together, tell dirty jokes, and sometimes even talk about important things. The only limitation is that they cannot love each other. For males to be friends, they have to prove to society that they are more attracted to women than to men. They can neither cry—nor comfortably kiss in public.

Friendship—or, as I understand friendship in America—

makes little sense, does little good. We fail to take seriously the sometimes special world of women or of men, we fail to grant the trait of humanness to most of those who are black or red or yellow or brown.

In doing so, we seem to define the world as violent—as unemotional and masculine, as unsentimental and white.

Toward the Last Chapter

He swallowed a whole lot of wisdom, but it seemed as if all of it had gone down the wrong way.

James Thurber wrote that a moth never burned its wings by flying toward the stars.

There is little reason for one to bother reading this "Toward," as it does not rightly belong to the preceding chapter, or to the one that follows. It has to do with some of what goes into—but rarely comes out of—writing.

Like many endeavors, writing consists of a series of traumas; with a book, these traumas are numbered in chapters. I suppose a ten-and-one-half chapter book is not so traumatic. It is hard to imagine a twenty-three chapter book. But that is not the whole point. The point is that The Last Chapter is somehow different from the others. It is (or, maybe, should be) different for a number of reasons.

The Last Chapter is the final chance to make whatever point one has been trying to make throughout the book. It is the last, best, and only chance one has left. It is the obvious place in which to sum up, to make clear, and to explain precisely. That should be pressure enough, but there is more.

The Last Chapter is the place to right all the wrong things that have been implied, to apologize for the tricks employed, or the shoddy arguments, or whatever. Some of that is easy enough to do, if one is so inclined.

It seems to me, though, that there is a great urge to come up with The Final Answer in The Last Chapter. To write is often to make up both the answer and the question (the order is not terribly important) and to create an illusion that things are thereby better, or that they soon will be. This book is probably in that tradition. The only problem is that I am still not quite sure about either the answer or the question.

Certainly there have been "answers" in almost every chapter. Just by dealing with this particular set of problems, I have assumed much. But it seems unlikely that this textbook should end with a neat series of solutions, have a Last Chapter which contains "strategies" for completely renewing society. It is not that I believe that all is well; indeed, complete renewal may be the minimum we need. The problem is: I do not know of a neat plan to solve our problems.

The *real* problem is this:

I do not believe in neat plans.

The last chapter does a little of all those things I have mentioned. There is a summing up, a final point making, and some apologizing. For certain, it does not reflect the wishes I had for it, which is my last apology.

> Today is gone. Today was fun.
> Tomorrow is another one.
> Everyday,
> From there to here
> From here to there
> Funny things are everywhere
> From there to here
> From here to there,
> Funny things
> Are everywhere.[1]

---

[1] From Dr. Seuss, *A Cat in the Hat* (Random House, 1957). Reprinted by permission.

The Last Chapter

10

There was once a company of six dancers who were part of a circus in the local village. Five of the dancers could leap about three feet. The villagers followed these five closely, knowing just how high each could jump. They would applaud enthusiastically at the dancer who would leap just a few inches higher than the others.

The sixth dancer could leap almost six feet. The villagers ignored him, wishing to reward the others in his company. When asked why he continued to leap so much higher than the others, while being unappreciated, he replied simply: "Because the other dancers understand."

SOREN KIERKEGAARD

Happiness is a warm gun: Bang, bang, shoot, shoot.

THE BEATLES

Happiness

It seems fairly obvious that if we had our choice, we would choose to be happy rather than unhappy. We want to be happy; we aim at it and plan for it and sometimes even strive toward it. But it seems to me that we have more of a passion for happiness than we have knowledge about it. As with so many seemingly important things, the greatness of our wants is equalled only by the greatness of our ignorance.

Happiness seems a reasonable topic to discuss when one considers the preceding topics. Maybe *all those other things* really do have some relationship to the ways we act and to how we feel. Maybe those things can make us happy, or unhappy, without our even knowing it. Maybe not. But happiness is a subject that should be explored.

Happiness is not *the* goal of humanity, or even of politics, and I do not want to argue that it is. I would simply like to suggest that to begin to think about how we think about happiness may help us to understand not only what we have but possibly what we don't have. By exploring happiness, we may be able to see more clearly how to get what we want, and also to ask ourselves if what we want is worth getting. To begin with, we should try to understand a little of what happiness consists of in ourselves and in our relationship with society.[1] Then, we will explore different ways of dealing with society.

There is no obvious beginning point to a happiness discussion. No point that is so natural a place to begin that it cannot be ignored. Dictionaries may help; so too may Aristotle or Augustine or Jesus. But a discussion that thorough may serve to confuse as much as to make clear.

For a laugh, we could start at an unlikely place—with the Puritans. They serve as models for many things, but I doubt

---

[1] The following discussion is based, in large part, on an unpublished article by John Schaar, entitled "... And the Pursuit of Happiness." The overstatement of the case is my, not his, doing.

that they have ever been a model for happiness. H. L. Mencken once wrote that Puritanism was the gnawing feeling that someone somewhere might be happy.

So much for the Puritans.

By the time of the Constitution, we had already decided that happiness—at least the pursuit of it—was something "originally" guaranteed. The apocryphal story goes that when Thomas Jefferson was drafting the Declaration of Independence, he wrote about the right to life, liberty, and property. That is said to be the true phrasing of the thought, but it was not much artistically. So Jefferson rewrote. He changed it. Instead of pursuing property we were to pursue happiness. The point is an obvious one: In many American minds, there is no difference. Any subtle distinctions are unclear. They are the same—property is happiness, is property is happiness.

But what does that mean now? What does it mean to us? One could easily imagine that it means something like this. Before, to have property was enough. An individual was thought to be more or less happy if he or she owned things. But times have changed. We have changed. We have sophisticated our tastes, modified our styles; now, we consume. Maybe happiness is no longer just the pursuit of property.

Maybe happiness in America is to buy things we won't use, use things we don't need, and waste things we don't want. To consume is to destroy, yet our happiness is in the consumption. Our credit revolves as our purchasing power increases, and the dynamic is to bring smiles to our faces and happiness to our hearts.

Of course, as middle-class, cared-for, mostly pampered college people, we think the consumption formulation vulgar and offensive. "No," you think, "that is for the others. *They* have to buy to be happy. Not me. Not us. No sir. For us to be happy, we just have to have fun."

So that is what you do: run after fun. Have a drink, smoke some dope. Now that is fun. Or you might ski. Or you might play bridge. Or you might go out and kill animals. Now that is really fun. What *more* could we want? Aren't we all happy now?

But is happiness just fun? Fun is cheap. Fun may be little more than a way to fill empty hours, or it may be a way to achieve status and social approval. In the final analysis, fun may have about as much to do with happiness as buying things does. Buying and having fun may simply be methods of display, motion, and instant reward.

If we look around for happiness, or even for fun, it is reasonable to assume that we will continue to be disappointed. The fact seems to be that society gives us few choices. We watch dull television, or the beautiful people in movies, or read *Penthouse* or *Mademoiselle*. And we think that is cool, and so we accept it and think ourselves happy. But that is little more than a sophisticated, societal lie.

The Madisonian man or woman in us will be content with new dresses or pictures of naked men and women, and we shall feel a little guilty and a little good, and go harmlessly on our way.

We somehow squander our right to pursue happiness for the security of mindless, inoffensive fun. We confuse internal pursuits—beauty, nobility, excellence—with the pursuit of happiness understood as the fulfillment of desire. We are too well trained in our own evilness and too used to our own self-interest to accept the task of trying to be happy while living with other people or while seeking values that do not have an obvious, tangible reality.[2]

Maybe there is no such thing as happiness in our society. The harder we look, the more hopeless we become. We grow further apart and pretend somehow that loneliness is happiness. We consume, and we kill, and we read and watch things which only limit our perceptions, dull our imaginations.

To begin to think hard about happiness is to begin to feel cheated. It is to feel that there is an empty space where fullness should be. The more we pursue happiness in a society based on the presumption of our own evilness, the less well off we are as human beings.

But to end "happiness" in great despair does not make much sense, at least not much good sense. If I really agreed with Archbishop Whately that happiness was no laughing mat-

---

[2] I would like to share a curious fact in the form of a question: Why are so many people so willing to share unhappiness but unwilling to even acknowledge happiness? Curious, huh?

ter, I should be forced to believe that happiness was probably not worth the trouble of figuring out. No, I want to argue that I have seen people happy, and have even felt it, and certainly enjoyed it. Not only that, happiness might be important. It was Hawthorne who suggested the likeness of happiness to a butterfly, which flits away when chased but which may come and light on your hand if you will only sit quietly, occupied with something else.

It is wholly possible that we have been searching in the wrong place, pursuing the wrong question. If we take Hawthorne seriously, it may be best to occupy ourselves with that "something else."

Beyond Butterflies

I have no desire to set out a reasoned and reasonable argument about what one should do, about what that "something else" would look like if we wanted to have the butterfly light on our hand. Indeed, the implication of my remarks up to now is that happiness may simply be a nice by-product. It may not be worth pursuing in its own right.

Nor do I wish to agree fully with Hawthorne. While his insight into the chase seems a good one, his analogy is not quite accurate. Just sitting may be good for butterfly landings, but I am not certain that it is the best condition for happiness. Indeed, happiness may be, in some part, the connections between one's self and others and society. It may have to do with how one thinks and sees and acts, not with how well one sits still.

If what has been said so far is right—if a portion of happiness is both personal and societal, and if our society is more limiting than fulfilling—then we must consider some general notions of what might be done. No plans (specifically); no Final Answer; nothing that hasn't already been suggested. Certainly each chapter has contained ideas about how we might begin to politicize our politics and possibly take our public selves and actions more seriously. No need to repeat that.

It is important to understand a little more about how to deal with what is going on now. If the preceding chapters have been at all successful in defining the present—and how we got here and where we are logically heading—then something should be said about the ways in which this "reality" might be confronted. It seems clear that almost everyone can get along, that most can cope, and that many can even "succeed" according to the present rules. But, if what has been said is correct, then that seems a foolish option to take.

What we must do is to talk about the different ways of facing the problems of now, of the different options for everyday life, and make those ways free from the conventional definitions of "success." There are at least three ways.

Way One: Do Not Do It

There may be a point, for some people, when it seems impossible or unlikely that what has been going on can keep going on. A point at which all seems hopeless or insane or inane, wicked or vile or cruel. A point when they just cannot continue doing whatever it is they have been doing. There are those who believe that nothing they do is getting them anywhere, yet who cannot quite figure out the next move.

One next move might be this: Stop doing those things that are not helping. Begin to understand—and don't do—the things "they" do.

What follows is an elaborate story that helps illustrate the point. It is suggested as an obvious move if what you are doing doesn't seem worth much. It is just a suggested move, not a stance toward life or an ultimate political action. It is simply a story of breaking away. The story is about Ken Kesey and a speech he once gave to protest the war in Vietnam.

Before beginning, a word about Kesey. He is a fine (I would vote for "great") American author. *One Flew Over the Cuckoo's Nest* and *Sometimes a Great Notion* are beautifully written, powerful books. Kesey was heavily involved with LSD and now writes and farms and does politics in Oregon. To understand his acid life-style of the mid-sixties, read Tom Wolfe's *The Electric Kool-Aid Acid Test*. But that is, mostly, beside the point. One can learn from Kesey without using heavy drugs. He can conceptualize important things fantastically well. Enough background.

In 1965, Ken Kesey was invited to a teach-in held by the Vietnam Day Committee at Berkeley. According to Wolfe, no one was sure just why he was invited, but he was and he accepted the invitation. So Kesey and his friends dressed up in funny war costumes, painted themselves and their big old school bus in bright Day-Glo colors, took horns and electric guitars, and went to Berkeley.

When they arrived, a whole series of speakers were talking about "genocidal atrocities" and the need for great marches in the streets. Pretty soon it was Kesey's turn and this is what he had to say:[3]

"You know, you're not gonna stop this war with this rally, by marching... that's what *they* do... they hold rallies and they march.... They've been having wars for ten thousand years and you're not gonna stop it this way... ten thousand years, and this is this game they play to do it... holding rallies and having marches... and that's the same game you're playing... their game."

Kesey stopped talking. According to Wolfe, he reached "into his great glowing Day-Glo coat and produced a harmonica and start(ed) playing it right into the microphone, '*Home, home on the range, hawonking away on the goddamn thing— Home... home... on the ra-a-a-ange hawonkawonk....*'"

And his friends behind him began to play their guitars, and dance, and blow their horns. But the crowd—the Berkeley serious people—could not quite understand. This was a serious thing: the teach-in before the march. Home, home on the range? "We know about that *home!* We know about that *range!* That rotten U.S. home and that rotten U.S. range—" Maybe that is what the audience was thinking; but they just misunderstood. Kesey stopped playing and began to speak:

"I was just looking at the speaker who was up here before me... and I couldn't hear what he was saying... but I could hear the sound of it... and I could hear *your* sound coming back at him... and I could see the gestures and I could see his jaw sticking out... and you know who I saw... and who I

---

[3] As reported by Tom Wolfe, in *The Electric Kool-Aid Acid Test* (New York: Farrar, Straus & Giroux, 1969).

heard? . . . Mussolini . . . I saw and I heard Mussolini here just a few minutes ago . . . Yep, you're playing their game. . . ."

Most of the crowd simply was not with Kesey or his friends. Some booed, most were just confused. That changed nothing on the stage. There was more music and more talk, more guitars and more "Home on the Range." The message was always the same: You're playing their game. And then another message:

"There's only one thing to do . . . there's only one thing's gonna do any good at all . . . and that's everybody just look at it, look at the war, and turn your backs and say . . . Fuck it. . . ."

"—hawonkawonkawonkawanka—"

Then the music got louder and madder and the Day-Glo crazies were really into playing and dancing and strutting to variations of the old classic "Home on the Range." And the Berkeley people weren't ready, and were a little shocked, and maybe a little drained of their desire to march, of their desire to "be like them." And Kesey repeated his message—and our first way out:

"Just look at it and turn away and say . . . Fuck it

—hawonkawonkawonka blam

—fuck it—

Hawonkafuckit . . . friends. . . ."

Way Two: Do It

It is not at all difficult to imagine some people's unhappiness with the above advice. For a whole group of individuals, both the style and the substance are potentially as distasteful as they are disagreeable. The style is a matter of taste, which is important—but not necessarily to this discussion. To walk away takes a good deal of understanding and nerve; but it is not necessarily the way for everybody. Some people want to know where they are going, just what they are getting into. They ask the naturally conservative (but reasonable) question: Will it be better than what we have?

To cling to that question is to limit what will be to what one is sure of, to what one knows. While Kesey's advice is precise, it is limited. He has no thoroughgoing view to offer us. It seems to take a certain kind of person to leave what is, without really knowing what will happen. In part, it takes an individual who knows that what is is not enough, is lacking something, is wrong; and who, because of that, is willing to try to create something else. Leaving—or not doing—something that seems wrong is not necessarily a negative act.

But it is clear that most of us, most of the time, need more than the advice to leave. We need some kind of direction. Moreover, we want that direction to be built on a rather explicit view of the world. Given that, Kesey is not our man. Possibly, Georges Sorel is.[4]

In order to get any meaning out of Sorel, in order to understand his politics and his influence, it is necessary to talk about some of his ideas of society. Basically, Sorel believed that societies ebbed and flowed; they were founded and destroyed, they decayed and were renewed. There was no permanent answer, no state of peace. There were just continual cycles of change.

Europe, at the turn of this century, was in what Sorel believed to be a state of decline. Indeed, he thought the people bland, compromising, and corrupt. The institutions were as bad: both Church and State seemed to him decadent. We are familiar enough with more contemporary versions of this kind of analysis to see why Sorel may be of some use, why he may illuminate some points.

The problem of Sorel—to oversimplify—was this: How can things be reformed and renewed? How can the decadence and the old ways of acting be cut out, be changed? His goal was a new style of being, a new way of acting. He wanted people to involve themselves in creating new societal forms, and he wanted this done in a new atmosphere of liberty. These were no modest aims.

What Sorel tried to do was involve the majority of the people—in his term, the proletariat—in the change. To his way of thinking, there was a slave morality and a master morality. It was only the master morality that was noble enough to cause heroic action. It was the master morality that the people had

---

[4] See Georges Sorel, *Reflections on Violence* (New York: The Free Press, 1950).

to acquire. Moreover, this morality had to be shared, had to be public, had to be political. If society was to be renewed, there had to be a collective force stronger than society. There had to be political action of a great mass of people.

Sorel proposed that people be reeducated—but with a difference. People were to be taught through a concept of their own hope. They were to be given a new myth, a new ideal of what might be, a new vision to do battle for. It should be made clear that this myth cannot be characterized as a single idea, or as a series of small changes, or as a blueprint. It isn't logical or rational or open to critical analysis. The new myth is a complex of pictures and images of what we believe. It contains what we hate and what we want and what we will fight for.

We have a myth of America. It may or may not be worn out. If it is old, out of date, decadent, then, according to the teachings of Sorel, we must create a new myth. The new one will be built on our hopes, on our own best thoughts.

The idea of the myth is important in understanding Sorel, and in understanding what we must do. For at the heart of his myth is a commitment to violence, a commitment to starting afresh. Through this commitment, people begin to take action, to reeducate others by their example, and to develop a sense of the master morality. In the creation of the myth and through commitment to it, an individual will turn more and more to the interests of the community and to the fate of his fellows.

In the end, the state is destroyed and a new one created. But according to Sorel, the individual is not only creating a state, he or she is also creating virtue. To take it to the next step, the individual is achieving a remarkable aim: By creating virtue the individual is also helping to create himself or herself.

The themes of Sorel are instructive; he is able to help us understand that the state and politics are beyond the rational, the routine, the bureaucratic. The whole idea of remaking —indeed, of creating—through political action enables us to glimpse an important vision we now lack. It is, in part, to begin to know that change is connected with the creation of, and then the substitution of, one way of looking at the world for another, of one myth for another myth. Finally, Sorel teaches us that there is a close tie between the development of the political and the individual, and that ultimately, the virtue of the one is tied to the virtue of the other.

For those who do not want to walk away but who believe that the state of the state is beyond repair, Georges Sorel might point the way. Certainly his arguments are too powerful to simply ignore, his aims too grand to put aside. Sadly, he may have been wrong about us: It is possible that we are *all* corrupt, all bland and compromising. Maybe we are slaves to a morality which effectively blocks us from the new myth —from the Myth of the General Strike.

But that is off the point.

Way Three

With Sorel, as with Kesey, one can imagine criticism; it is not difficult to anticipate. It is hard enough to break away from what we have, if for no other reason than the combination of training and inertia. But to accept a new myth that will regenerate society may well be beyond what most people can do. Whether Sorel is correct or not, it would seem that only some are able to carry his ideas to the point of action.

There is a Way Three, which is not obvious enough to sum up in a catchy phrase. In a sense, this third way counsels us to do the best we can, no matter. Although it might seem pessimistic (it counsels that, no matter what, we all die and rot), I do not believe it is. While not as obviously political as Sorel or as direct as Kesey, this way does provide a basis for action. While it comes from the Bible, from Ecclesiastes to be precise, it certainly is not religious. Indeed, it pretty much ignores the God-problem. It involves what we should do, if anything, and why. It involves the same questions raised in the discussion on happiness and by Kesey and Sorel.

Vanity of vanities, all is vanity.

Ecclesiastes was written by the son of David, the king of Jerusalem. The best guess is that Ecclesiastes was written by King Solomon, a person reputed to be wise, just, wealthy, and virtuous. An impressive combination. It is from this vantage point that he writes his advice, that he tries to explain their merits in accordance with what he understands to be the human condition.

First, Solomon explains that we cannot count on being different than we are; we cannot count on having something new. All has happened, all will happen again. We will continue unsatisfied, unfulfilled, if we continually expect something new. "I have seen all the works that are done under the sun; and, behold, all is vanity and a striving after wind."

But there are goals other than trying to be different. There is wealth: "I made me great works; I builded me houses; I planted me vineyards.... I acquired me man-servants and maid-servants, and had servants born in my house.... I gathered me also silver and gold and treasure.... So I was great ... and whatsoever mine eyes desired I kept not from them; I withheld not my heart from any joy, for my heart had joy of all my labour; and this was my portion from all my labour.

"Then I looked on all the works that my hands had wrought, and on the labour that I had laboured to do; and, behold, all was vanity and a striving after the wind. ..."

Verses can be repeated, about wisdom and about virtue, and the conclusion is always the same: All is vanity, a striving after the wind. That is a part of our condition we cannot ignore. It is a part of our condition in part, because we all must die.

"... There is one event to the righteous and to the wicked; to the good and to the clean and to the unclean; to him that sacrificeth and to him that sacrificeth not; as is the good, so is the sinner ... there is one event unto all ... the heart of the sons of men is full of evil, and madness is in their heart while they live, and after that they go to the dead."

And when we "go to the dead," that is it.

"For to him that is joined to all the living there is hope; for a living dog is better than a dead lion ... the dead know not anything, neither have they any more a reward; for the memory of them is forgotten. As well as their love, as their hatred and their envy, is long ago perished; neither have they any more a portion for ever in anything that is done under the sun."

No heaven, no hell: just vanity and chasing the wind. Then, no more a portion for ever in anything. But this third way—

this advice of Solomon—is not depressing. These are not grounds for despair. The advice is twofold: First, enjoy life. "Eat thy bread with joy, and drink thy wine with a merry heart . . . let thy garments be always white; and let thy head lack no oil . . . . Enjoy life with a wife when thou lovest . . . whatsoever thy hand attaineth to do by thy strength, that do; for there is no work, nor device, nor knowledge, nor wisdom, in the grave, whither thou goest."

Second, be with people. "Two are better than one . . . if two lie together, then they have warmth; but how can one be warm alone? And if a man prevail against him that is alone, two shall withstand him; and a threefold cord is not quickly broken."

Enough Bible. Maybe too much. But the points are sufficiently important to be made explicitly. For some, Kesey's advice was obvious and good; for others Sorel was good. Yet there are many who cannot quite make blind leaps, who are not ready for an ideological stand, who just have to think things through as far as possible. That is the point here: To understand vanity and death is not to be immobilized, is not to despair, is not to avoid action. It is to do all these things— to act, and to move, and to accept happiness. It can easily be the basis of politics, for it is all we have; and if Solomon is right, we only have one chance at it.

So the third way is the most vague of all, but maybe the most urgent.

Where to Begin: What to Talk About

Freedom is fire, overcoming this world by reducing it to a fluctuating chaos, as in schizophrenia; the chaos which is the eternal ground of creation. There is no uni-verse, no one way.

We are always in error
Lost in the wood
Standing in chaos
The original mess
Creating
A brand-new world

Thank God the world cannot be made safe, for democracy or anything else.

NORMAN O. BROWN

Before ending this chapter, it is necessary to explore one more problem. Where do we begin to talk about politics? By where, I simply mean to ask what the logical entry point for a discussion of politics is.

It is clear that, for some, the "real" concerns of politics have not even been mentioned, or that they have been mentioned only in passing. Many would think that any discussion of politics should inevitably center on "real-life" issues: schools, health care, income distribution, and the like. *Those* are the problem areas, those are the concerns of politics and political science. To concentrate on alienation, aloneness, or privatization is, for many political scientists, to concentrate on all the wrong things.

In a sense, it is difficult to disagree. It would be hard to say that better health or better schools or more food were not really the point. Of course, they are the point. They represent, in great measure, the concerns of society and are the issues any political system must deal with. Yet we should know by now that to deal exclusively with such problems is to doom the search to only one dimension and to almost certain failure.

We must understand the reasons for the problems, in what way we are involved, and how these two things are connected. We must ask how the problems are going to be solved and whether the proposed solutions involve change or just more of what we have. We must be constantly aware that there are "solutions" which are even worse than the original problems.

Put another way: There are a number of fundamental questions we must come to terms with before we can answer the "better health" problems of everyday, obvious politics.[5]

In order to get to a more fundamental level of discussion, we must first ask what we can expect from the political system and from politics. It seems to me obvious that we have been taught to make unnecessary distinctions. That there is any tension between the "cultural" problem of aloneness and the "political" problems of food and money may, in part, stem

---

[5] For two examples of works which consider the question of how people should organize themselves so as to produce better actions and better decisions, see Martin Buber, *Paths in Utopia* (Boston: Beacon Press, 1970), and Erich Fromm, *The Revolution of Hope* (New York: Harper Colophon Books, 1968).

from the very narrow view of politics we have been brought up on. A view that is limiting in subject matter as well as scope, one that is set off from rather than inclusive of the idea that political action can be the resolution of the creative tension between individual and societal virtue.

Before discussing the "real" problems, it is necessary to understand the context of the discussion. It is necessary to realize that until the context contains a definition of politics that includes the qualitative values of those involved, the solutions to the problems will only be "tricks," only variations on the themes that helped bring about the problems in the first place.

I am suggesting that the study of politics is twice the work some think it is. First, we must define politics in such a way that it helps us to define who we are. We must understand politics as a creative process—both for ourselves and our society. Second, with that definition, we must try to solve the critical problems around us. But we can't do the second until we have done the first. It is necessary to understand that to talk about politics is to talk about both the process and the problem, about both the individual and the outcome.

In one sense, this whole book has tried to get at the "normal" context of politics and to suggest why that context is inadequate. An effort has been made to look at the obvious as a carrier of an ideology. But this discussion is best set off by itself; it is, indeed, the last topic.

On Trying to Understand the Whole Book

This is meant to be an introduction to politics, some ideas that may lead one to begin to understand a few important problems.

What was done seems reasonable enough to do at a beginning level. An effort was made to try to understand the elements of politics. Pretty obviously, the book has been concerned with much more than how a bill becomes a law or how to be elected mayor or president. Simply and reasonably and logically, we have found that politics is prior to and more important than our governmental apparatus.

In many ways, politics is a function of how we think of each other and of how we relate to the whole. It is us and them, and we and me, and I and thou, in all combinations. To understand that, we began at the beginning.

The beginning was a simple search into how we related to each other, into how society wanted us to understand ourselves, and—somewhat closer to the root of the matter— into how much we counted. So we read *Federalist* No. 10 and tried to figure out what it means and how we acted according to it. The conclusion was unhappy, but fairly accurate: Madison's account of society—of us—was true. We Americans built a society on the evilness of us all. Somehow we chose to emphasize those things least desirable in ourselves. We discovered that we believed each other to be evil, and that our belief had become a self-fulfilling prophecy.

There was the whole question of how we know things, of what things are real. The conclusion was rather an odd one: we found that we believed knowledge was something that could be touched, or felt, or seen. We believe that we know things by rationalizing them, by objectifying them. So there is little opportunity to think about "unreal" things, about knowledge that is neither wholly objective nor rational.

A world in which all things were rational and objective would be a world without humans, it would be mute testimony to our own stupidity.

So we hunted hard for our own humanity. We began to realize that the political state was more than laws and elections, that politics had something to do with who we were. So we tried to be free but saw that we were made to be alone; we tried to understand justice but could only talk about being judged.

And for me the whole thing was depressing. To work through the problems and to think about the answers was often no fun. But it seemed to make sense to begin the study of politics by talking about what politics is doing to you. And, just as importantly, about what you are allowing to happen to you simply out of ignorance.[6]

·Everything means something; nothing is entirely obvious.

---

[6] For a brilliant description of going through life normally, and just what that might mean, see Kurt Vonnegut, Jr., *Mother Night* (New York: Avon Books, 1961).

So we tried to understand what was happening and how it happened. There were discussions about how groups could pressure you, freedom isolate you, voting degrade you, and happiness sadden you. It was no mistake that we reached the conclusions we did.

What was discussed, much of what was decided, are real, hard, true facts. They are, to some degree, the facts with which we have lived up to now. They seem imprecise simply because they are difficult to measure; but, in the long run, they are much more important than most things easily quantifiable.

The study of political science—of politics—can be the study of these facts. I think it can, at its best, be an attempt to understand how to relate to our society in a public, open —indeed, political—manner. My bias is obvious: It seems important to understand what is happening, which things must be kept, and which things should be changed. We are free to study any aspect in any manner; but it seems a great loss when we fail to relate what goes on to our human condition. To discuss politics without people seems as silly as discussing economics without goods and products, or history without the past.

If anyone asks: There are 100 senators, there are presidential elections every four years, and we are who we were in the context of who we will be. Tell them, beyond that, the answers get much more complicated and difficult—but possibly much more meaningful.

Ask them on the bus.

Once there was a flock of geese. They were kept in a wire cage, by a farmer. One day, one of the geese looked up and saw that there was no top to the cage. Excitedly, he told the other geese:

"Look, look: There is no top. We may leave here. We may become free."

Few listened, and none would turn his head to the sky.

So, one day, he simply spread his wings and flew away— alone.

SOREN KIERKEGAARD

3 4 5 6 7 8 9 0